An Introduction to Internet-Based Financial Investigations

An Introduction to Internet-Based Financial Investigations

Structuring and Resourcing the Search for Hidden Assets and Information

KIMBERLY GOETZ

GOWER

Published by
Gower Publishing Limited
Wey Court East
Union Road
Farnham
Surrey, GU9 7PT
England

Ashgate Publishing Company
Suite 420
101 Cherry Street
Burlington,
VT 05401-4405
USA

www.gowerpublishing.com

British Library Cataloguing in Publication Data
Goetz, Kimberly.
 An introduction to Internet-based financial investigation :
 structuring and resourcing the search for hidden assets and
 information.
 1. Forensic accounting. 2. Investigations--Computer
 network resources. 3. Internet searching.
 I. Title
 363.2'5'0285'4678-dc22

 ISBN: 978-0-566-09190-2 (hbk)
 ISBN: 978-0-566-09191-9 (ebk)

Library of Congress Cataloging-in-Publication Data
Goetz, Kimberly, 1971-
 An introduction to internet-based financial investigation : structuring and resourcing the search for hidden assets and information / Kimberly Goetz.
  p. cm.
 Includes index.
 ISBN 978-0-566-09190-2 (hardback) -- ISBN 978-0-566-09191-9 1. Fraud investigation. 2. White collar crime investigation. 3. Internet. 4. Business ethics. I. Title.
 HV8079.F7G64 2010
 363.25'968--dc22

MIX
Paper from
responsible sources
FSC® C018575
www.fsc.org

Printed and bound in Great Britain by the
MPG Books Group, UK

Contents

List of Figures

List of Abbreviations

The following abbreviations are used in this book:

AFIS	Automated Fingerprint Identification System
AG	*Aktiengesellschaft* (German business designation)
AKA	Also Known As
AOL	America On Line
BBB	Better Business Bureau
CPA	Certified Public Accountant
DBA	Doing Business As
DBE	Disadvantaged Business Enterprise
DOT	Deed of Trust
DPA	Durable Power of Attorney
DPAHC	Durable Power of Attorney for Health Care
EBIT	Earnings Before Interest and Taxes
EBITA	Earnings Before Interest, Taxes, and Appreciation
EDGAR	Electronic Data Gathering, Analysis, and Retrieval
EPA	US Environmental Protection Agency
FASB	Financial Accounting Standards Board
FBI	Federal Bureau of Investigation
FEIN	Federal Employer Identification Number (same as TIN)
FinCEN	Financial Crimes Enforcement Network
FINRA	Financial Industry Regulatory Authority, Inc.
FKA	Formerly Known As
FOIA	Freedom of Information Act
GAAP	Generally Accepted Accounting Principles
GmbH	*Gesellschaft mit Beschränkter Haftung* (German business designation)
GP	General Partnership
HCD	Health Care Directive (Advanced Directive or Living Will)
ICANN	Internet Corporation for Assigned Names and Numbers
IRA	Individual Retirement Account
IRS	Internal Revenue Service
JDLR	Just Doesn't Look Right
JTWROS	Joint Tenancy with Right of Survivorship
LLC	Limited Liability Company
LLP	Limited Liability Partnership
LP	Limited Partnership
NADA	National Association of Automobile Dealers
NAIC	National Association of Insurance Commissioners
NAICS	North American Industry Classification System

NASDAQ	National Association of Securities Dealers Automated Quotation
NCIC	National Crime Information Center
NKA	Now Known As
NYSE	New York Stock Exchange
OBO	On Behalf Of
PACER	Public Access to Court Electronic Records
PLLC	Professional Limited Liability Company
PLLP	Professional Limited Liability Partnership
POD	Pay on Death
QCD	Quit Claim Deed
REIT	Real Estate Investment Trust
RV	Recreational Vehicle
SA	*Sociedad Anónima* (Spanish company designation)
SA	*Société Anonyme* (French business designation)
SEC	Securities and Exchange Commission
SEDAR	System for Electronic Document Analysis and Retrieval
SIC	Standard Industrial Classification System
SLAPP	Strategic Lawsuit Against Public Participation
SOS	Secretary of State
SOX	Sarbanes-Oxley Act
SSDI	Social Security Death Index
SWD	Statutory Warranty Deed
TIN	Taxpayer Identification Number (same as FEIN)
UCC	Uniform Commercial Code
VPN	Virtual Private Network
WD	Warranty Deed

About the Author

Kimberly Goetz is currently the Financial Assurance Officer for the Washington State Department of Ecology's Hazardous Waste and Toxics Reduction Program. She oversees the implementation of financial assurance programs for facilities handling hazardous or dangerous waste in Washington State. She also handles corporate finance, economic, policy, and statistical analysis and coordinates legislative issues for the program. Prior to joining the State Department of Ecology, Kimberly worked for approximately five years conducting business investigations and more than eight years as a legal assistant and paralegal working in the areas of complex litigation, estate planning/probate, and business law. She is a former member of the Washington State Bar Association's Disciplinary Board and the Thurston County Teen-Works Advisory Board; she is currently a member of the Board of Directors of Sean-nós Northwest. Kimberly's BA in Political Science (International Relations) and Global Studies (Development and Social Justice) is from Pacific Lutheran University in Tacoma, Washington and her MPA (Public Policy) is from The Evergreen State College in Olympia, Washington.

Preface

I would have loved to have a book like this when I started doing investigations. My initial training consisted of a two-day investigator course and a one-day legal education seminar about fraud. While I had an extensive background working for attorneys in a variety of fields of law, I really didn't have a clear idea about how to look for information or how to understand what I found. I could do legal research and I could do library research, but Internet research was something new. I had some successes, made some mistakes, and learned a lot in those first few years. This book is a summary of everything I ended up teaching myself.

Please note that the materials in this book are not intended to be legal advice or instruction. Information about laws and legal documents is presented from the perspective of an investigator, not a lawyer. A lawyer would probably disagree with some of the explanations I provide. The information presented is only a general guide based on my personal experiences. Laws, regulations, and standards may be different in each jurisdiction. If you have questions about legal issues, you should address them to an attorney or other relevant expert in the appropriate country, state, or county. My explanations are not "legal" explanations—they are intended to be "real world" explanations.

This book not only summarizes my opinions and experiences related to financial investigations but it also reflects my strong belief in making information understandable and accessible. I firmly believe that information should be presented in a way that the audience is most likely to understand. The language in this book was chosen to enhance the reader's understanding, irrespective of whether that language is "standard" English. When faced with a choice between plain English and proper grammar, I default to plain English. Good grammar may be important, but not at the expense of communication. As Winston Churchill is reported to have said, "This is the sort of English up with which I will not put." I wholeheartedly agree. I also wholeheartedly recommend that investigators and other regulatory employees adopt a similar attitude. "Legalese" and "bureaucratese" may be technically correct (and are sometimes necessary), but they don't do a very good job of communicating a message. I sincerely hope you understand every paragraph in this book the first time you read it. I also hope that this book helps you write investigation reports that are easy for your audience to understand the first time. When in doubt use short sentences and active voices. Avoid using jargon and acronyms as much as you possibly can.

While the majority of this book is focused on Internet-based investigations, parts of the book also apply to other types of investigations. Not every part of the book will apply to every investigator. It is still a good idea to read the parts that don't necessarily apply to you and your job. It is possible that one day your job will include these activities. You could be asked to assist on an investigation that differs from the kind you are accustomed to performing. Either way, it is advantageous for you to know how other investigators do their work and how that work differs from your own.

Finally, please keep in mind that the tips and suggestions I present are based on my own personal experience and work for me. You may view a situation from a diametrically opposing position—and that's OK. No two investigators will conduct identical investigations. What works for me might not work for you. The suggestions in this book are exactly that: suggestions. They are not rules. They are not laws. They are just good ideas. Feel free to take them, leave them, or change them to suit your own needs, personality, and investigation style. I hope the ideas and advice in this book help make your job easier and your investigations more effective.

Kimberly Goetz

1 *Introduction: Why and Where to Start*

Many public sector employees find they need to perform financial investigations even though they have no financial training or expertise. Perhaps you are a new employee who has simply been told, "Here are the program rules and some applications. Figure out which ones are eligible and which ones aren't." Alternatively, you might be an engineer who oversees the cleanup of a toxic waste site and you need to track down the companies that contributed to the pollution so they can help to pay for the cleanup. Maybe you're reading this book because you work for a quasi-governmental agency and you've received a complaint about an attorney mishandling a client's money. Alternatively, maybe you're an attorney and need help finding the assets absconded by your client's former spouse.

Training about investigation techniques and resources tends to be very limited, even in law-enforcement agencies. In my experience, training on how to find information without incurring significant expense is virtually nonexistent. Employees who find themselves in these types of situations frequently resort to on-the-job training. This book is intended to help fill the void for those employees. It will provide practical tips on how to conduct a financial investigation—the type of information that new investigators usually have to learn through trial and error. The book is specifically designed for beginning investigators and regulatory employees who conduct financial investigations as a portion of the job. It is not targeted at forensic accountants or others with extensive investigation experience.

If you suspect that you don't have the full financial picture, how can you go about finding more information? More importantly, how do you find that information in a timely manner for little or no cost? Frequently the answer is the Internet. If you know where to look (or, perhaps more importantly, *how* to look), you can find considerable information about most companies and individuals in the United States. By starting with some basic information, you can frequently learn more than you ever thought possible. These materials will provide you with a rough guide to finding information on the Internet—both what questions to ask and how to start looking for the answers. If you're new to investigations or need some help using Internet-based methods, these materials will give you a good start.

For the purposes of this book, I will simply refer to the target of your financial investigation as the "subject." This may include program applicants, potentially liable parties, companies that may have committed a regulatory infraction, and other related individuals and businesses. The term "subject" is not intended to be limited to the applicant or respondent in an investigation; it is merely a catchall term used for the sake of simplicity.

In addition, it's important to know that this book is intended primarily for investigators in the United States. The terminology is specific to US companies and subjects (as are date and currency notations). However, other countries should have equivalent documents or similar legal concepts even if they have different names. If you are investigating people or businesses in other countries, you may need to do additional research to find out what those equivalent documents or concepts are called.

Why Use These Techniques?

There are many situations when these techniques may be useful. While some investigators may have access to paid databases such as Dun & Bradstreet, LexisNexis, or Westlaw— expensive subscription products that can provide a vast quantity of data—most of us are not that lucky. The techniques explained in this book are intended to assist employees from federal, state, or local agencies who do not have access to paid database resources and are looking for a free or low-cost alternative. Even if you have access to information from paid databases, you may want to try these techniques when you want (1) to verify information you have obtained from another source, (2) to obtain information not available through paid database sources, or (3) to try to find information that you don't know to search for in paid resources. The same basic techniques can be used in each of these situations.

The first example of when to use these techniques is if you don't have access to paid databases. Access to resources like LexisNexis, Westlaw, and Dun & Bradstreet reports is very expensive and as a result, many agencies and organizations do not have routine access to these databases. If you work for a state agency, you may have access to some or all of these paid resources through another part of your agency, a regional association of state agencies, or an organization in which your agency is a member. (If you don't know whether you have access, check with your agency's regional contact person or membership coordinator.) If you work for a local government entity, a nonprofit organization, or some other type of company, it is still possible you might have access to paid database resources. If your organization has a fundraising or development office, they may have purchased database access. Your organization may also belong to a group that provides access to paid databases. If none of these opportunities are available to you, you may be able to purchase access to one or more databases on a limited basis. Your organization may also have an existing partnership with another company or organization that has access and may be willing to assist you on a limited basis. However, if none of these situations applies, you may need to look for other methods of finding information.

The second situation when these techniques will be useful is to verify or further explain the information you obtained from the subject or a paid database. Just because a credit bureau reports an outstanding debt or judgment doesn't mean it really exists. A paid database might report that your subject owns a house in another state—is that true, or did the subject just co-sign the mortgage and is listed on the title as a result? Or does the subject's tax return show a deduction for mortgage interest paid, but the database report not show a corresponding parcel of real estate? These are the types of situations where paid databases are not as reliable as they might otherwise appear. Independent verification of the information you obtain from a paid database is very important, especially if that information is the basis for a fine, penalty, or legal action.

The third situation is when you want to access information that is not available through paid databases. This includes information in many government databases, including professional licenses and other business information. While it may not seem like information that is typically applicable to a search for assets, a professional license or other certification may give you a clue about who your subject is and possibly even other businesses they may own. You may also obtain information from a subject's tax return, insurance policy, or similar documentation that is not verifiable through a paid database, such as ownership of an important piece of art or valuable collection.

Finally, you may want to use these techniques to search for other information you don't know about. Paid databases can be great, but they don't incorporate the "human" factor that is critical in conducting investigations. Take a hypothetical situation: say you are investigating a firm whose owners say they lease their business location rather than own it. Their monthly lease payments are made to an unrelated property management firm. When you look up the name of the property owner, the county says it belongs to "The Bachbeet Family Trust." Neither the lease nor the agreement establishing "The Bachbeet Family Trust" has been recorded with the county, so you don't have a copy of either document. There is no public record except the deed that even mentions "The Bachbeet Family Trust." A paid database will stop there. It doesn't have the ability to see the connection between the name "Bachbeet" and the subjects of your investigation: Mr. Bach and Mr. Beethoven. As long as they are careful about how they set up and use the trust, there may never be a clear connection that any paid database will ever find (even on an "associated names" report)—but your human intuition can make enough of a connection to help you find relevant information.

The Skills You Need

Looking for hidden assets is not the purview of any single discipline. You need to know at least a little about accounting, law, finance, banking, business, public records, and investigation techniques. In other words, it requires you to use both your logical left brain and your creative right brain. Because of the diverse skills required, it may take more than one person to investigate a hidden assets case to the fullest extent possible. This book is not intended to be a comprehensive investigation manual; it is intended to give you an idea about what information is available for no or low-cost and how to use that information to tell a story. You may want to use some of these techniques just so you can say you personally reviewed a document before you have to testify about a case in court. You can also use these techniques as a screening tool to do a cursory review of a subject's finances to figure out whether it is worth contacting a trained investigator for further assistance.

For many investigators the most successful approach to fraud investigation is to place yourself in the subject's position: if you had a particular asset, how would you hide it? What evidence would you leave behind? (Just don't be surprised when they manage to think of ways you never would have dreamed up.) You may find inspiration in the most unlikely of places. Financial investigation and forensic accounting texts usually focus on frauds committed by employees against businesses. Corporate fraud texts usually focus on Enron-like deceptions related to hiding losses and financial instability. However, the techniques that can be used to disguise thefts or business losses can probably also be used to hide business profits. Financial schemes that employees can use to steal from their employer can also be used by business owners to covertly divert profits from the company to their personal accounts. So the next time you read a news article or see a television special about financial fraud or identity theft, ask yourself how a subject could use the same technique to hide assets from you.

Where to Start: Beginning an Investigation

This book is intended to be an introduction to using the Internet to conduct financial investigations. However, searching the Internet for information is neither the first nor the last step. Before you begin an investigation, think about the resources that are available to you through your employer, resources provided by organizations you belong to, and resources that are available to the general public.

The first place many of us overlook is our public library. Not only do librarians have access to vast amounts of information, they have special training on how to access that information. If your local public library does not offer the resources or assistance you need, check with your local university or state library. If you went to school at a local university, you may have alumnus privileges. Even if you can't borrow from the library, it can still be an excellent source of information.

The second source of information that can be easy to overlook is a personal visit. For many investigations, an on-site visit is a routine part of the investigation or review. Even if it is not required, you may find a visit very helpful for some cases. You may find a business with someone else's name on the door. You may find the last parcel of vacant land in a newly developed industrial area. Or you may find exactly what you are supposed to find—a legitimate company going about their business just as they claimed.

Finally, remember to take advantage of experts you work with or that you may know though other professional relationships. Does your agency have an economist on staff? Need an expert in accounting? Try your organization's bookkeeper. Need some legal information? Try contacting the manager down the hall that went to law school (even though they never practiced law). While these experts may not be able to answer all your questions, they may be able to provide answers to some of your most basic questions and help guide the direction of your investigation.

Before you start searching the Internet, it is also important to collect and organize all of the information you already have related to your subject. What is the purpose of your investigation? Who is your subject? What type of investigation are you conducting? What will be the final result of your investigation? Are penalties or sanctions possible? Is your work purely administrative, or could there be criminal charges filed? Each of these questions will affect what steps you take, what resources you use, and how you report your findings.

Filling in the Holes

One way that Internet-based financial investigations differ from other types of investigations is their focus. You can't use the Internet to audit a company's books or conduct a credit check. Information you find on the Internet can instead help you fill holes in your investigation. For example, perhaps you're wondering why a parcel of real estate shows up on a subject's financial statement one year, but not the next. You can use the Internet to try to find an explanation—like a divorce filing and a deed transferring the property to the subject's former spouse. Or perhaps you're wondering why the subject's company laid off half its workforce. Finding the minutes of the local city council meeting where the council members voted to cancel the company's city contract might be the answer you're looking for. While those documents can (and sometimes must) be obtained in person, using the Internet can save time and avoid false starts. You can find more information in less time when you don't have to leave your desk.

Finding more information in less time also has a significant downside: numerous false leads. You might not think "Kimberly Goetz" is a particularly common name, but I'm not the only one out there (as I periodically have to remind the various credit bureaus). A name is only one piece of the puzzle.

Contrary to what you see on television, there is no "magic" database that will tell you every company a subject has a contract with or every bank where they have a safe deposit box. Regardless of what conspiracy theorists might believe, the government cannot track your every movement or how much money you have in your wallet at any time. There is simply too much information to collect, store, organize, and access for that to be the case. If a "magic" database actually did exist, there wouldn't be any need for the FBI's "Most Wanted" list—law enforcement could simply round up criminals at will (just like they do on television).

There are many resources available where you can find extensive information in furtherance of your investigation, but those resources are limited by what information is digital. The odds that a subject's yearbook photo is available on-line are directly affected by how recently that photo was taken. The chances are extremely slim that a high school or college graduation photo or permanent student record from 1953 has been scanned, indexed, and annotated. No hacker, regardless of skill, can access information that has not been stored digitally. If the information only exists on paper, you're not going to find it on the Internet (despite what you see on television).

"There's No Such Thing as a Free Lunch"

Perhaps a better warning is: "you get what you pay for." Most of the resources discussed in this book are available at no cost, while a few may charge nominal fees of a few dollars. Why aren't more sites free? The question you should actually ask is, "Why aren't fewer sites free?" When using free and low-cost Internet sites, it's a good idea to consider why the information is available for free. Government sites may make information freely available to meet legal obligations under federal and state Sunshine laws; they can save time and labor costs if customers can access documents directly instead of asking a government employee to access it for them. Some companies may also make corporate documents available on-line to enhance customer service or meet financial disclosure obligations.

Private websites, however, are likely not under any obligation to provide any information to the public of any kind. So why do they? A nonprofit entity may receive grants and donations to fund website maintenance, but a business needs to make money. How do they make money while providing you free information? Depending on their business model, the company might rely on advertising or sponsored links. They can require a free registration and subsequently sell the personal information they obtain. Or they could provide you with limited free information in order to get you to purchase more complete records. Regardless of which method these sites use, remember that you are helping them to make money even if you don't pay them with a check or credit card.

If you have found a link to important information from a private website, especially one that requires a subscription or payment, stop and consider where *they* get their information. Many commercial websites earn their money by creating their own paid version of free information. Some of these for-profit companies are doing exactly the same type of thing you are doing—they're just doing it bigger and faster. Always consider the ultimate source of the information you are accessing. If you are looking at recorded documents from the local county office, consider how the paid service obtained those records. Did they pay the county to obtain copies of the documents, spend employee time scanning those copies, and create their own database of all the scanned documents? Or does their database merely search a database you can search yourself for free?

It is very important to understand the source of documents you access on the Internet. This information can help you judge the credibility of the documents and evaluate whether payment for those documents is appropriate. Understanding the source of documents will also be important as part of authenticating those documents if you use them as part of the basis for your final determination or recommendation.

Case in Point

I routinely check my credit report and I strongly recommend everyone else does as well. Mistakes happen: a payment might not be posted correctly or the wrong account might be referred to collections. Identity thieves may apply for (and be granted) extensive credit in someone else's name. Unfortunately, identity thieves can also steal your good credit (and burden you with their bad credit) with amazing ease. I know because it happened to me.

While I'm not going to describe the method used, I will say that the woman who stole my credit did so with relative ease. She didn't have to rifle through my garbage or steal my mail. As far as I know, to this day she doesn't have my Social Security Number. And yet her bad credit, collections, and judgments periodically show up on my credit report—presumably, my good credit shows up on hers as well (otherwise I doubt she ever would have qualified for the mortgage or car loan that recently appeared).

Information from the credit bureaus is commonly included in many paid database reports. In my case, that information may be wildly incorrect and completely unreliable. That is why it is a good practice to verify the information you obtain from paid databases. Otherwise, you could be embarrassed when your subject publicly corrects you in front of your boss or a judge.

2 *Before You Start: Ethical Considerations*

All of the advice and website resources discussed in this book are available to anyone, mostly for free or for a negligible cost through the Internet, the local library, or a local government office. Does that mean you should collect any and all information you can, or are there limits on what you can and should do? There may not be a universal answer to that question, but there are some important points to keep in mind when conducting an investigation.

Types of Ethical Issues

Ethical concerns in financial investigations generally fall into three categories: legal issues, privacy issues, and disclosure issues. It is important to remember that with our society's constantly changing technologies, issues related to privacy and disclosure are in a constant state of flux. However, as a government employee, you have a fiduciary responsibility to the citizens of your jurisdiction. You work for *them*, and your actions must be for *their* benefit—not your benefit, not your manager's benefit, and not your agency's benefit. If you do not work for a government agency, your behavior must still be ethical, even if for no other reason than the trouble you may find yourself in if you engage in questionable behavior.

LEGAL ISSUES

The first legal issue to consider is the extent of your authority. What law, rule, or regulation gives you the authority to snoop around in someone else's private affairs? That authority may or may not have clearly defined limits. If you work for a law enforcement agency, there is likely a bright-line rule about what you may or may not pursue and what may require a warrant, subpoena, or court order. Employees of regulatory agencies may not be so lucky—there may not be case law to tell you where the dividing line is.

If you are unsure what information you are authorized to collect, limit yourself to public information that anyone could obtain. While a subject may believe that the documents related to their home should not be public records, that belief is not your immediate concern. Those documents *are* public records that anyone can obtain. There is no ethical reason why you may not obtain a copy of those records if they are germane to your investigation. Access to some types of records is restricted and can only be obtained through a waiver, subpoena, court order, or similar legal document. If you are unsure whether to collect these types of records, consult your agency's attorney for assistance. Medical and other legally protected records should never be acquired without a specific reason and without the express consent of the subject (or a legal document such as a court order authorizing collection against the subject's wishes).

The next legal issue you may face is what to do if you discover a legal violation that falls outside the scope of your authority. For example, what if you work for a state regulatory agency and your investigation shows the subject lied on their federal taxes? Should you contact the Internal Revenue Service and let them know? What if you learn the subject regularly hires undocumented workers? Are you obligated to contact Immigration Services? In some cases, such as suspicions of child abuse, you may be legally obligated to report your discovery. When that is not the case, you might be lucky enough to have an employer who has an established policy covering these circumstances. If neither of those situations applies, you may need to make that decision for yourself. If you find yourself in this unenviable position, there are steps you can take to determine the best course of action:

1. Consult a more experienced employee in your organization who has handled a similar situation. Find out how they handled it. Not only can this information help guide your decision making, but it also provides a basis for comparison. Consistency and proportionality with previous determinations are important components in making a proper decision. It increases the likelihood that your decision will be fair and that it will be perceived as fair if it is subsequently reviewed by a judge or other decision maker.
2. Consult an outside expert. This might be the attorney general or prosecutor assigned to represent your agency, a criminal or civil investigator from a related agency, or an outside consultant you've worked with on other cases. When consulting an outside expert, do not reveal specifics of the case unless the expert can legally keep that information confidential. Revealing information to the attorney who represents you is probably fine; no one else should be given specifics like the name of the subject or the specific legal violation you have discovered. While these outside experts may not be able to help you make your decision, they can probably give you advice about what the law requires you to do, what the law allows you to do, and how your decision might be perceived by a judge or other parties.
3. Check professional rules, even those that do not apply to you. You do not need to be a CPA to find out what an accountant would do in your situation. You do not need to be a lawyer to check the ethics rules for attorneys. Many professional organizations, including the Association of Certified Fraud Examiners and the Council of International Investigators, maintain codes of ethics that might be informative. Finding out what a professional would do in your situation may provide the best guidance.

Finally, remember that everything you do must be completely and totally proper, legal, and ethical. There is no "grey area." Do not attempt to obtain information under false pretenses, including lies of omission. The same thing applies to having someone else do something unethical on your behalf. In some very limited cases, subterfuge ("the use of pretext or deception about who you are in order to obtain information that may not otherwise be forthcoming") by an *expert* investigator or forensic accountant *may* be an acceptable investigative technique (Golden & Dyer 2006: 364). However, subterfuge or other deceptive practices are *never* acceptable or advisable for a casual or amateur investigator. If you believe that relevant information can only be obtained through subterfuge, you should assume that the case exceeds your investigative skill level and you should involve experienced investigation staff. Failing to abide by this restriction is likely to seriously damage your credibility as an analyst or expert, and will probably destroy your case.

PRIVACY ISSUES

Privacy seems to be a disappearing commodity. Just what is "private" information anymore? How much you earn, how much you paid for your house, your unlisted telephone number, or your criminal history? Much of this information may be legally available to anyone who wants it—sometimes for free, sometimes for a price. Nevertheless, just because something is available, does that mean you should collect it? Your state may have regulations about what information is public and what is not. Your agency may also have policies, procedures, or guidelines about what information is "fair game" and what isn't.

When thinking about information that is available on the Internet, I usually classify the sources into three categories: public, semi-public, and private. Each category of information is determined by who can access the information and how they go about gaining that access. The source of information can help guide you as to its proper use and application.

Information that is "public" is that which is generally available to anyone searching the Internet. If there are no restrictions on who can view or otherwise access the information, then you can consider the information public and it is probably acceptable to collect and use it. Many websites fall into this category, including results from search engines, personal and business web sites, and Internet resources such as Wikipedia and the Internet Archive.

"Semi-public" websites are those that restrict access to certain users, but allow almost everyone to become an eligible user. A common restriction for semi-public websites is payment of a fee; the information is restricted to those who pay a specified fee, but anyone who pays the fee can access the information. Another common restriction is a free membership; you must be a member to access the site's information, but anyone is allowed to become a member. Semi-public information is usually going to be acceptable, but be careful of sites that engage in discriminatory practices (e.g., only women can access the information, only members of certain religious organizations are eligible to become members, etc.) Examples of semi-public websites include business information sites like Hoovers and Dun & Bradstreet, public records compilation sites like KnowX, and social networking sites such as Myspace or Classmates.com.

Finally, some information will only be available on "private" websites. Private websites are restricted to certain groups and do not have open membership. Payment of a fee may be involved, but is not a requirement to classify a website as private. Some private websites restrict access based on employment, such as those that are only available to law enforcement officers or regulatory employees. These sites are private and not semi-public because only certain professions can access the information—you can't simply become a sworn peace officer so you can access the website. If information is restricted based on employment, make sure you are actually eligible to access the information and that you don't violate the terms and conditions of the website before basing your case on the information you collect. Examples of private websites include a company's virtual private network (VPN) or intranet, law enforcement databases such as the National Crime Information Center (NCIC), or scholarly databases such as JSTOR and EBSCOhost.

Depending on privacy settings, some websites may fall into more than one of these categories. Facebook is probably the best example of a site that limits information in such a way that it can be public, semi-public, or private. If a Facebook user sets their permissions to allow "everyone" to see their information, it is accessible to anyone who is a member of Facebook and may even be partially visible through public websites such as Google. If a Facebook user sets their permissions to allow "only friends" to see their information, you will need to have that person confirm you are their "friend" before you will be able to see the information, making the information "semi-public." If the user restricts access to only certain people, that information will probably fall into the "private" category.

What should you do if you don't have a law, regulation, or policy about what information you are allowed to collect? As explained above, you must first determine whether you can legally obtain the records from someone other than the subject. Keep in mind that some institutions no longer keep long-term records because they don't want to be legally obligated to produce information they deem private. The best example of this is libraries that delete borrower records after the material has been returned, rather than possibly being required to produce those borrower records in accordance with the Patriot Act. "At the end of each day, Schaumburg, Ill., library employees delete the names of those who have used computers" (Orecklin *et al.* 2003).

Second, ask yourself if the information is actually germane to your investigation. Where a business owner went to high school might or might not be applicable. If it was at the same school and timeframe as the person who allegedly purchased a significant company asset for far below market value, it's probably relevant. If not, it probably isn't. Divorce records detailing adultery allegations are probably not relevant unless they indicate how a business owner's paramour helped hide their assets from the jilted spouse. If it's not directly relevant to your investigation, you probably don't have a legitimate reason for collecting the information even if it is readily available. The mere fact that the information is easy to find does not justify collection.

Third, ask yourself if you would object to a stranger having the same information about you. While this is an admittedly "loosey-goosey" guideline, it is a reasonable question to ask. Some of us may object to others knowing what brand of toothpaste we use, while others wouldn't mind discussing the most intimate details of our lives. If you can't honestly say that you would consent to releasing that information to someone you didn't personally know, you should at least ask yourself whether you should be collecting that information about someone else.

DISCLOSURE ISSUES

Once you actually collect information, you may be faced with possible disclosure issues. If you work for a government agency of any kind, you work for the people—and the people generally have a right to know what you're doing and how you're doing it. Even if you don't work for the government, you may still be required to disclose the information you uncover because of a lawsuit, subpoena, or court order. Your investigation will produce evidence that someone else may want to obtain.

If your investigation is related to possible criminal charges, civil charges, or financial penalties, the documents may be eligible for an exemption from public disclosure because they are related to enforcement actions. During the course of your investigation, documents may likewise be exempt from disclosure because they are related to an on-going investigation. There is a good reason for these types of disclosure exemptions: you don't want to tip off the subject and give them a chance to cover their tracks before your investigation is complete. Just remember that even these "enforcement sensitive" documents will eventually have to be disclosed, either as proof of wrongdoing or as exculpatory evidence in future proceedings. Of course, after the conclusion of an enforcement action, all documents will likely be subject to disclosure unless protected by a court order or other legal document.

If the information does not qualify as enforcement sensitive or if it is not otherwise exempt from Freedom of Information Act (FOIA) or other public disclosure requirements (such as your state's "sunshine" laws), you may be legally obligated to share it with people unrelated to the investigation. If your investigation reveals that the subject has been surreptitiously substituting substandard parts to increase their company's profit margin, should you disclose this information to their customers and competitors or protect it as "confidential business information?" If you find a bank account the subject failed to disclose, should you tell their soon-to-be-former spouse? If you learn where a business owner lives and their unlisted phone number, are you obligated to disclose that information to their former boy/girlfriend who might be stalking them? On the other hand, doesn't the public—for whom we all work—have a right to know what we are doing on their behalf with their money?

You will likely need to decide which information should be subject to a FOIA request and which should be exempt on a case-by-case basis in accordance with appropriate regulations and agency guidelines. However, information from websites in the "public" category and other information that is generally available for free on the Internet (such as information from semi-public sites requiring a free registration) are likely *not* going to be exempt from disclosure. Once information is part of the public domain, it is virtually impossible to "put the genie back in the bottle." Information from paid databases or that which is legally protected is likely the only information that could be non-disclosable. In other words, if you found it through Google, then you probably can't protect it. If you paid for the information, you might be able to protect some of it but still be required to explain where and how you got the information. Depending on how stringent your state disclosure laws are, you may even be required to disclose information you paid to obtain or which you believe should be confidential. This requirement may play a role in whether you choose to collect sensitive information.

Not all organizations have similar attitudes towards disclosure. From my personal experience, I can attest that some organizations try to restrict access to any and all information in their files while others disclose information that is actually protected. The best course of action is to follow the law that applies to you, whether or not that law favors disclosure. Do not mark documents as being "enforcement sensitive," "privileged," or otherwise exempt from disclosure if there isn't clear justification for doing so. For example, you shouldn't assume an email is subject to attorney-client privilege just because a lawyer was cc'd on the message; not every communication with a lawyer is exempt from public disclosure. On the other hand, you want to carefully review documents for confidential information such as Social Security Numbers, bank account numbers, or credit and debit card numbers and redact any highly sensitive or personal information that is protected by law.

If you don't know whether information is protected, check with your public records officer or the attorney representing your organization. Courts in your state may have interpreted your public disclosure laws in a way you didn't expect, or the public records law in your jurisdiction might not be well written or easy to understand. Someone with specific training can help you make a legally sound and defensible decision about releasing information.

"Let's Be Careful Out There"

Staying safe is more than just good common sense. When conducting an investigation, especially when doing so in person, you have an ethical obligation to keep yourself out of harm's way. As a government employee, you are covered by the government's insurance and worker's compensation programs when you are on the job. Those programs are paid for by taxpayers. If you are injured while conducting an investigation, you are likely going to cost the taxpayers money. Sometimes that cannot be avoided. Other times, a few simple steps can help avoid harm to you and cost to the taxpayers.

The first and most obvious way to prevent harm during an investigation is to avoid confrontations whenever possible. That may mean not pursuing a lead or stopping an investigation before you have finished so you can remove yourself from a potentially dangerous situation. If you are confronted by anyone who threatens your physical safety, the best course of action is frequently to simply leave.

Unfortunately, leaving is not always possible. In those cases, having support from a fellow investigator may be helpful. Law enforcement personnel are trained to call for backup when needed; regulatory employees may need to do the same. The presence of another person can help defuse a confrontation. A subject who might otherwise be willing to engage in physical violence may reconsider due to the presence of a witness.

If you choose to take someone with you while investigating, you need to avoid making the subject feel as if you are ganging up on them. Being on the short side of two against one is not a comfortable position. In some circumstances, bringing backup may actually escalate a potentially dangerous situation. To avoid this, you may want to consider using one of the following techniques.

1. "Good cop/bad cop." Having another investigator present can allow you to "play good cop/bad cop." This strategy can help defuse a potentially harmful situation by providing the subject with an ally; instead of being two against one, it becomes one against one, with the "good cop" acting as mediator between the two. Using this technique requires both investigators to have extensive knowledge of the case and to plan ahead for the possible twists and turns that may develop during the course of an interview or other investigation.
2. "Meet the new guy." Having your backup fulfill the role of a trainee can also be an effective investigation technique. The backup is there to learn, not to actually investigate the subject, so they are not a significant threat. The trainee can ask questions in a non-threatening way because they are not familiar with the specifics of the case. Having an experienced investigator ask a subject why they took a particular

action can be threatening, while the same question coming from a trainee may be perceived as naïve or inexperienced. If you choose to use this technique, make sure you do so in an honest manner. Don't take the most experienced investigator in your office with you and try to pass them off as a "trainee." The best choice for this technique is a new employee that actually needs the experience. Barring that possibility, use a less-experienced investigator who is unfamiliar with most of the specifics of the case. Brief them only on what they need to know ahead of time. Leave the rest for after the interview.

3. "Meet my boss." Bringing a more seasoned investigator with you can also be an effective technique. In this case, your backup might be presented to the subject as someone who is there to observe and/or evaluate your investigation and interview techniques. Again, the backup is less threatening to the subject because they are not an adversary. Just as in the "trainee" technique, the "evaluator" technique should only be used if is passably true: don't try to pretend an inexperienced employee is there to give you advice on how to do your job better. At the conclusion of the interview, the evaluator should attempt to give you constructive feedback on how to improve your performance, even if that feedback is not official or made a part of your personnel record.

One last consideration in taking backup with you is the protection of the subject. That person is a member of the public as well—you work for them just like you work for the rest of your community. They also deserve protection, even if it is from themselves. If taking backup with you on an investigation helps prevent a subject from physically harming you, both you and the subject are better off: you don't have to recover from an injury, and the subject won't have to face criminal charges for assaulting you. As long as you don't unintentionally inflame the situation, bringing along another person does both of you a favor.

Protecting yourself is not limited to situations where you are physically confronted by the subject of your investigation. As you will discover later in this book, a seemingly insignificant piece of information can lead a skilled investigator to all sorts of personal information. Protecting yourself means not only protecting yourself against a physical assault, but also against identity theft, cyberbullying, and stalking. Never use your home address, home or personal cell-phone number, or your personal email address when conducting an investigation. If you need to register in order to access information on a website, use your work contact information or a dummy registration. If the work you do is at all controversial, it is probably a good idea to keep your personal phone numbers unlisted and, if possible, your home address disguised. Don't divulge personal information to the subject or others associated with your investigation. Don't let them know where your kids go to school, your dog's name, where you went to college, or other unique information. While the odds of a subject doing something harmful with that information may be remote, your safety and the safety of your family are too important to take a chance.

Additional Requirements

If you have a special license or certification, you may be subject to additional ethical requirements beyond those of a normal regulatory employee. Attorneys, accountants, law enforcement officers, and private investigators are just some of the professions that may impose standards of professional behavior. Some voluntary groups also impose additional ethics requirements on their members. If you belong to a group or profession that imposes additional or more stringent behavior requirements, make sure you follow those requirements even if you are not doing work directly related to that group or profession. That means if you are an attorney, follow the ethics rules governing attorneys even when you are not doing law-related work. Failure to do so may expose you to professional discipline or other sanctions, even though you may not see a connection between your behavior and an ethics rule.

Potential Liability

There are a number of potential consequences you could face if you engage in unethical behavior: reprimand, suspension, and termination from your job are just the most obvious. While most public employees are protected by law from private lawsuits, unethical behavior may fall outside protected activities. Not only can you be sued, your employer might not pay for a lawyer to defend you. If your behavior crosses the line from unethical into potentially illegal, the odds are very good that you may need to hire your own defense attorney. "Official misconduct" is a broad category covering many offenses that should be avoided at all costs. As a public servant, higher standards apply to you than to your private-sector colleagues.

Power Corrupts, Absolute Power Corrupts Absolutely

It is important to keep a realistic perspective on the rules you enforce, the subject you are investigating, and the proper use of your power. It can be easy to lose perspective during an investigation; mountains and molehills become interchangeable. Some actions should be avoided even if they are legal and arguably ethical.

The distinguishing characteristic of government is the legal power to use coercion. Sometimes that coercion takes the form of violence (e.g., the death penalty) and sometimes it takes the form of compulsory behavior (e.g., paying taxes). While coercion may not be inherently unethical, its indiscriminant use is. Thomas Jefferson advised that, "The government is best which governs least." That statement is frequently misinterpreted as an indictment of big government. Actually, it is an indictment of tyranny—that is, coercive government irrespective of size. Whenever possible, cooperation and voluntary compliance should be your first strategy. Reliance on authority should be limited to cases where it is absolutely necessary.

As an employee of a regulatory or law enforcement agency, your actions may be perceived as a form of coercion. Courts in the United States have found that when law enforcement officials ask questions, it might be inherently coercive.[1] Regulatory employees, attorneys, and private investigators all operate with some legal authority that can be perceived as threatening. It may seem routine to you, but it is possible the subject will not agree. The determining factor is whether an outsider will agree that your actions were reasonable and necessary, given the specifics of the investigation. This is even more important when the outsider is a judge:

> [T]here is nothing more reprehensible to the law than an agent of the government causing unnecessary and unreasonable damage to the person or property of a person while performing— or purporting to perform—a government function. It is not necessary that the State and its agents choose the means that causes the least damage, so long as the means chosen is reasonable under all of the circumstances. There may be a legitimate basis for breaking down doors the owner stands ready and willing to unlock. But that use of force should be subject to scrutiny. The State must be prepared to show it was reasonable under all of the circumstances Brutsche v. City of Kent, 164 Wn.2d 664, 686, 193 P.3d 110 (2008) (Chambers, J., dissenting in part).

Whether it is breaking down a door or snooping in bank records, our society is based on the premise that the government should avoid using force whenever possible. When you find yourself losing perspective, keep in mind that it is not your job to punish anyone. You're not there to "get" the bad guy by playing judge and jury. Your role is to assemble the facts and find the truth so judges and juries can make the best decision possible. When you allow an investigation to become personal, you run the risk of crossing that very important line.

Remember the Repercussions

Remember that your investigation will have long-ranging effects that you may not be able to predict. At the very least, your investigation will create a paper trail that may be consulted in future proceedings. A business competitor may request a copy of your investigation file and use the information to gain a competitive advantage over the subject. Your findings could lead to criminal charges, civil lawsuits, or financial penalties. If you are not careful, you can unwittingly damage an innocent person's good name and reputation beyond repair.

You may also damage your own good name and reputation. Having a reputation as a "loose cannon" makes it harder to do your job. Decision makers won't trust your work. Opposing counsel can more easily discredit your findings. Your colleagues will hesitate to consult you or assist you on a complicated investigation for fear of being "tainted" by your reputation. Establishing and preserving a reputation as an honest and accurate investigator will help you be better at your job.

That means there is one overriding ethical imperative: *get it right*. Decisions will be made based on the information you obtain and the story you eventually tell. If you confuse one person for another, one company for another, or who owns a particular asset, you can inadvertently cause significant problems. Part of getting it right means using all the information you find instead of "cherry-picking" the evidence that best fits

---

1   See, for example, *Miranda v. Arizona*, 384 U.S. 436 (1966).

your preconceived notions. The point of conducting an investigation is to *investigate*, not to simply collect information that proves a predetermined conclusion.

One final caution: if you are still not convinced about the need to maintain ethical behavior at all times during an investigation, check out what can happen to you if you do not. Try using the techniques you learn in this book to research former Hewlett-Packard Chairman Patricia Dunn. It will give you a real world example of what can happen if you choose to ignore this warning.

Case in Point

In 2009, the Philadelphia Bar Association Professional Guidance Committee issued an ethics opinion regarding the potential use of subterfuge in a legal matter. A lawyer inquired whether he could ask his paralegal to "friend" a potential adverse witness on her Facebook account and possibly gain information that could be used to discredit her testimony. The paralegal intended to use his real name and information, but conceal his relationship with the law firm. The Professional Guidance Committee determined that even though no false information would be given, the situation would still be unethical. "Deception is deception, regardless of the victim's wariness in her interactions on the Internet and susceptibility to being deceived" (Philadelphia Bar Association 2009: 3).

Luckily, the lawyer asked for advice *before* he proceeded. If he hadn't, he could have faced both professional disciplinary charges as well as having his evidence thrown out. In this specific case, the information may have fallen into the "semi-public" category, but the only way the lawyer could have joined the group entitled to access the information was through omitting key details. Since attorneys are required to be fully honest when dealing with non-represented individuals like witnesses and other parties,[2] failing to disclose his or his employee's lack of neutrality would have violated the rules applicable to his profession. Even if you are not a lawyer, following the same guidelines can be a good way to protect yourself from problems when presenting your investigation results or defending your final recommendations

---

2   See, for example, the American Bar Association's Model Rules for Professional Conduct Rule 4.3: "In dealing on behalf of a client with a person who is not represented by counsel, a lawyer shall not state or imply that the lawyer is disinterested. When the lawyer knows or reasonably should know that the unrepresented person misunderstands the lawyer's role in the matter, the lawyer shall make reasonable efforts to correct the misunderstanding ..." The Model Rules are available at http://www.abanet.org/cpr/mrpc/mrpc_toc.html.

3 *Thinking About Financial Fraud and Investigations*

Part of detecting deception is consciously moving beyond our preconceived notions. Many of us (including many business owners) frequently associate crime with poverty, lack of education, and lack of opportunity. However, the evidence does not support these assumptions, especially when it comes to financial crimes. White-collar criminals are more likely to be highly educated, married, and religious and less likely to have histories of substance abuse, psychological problems, or criminal records (Silverstone & Sheets 2004). In other words, they're more likely to have a lot in common with you (the investigator) than with your preconceived idea of a "criminal."

The first step in conducting a financial investigation is acknowledging and trying to work around the stereotypes that we all have. Stereotypes and preconceptions don't always mean you assume the worst—presuming someone is telling the truth simply because she's a sweet-looking little old lady who reminds you of your favorite grandmother is making a determination based on a preconception. Assuming someone wouldn't lie to you just because they share your culture, religion, or educational background is also a form of stereotyping. We all want to believe we aren't prejudiced, but we need to acknowledge that some people just make us feel awkward or tense. Be objective and honest and be willing to admit (at least to yourself) when you just aren't comfortable with someone because of their ethnicity, religion, political philosophy, gender, sexual orientation, socioeconomic class, personality, or some other factor. It's also possible that you may be the object of discomfort—your subject may not be able to deal with you fairly because of your gender, ethnicity, religion, etc. If you can't set those feelings of discomfort aside, you may need to consult with a manager to help you assess the situation. In the worst-case scenario, you may need to transfer the case to a co-worker or work with a more experienced colleague to develop a strategy for helping you deal with your discomfort.

The next step is clearly establishing the goal and parameters of your investigation. What are you trying to accomplish? Your review should be limited to the information that is relevant to that goal. The subject of your investigation may be a truly vile human being who beats his dog, disrespects his mother, and cheats at cards. Unless that information is somehow relevant to your inquiry, it falls outside the parameters of your investigation. It is a good practice to clearly identify both your goal and limitations as part of your investigation plan before you start.

Standards of Proof

It is always important to clearly identify the applicable standard of proof before you start your investigation. Taking this step at the beginning can guide your investigation and help you know when you have collected enough evidence to make a final determination. In the US, you'll probably have to meet one of the following standards to prove your case.

BEYOND A REASONABLE DOUBT

This is the standard that is used in criminal proceedings and is the most difficult to meet. If you must prove your case "beyond a reasonable doubt," that means a judge, jury, or other decision maker cannot have a doubt that the defendant is actually guilty of committing the crime for which they are accused.

PREPONDERANCE OF THE EVIDENCE

This is the standard that is used in civil proceedings. A preponderance standard simply means it is "more likely than not" that something happened or is true. In other words, majority rules. If six documents support conclusion A and four documents support conclusion B (assuming all the documents have equal weight and are equally trustworthy), conclusion A gets the nod.

CLEAR AND CONVINCING EVIDENCE

This standard is less common and falls somewhere between the other two standards. The law may require proof by "clear and convincing evidence" when someone is at risk of losing a right or property of great worth, such as parental rights or a license needed for work (like a medical license). Many administrative proceedings use this standard. I have never found a definition of "clear and convincing evidence" that I actually like. *West's Encyclopedia of American Law* states:

> *Clear and convincing proof means that the evidence presented by a party during the trial is more highly probable to be true than not and the jury or judge has a firm belief or conviction in it. A greater degree of believability must be met than the common standard of proof in civil actions, PREPONDERANCE OF THE EVIDENCE, which requires that the facts more likely than not prove the issue for which they are asserted (eNotes 2006).*

An easy (if non-technical) way of thinking about it is if "beyond a reasonable doubt" is being 100 percent sure, and "preponderance of the evidence" is being 51 percent sure, then "clear and convincing evidence" is somewhere in the neighborhood of being 75 percent sure. If you're only 60 percent sure the doctor sent out falsified billing statements, you probably don't have enough to take away their license.

Categories of Failure to Disclose

When starting a financial investigation, it can also be helpful to think about what type of deception or "failure to disclose" that you believe you are encountering. This might be based on the type of information being withheld, the subject's demeanor, or maybe nothing more than a gut feeling about someone. These are not hard and fast categories, but instead are meant to be fluid and flexible. You may need to re-categorize a subject based on their subsequent behavior, so don't get too locked into one or another.

NEGLIGENT OMISSION

The first group of subjects that fail to disclose their assets are those that do so negligently. Frequently, this subject simply does not understand what they are supposed to disclose or they inadvertently overlook disclosure of an asset. These subjects are not purposefully shirking their responsibilities—they may have simply forgotten that old savings account they never use or they didn't realize they were listed on the title when they helped their son or daughter buy their first car. Subjects in this category are typically honest people who simply made a mistake. I have found that assets in this category tend to have relatively small values, which may explain why subjects overlook them.

KNOWING OMISSION

The second category of subjects that fail to disclose their assets are those that do so knowingly. These subjects push the envelope of what is or is not acceptable. These subjects are trying to minimize their reportable assets but they will only do so if they can justify or rationalize their attempt to do so. For example, they may realize they are listed as an owner on the title but would argue that "it's really my husband's car, not mine" in an attempt to justify excluding it from their list of assets. Owners in this category will often consider themselves to be honest people, and when confronted with an omitted asset they may attribute the omission to an "oversight." In my experience, assets in this category are typically worth a moderate amount when compared to the subject's other assets and may include items the subject thinks are not easily traceable, like vacation homes in distant locales, personal watercraft, or airplanes.

INTENTIONAL OMISSION

The final category of subjects that fail to disclose their assets are those that do so intentionally—those who are willing to take extensive steps to hide assets. These subjects don't just flirt with the line of acceptable behavior, they completely ignore it. They may transfer ownership of key assets to other people, they may establish shell companies to disguise ownership, and they may set up trusts or similar vehicles in order to shelter their assets. In extreme cases, they may engage in blatantly illegal activities in order to disguise their wealth. While this category of evasive owners may be the most difficult to detect, you will frequently get the biggest payoff from finding this type of deception.

FULL DISCLOSURE

Depending on the nature of your investigation, you may not initially suspect any deception at all. That is important as well. Some financial investigations may be nothing more than a routine verification of eligibility—making sure all the Ts are crossed and the Is are dotted. The Internet is well suited to handle these types of investigations because you can quickly obtain third-party verification of needed information.

UNDERREPORTED VALUES VERSUS "TRUTHINESS"

One potential problem with all categories of omission is the "truthiness"[1] factor. Many subjects are surprisingly careless when asked to report their assets. Instead of checking their most recent bank statement, getting an asset appraised, or checking the Internet for the price of comparable items, they will simply guess how much is in their account or report how much they feel something is worth. In my personal experience, asking them to sign "under penalty of perjury" seems to have no effect of the accuracy of the document or the reported values.

Finally, you should keep in mind that a financial statement produced in order to obtain a loan may look very different from one produced to support a claim of poverty. You can call it "spin" or you can call it "tailoring," but a smart subject will customize a financial disclosure for the given purpose. If possible, try to compare similar types of documents submitted by the subject for different reasons. If the form they gave the bank says they have real estate worth $1 million, the form they give you should say the same thing. If they filed a Uniform Commercial Code (UCC) form showing a $500,000 loan was collateralized with the firm's company vehicles, they shouldn't suddenly decide that those vehicles no longer have any resale value.

When Disclosure is Not Required

It is extremely important to be careful of "contingent" assets and liabilities. Contingent liabilities are financial obligations that may or may not develop in the future. Co-signing a mortgage or other loan is a common contingent liability—the co-signer isn't obligated to pay on the loan unless the primary borrower defaults. These types of arrangements may create the appearance of legal ownership because the co-signer may be listed as an owner of the asset. They may also create the appearance of a liability that reduces the subject's net worth, even though that liability is only a potential liability. It is always important to review the underlying documents to determine whether an ownership interest is real and substantial and whether the debt is actually owed.

A Word of Caution

A final word of caution on failure to disclose: *always confirm ownership* before taking action based on a failure to disclose. Mistakenly accusing a subject of failure to disclose will not only harm your credibility as an investigator but will understandably make the subject less willing to work with you. Consider visiting the property (if feasible) or sending a letter to the subject to verify your beliefs before you take action. If you do visit the property, make sure you do not trespass or otherwise invade a subject's privacy. Taking photos from a public street or sidewalk may be legally different from stepping onto the property in question to take the same photo. When in doubt, err on the side of caution.

---

1   "Truthiness" is a word attributed to comedian Stephen Colbert and his television show, "The Colbert Report." The American Dialect Society named it their 2005 "Word of the Year" and says, "truthiness refers to the quality of preferring concepts or facts one wishes to be true, rather than concepts or facts known to be true." More information is available at *http://www.americandialect.org/index.php/amerdial/truthiness_voted_2005_word_of_the_year/*.

"Financial Profiling"

One investigation technique that deserves a brief mention is "financial profiling." This technique involves analyzing known assets and funds and comparing them against known sources. This is an advanced technique that is not typically something that you would use for a casual or occasional investigation and is not generally applicable to Internet-based investigations. However, financial profiling is an analysis technique that you should be aware of for two important reasons: you might be asked to assist with one and the basic principles can help guide your investigation on the Internet. There are three basic approaches to financial profiling: the "Net Worth" method, the "Expenditure" method, and the "Deposit" method. Each of these methods is an excellent way to demonstrate a subject has assets exceeding their reported means of support. Each can also provide excellent circumstantial evidence the subject has unreported sources of income.

NET WORTH FINANCIAL PROFILING

This method of financial profiling compares a subject's assets and equity and against their known income. For example, if your subject claims to only earn $40,000 annually, but they live in a home worth $3 million, there is a discrepancy between their assets and their known income. That discrepancy may have a legitimate explanation: they could have inherited the property, they could have won the home as a prize, they could have won the lottery and purchased the home outright, or maybe they received the home in a divorce settlement. Any of these explanations could legitimately explain how the subject's assets and income could be so disparate.

However, each legitimate explanation for a disparity between Net Worth and income leaves a documentary trail that you can follow using Internet-based investigation techniques. Remember that once it's in cyberspace, it's hard to eliminate. Internet auctions, classified ads, and newsletters all leave a permanent record. That means if a subject claims to have sold a valuable art collection on eBay, you may be able to find a record of the auction and what the final bid was. That will either confirm or refute the subjects claim to no longer own the asset in question and the amount of funds they generated from the sale.

EXPENDITURE PROFILING

This method of financial profiling compares a subject's expenditures against their known income. Similar to the "Net Worth" method, this technique examines whether there have been increases or decreases in assets, increases or decreases in liabilities, and the subject's living expenses for a given period. These increases, decreases, and other expenses are compared to known sources of income for the same timeframe. Assume your subject earning $40,000 lives in a $3 million home and you have been able to establish the subject received the home as part of a divorce settlement. If your investigation on the Internet reveals the property taxes for the home are $30,000 each year—more than the subject brings home after taxes—you have shown a discrepancy that still needs explanation.

In a "Net Worth" or "Expenditure" analysis, the explanation will leave a paper trail that you can follow, whether that trail indicates the subject has income they've failed to disclose or perhaps that someone else is helping to pay the subject's expenses. However, using the Internet to substantiate expenses can be more difficult. Although you may be able to find clues about a probable dollar range, it may be impossible to find exact costs for many items. Real-estate property taxes are one notable exception to this rule: you can usually determine the exact amount of property taxes paid in a given year, but you may have difficulty proving who actually made the payment.

DEPOSIT PROFILING

Finally, the "Deposit" method of financial profiling compares a subject's banking activities against their known income. This method requires full access to the subject's bank records and assumes that the subject can either spend their money in cash or spend it by running it through a financial institution. This method is less comprehensive than the other two methods and is not particularly useful in an Internet-based investigation. However, as with the other analysis methods, the Internet can help substantiate or refute claims made by a subject related to their income or expenses.

Case in Point

The truthiness factor can play a big part in whether your subject's report of their assets is accurate or vastly understated. During one investigation, I had a subject who didn't feel her personal assets were particularly valuable. She reported a respectable income, some investments and retirement accounts, a home with a market value over $300,000, and a vacation home. That was all she disclosed—no vehicles, no art, no collections, and no personal property of any kind. When I asked her to correct her disclosure statement to account for the missing personal property, she disclosed a couple of vehicles and $3,000 of household furnishings. Two very nice houses and $3,000 of furnishings? As a mere civil servant not long out of college with a very modest income, even I had more than $3,000 worth of furniture, electronics, china, books, and clothing.

This particular owner was an excellent example of a subject who knowingly underreported the value of some of her assets and negligently underreported some of her other assets. The subject's initial failure to disclose her vehicles and other personal property was knowing, but her undervaluing the property after it was disclosed is a good example of how truthiness comes into play. Did she really believe she only had $3,000 worth of personal property? Maybe at first; it was a comfortable story to tell herself and reaffirmed her mistaken belief that she wasn't a "wealthy" person. That belief was shattered when I pointed out the amount of insurance she had on her personal belongings. All I had to do was ask if she would be able to replace even a portion of her belongings if there were a fire or other disaster and her insurance company only paid her $3,000. When she finally provided a copy of her insurance policy, it actually covered almost $80,000 of personal property. Eventually, she dropped her appeal of my determination.

4 *What Can You Do With Money?*

"What can you do with money?" It may seem like a silly question, but it's not. What can you actually do with money?

Although it may not feel like it after paying the bills each month, money never actually disappears. It can move, it can change hands, and it can change form, but it never goes away. That means "money" isn't the same as "value." "Money" is a tangible object that comes in many forms: coins, bank notes, gold, silver, or anything else that can be exchanged for something of value. "Value" is intangible—it is an attempt to quantify a belief about relative worth. A dollar is a dollar. However, a dollar can buy more or less depending on how many dollars there are in the world.

If money is a tangible object that never disappears, what can you do with it? As it turns out, surprisingly little. There are basically four things you can do with money.

1. Give it to someone else for safekeeping ("D"eposit it in a holding account).
2. Give it to someone else for their use ("I"nvest it in a business venture).
3. Use it for your own purposes ("S"pend it on goods or services).
4. Keep it in your personal stockpile ("H"oard it).

Everything you can do with money falls into one of these four categories. The most common examples of each type of action are illustrated in Figure 4.1 and expanded below.

Deposit

The first thing you can do with money is give it to someone else for safekeeping. This type of arrangement often includes a contract or other agreement that describes the obligations and responsibilities of each party. This is one of the most reliable and common methods of storing assets.

CHECKING, SAVINGS, AND OTHER DEMAND ACCOUNTS

This category is probably the one we are all most familiar with. Money is deposited with a financial institution, held in a designated account, and the account owner can access the funds according to the terms of their agreement with the financial institution. Unlike what you may see on television crime dramas, there is no ultimate database where you can type in someone's name and find out all the banks where they've ever had an account

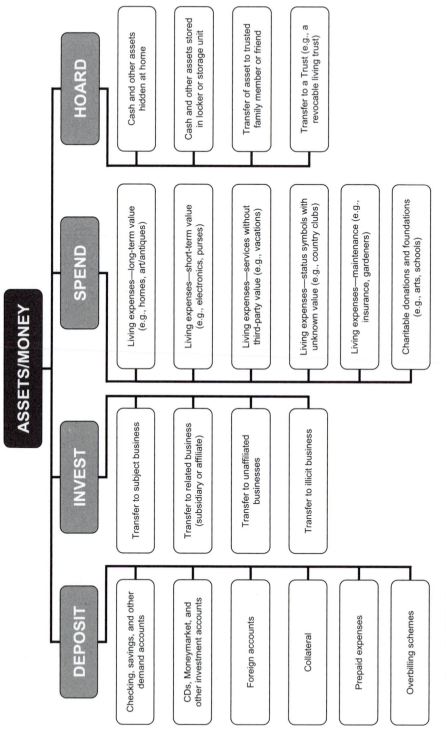

Figure 4.1 The "DISH" Model of Asset Disposition

and how much money they currently have on deposit. (Or if such a database actually does exist, the agency that created it isn't talking.) Your subject's banking information is not going to be available online. If you want this information, you need to request it directly from the subject or you'll need a subpoena or other legal authority to obtain it from the bank. However, information about interest rates and fees is typically available on many bank websites, so you can sometimes use the Internet to confirm or refute information provided by your subject.

Keep an eye out for designations such as "JTWROS" and "POD." The "JTWROS" designation stands for "Joint Tenancy with Right of Survivorship" and means that each listed owner of the account can access all the funds in the account, even if they didn't deposit any of the funds. If one owner dies, the other owner automatically owns everything in the account, even if the deceased specified otherwise in their will. The "POD" notation stands for "Pay on Death." In this case, the account owner is the only one who can access the funds in the account. After the account owner dies, the account passes to the POD beneficiary (again outside of probate and even if the deceased specified otherwise in their will). Depending on the circumstances, it might be appropriate to consider JTWROS accounts as assets belonging to the subject. However, if a subject is listed as a POD beneficiary only, you should not consider the account as an asset belonging to the subject because they do not legally own the funds in the account unless the account owner dies. This is a contingent asset only.

CDS, MONEY MARKET, AND OTHER INVESTMENT ACCOUNTS

Many people make investments in Certificates of Deposit, money market accounts, 401(k) accounts, IRAs, savings bonds, and similar accounts. These accounts frequently contain restrictions about when the account holder can access the funds in the account without paying a penalty or foregoing the interest earned. Like demand accounts, investment accounts may also have a JTWROS or POD designation. If so, they will work the same way as demand accounts.

FOREIGN ACCOUNTS

Thanks to television programs and numerous mystery novels, bank accounts in Switzerland or the Cayman Islands are what most of us think of when we think about foreign accounts. While these are certainly two possible locations, there are many other possible foreign depositories for subjects who are trying to hide or otherwise shelter their assets. Depending on the degree of anonymity desired and the lengths a subject is willing to go to, certain types of accounts in many other countries may allow subjects to hide assets with at least some degree of anonymity.

COLLATERAL

Usually people who offer an asset as collateral maintain possession of that asset—whether it is a vehicle, jewelry, or another valuable item. In order to document that the creditor has an interest in the asset being used as collateral, they file a "UCC" document. This gives other potential interested parties notice of the arrangement. That prevents the borrower from getting multiple loans all secured by the same collateral without each lender being able to find out about previous loans. Each state has an entity that handles these filings. You're typically most interested in filings of UCC-1 forms, but UCC-3 forms (amendments) can also be informative.

PREPAID EXPENSES

Credit card companies have historically been more than happy to take money anytime, even if the cardholder doesn't have a balance owing. They don't pay interest for the use of the money, so it doesn't cost them anything. Overpayment on credit accounts can be a very effective method of hiding cash if the credit card company, supplier, or other creditor allows it. It may even be better than having it sit in your checking account—you have instant access to it but it doesn't show up anywhere but your monthly credit card statement.

An overpayment would probably be done by check because some (if not all) credit card companies' websites will not allow an electronic payment for more than the current account balance. While many credit cards do not allow overpayment when making a payment online, they may not place the same restrictions on overpayments sent by mail or made in person to a bank teller. In the modern world of paperless accounts there might not be any obvious record of this asset. How many of us would think to ask a subject for a copy of their credit card bill if they aren't claiming it as a liability?

Similar to overpaying on your credit cards, you can also overpay your taxes. Just like creditors, the IRS is happy to take the money and hang onto it, especially since they're not paying you any interest on those funds. Let's say you are investigating a subject's claim that they are unable to pay a fine. To support their claim, they submit a copy of their tax return. In reality, the subject is trying to hide assets. In order to back up their claim of a considerable tax liability, the subject can file a tax return showing they owe a significant amount. After payment of the inflated tax bill, the subject provides a copy of the return to you to demonstrate their inability to pay the fine. After the appropriate paperwork has been filed, the subject then files an amended tax return to get back all the funds that were overpaid. Of course, the subject will conveniently forget to send you a copy of the amended return showing their real tax liability.

Overpayment on loans is another method of hiding cash, but is sometimes less convenient. Some loan agreements contain pre-payment penalties, so overpaying may not provide a substantial benefit to the subject. However, depending on the terms of the loan agreement, it may be extremely advantageous for the subject to prepay their mortgage, vehicle, or equipment loans. Whether the loans are personal or business, it is always a good idea to double-check the *current* amount owed instead of relying on an amortization table.

Finally, it may be worthwhile to inquire if a subject has a PayPal account. Many online merchants (not just eBay) accept payment through PayPal. Because PayPal accounts are pre-paid, you may want to consider asking a subject to verify they (1) don't have a PayPal or similar account, or (2) do have a PayPal or similar account and the amount of the current balance.

OVERBILLING SCHEMES

This technique is similar to the "prepaid expenses" method. However, in this case the subject intentionally overpays an invoice or other outstanding bill knowing the recipient will return the excess funds. When the refund is received the funds are redirected to someone other than the original payer. For example, say you are investigating ABC Company. They have an outstanding invoice to 1-2-3 Office Supplies for $10,000. Instead of sending a check for $10,000, ABC instead sends a check for $25,000. Because they want to ensure they get the money they are owed, 1-2-3 doesn't want to return the check. Instead, they deposit the $25,000 check, wait for it to clear, and then write a $15,000 refund check back to ABC. On receipt of the refund check, ABC's owner endorses the check to themselves and deposits it into their personal bank account. The owner has just successfully (1) decreased ABC's assets by $15,000 while simultaneously (2) increasing their personal net worth by $15,000. It is as if the owner had taken a $15,000 distribution or draw from the company, but you will never find it by looking at the company's check register.

This technique can also be utilized by sending multiple checks. Instead of sending a $25,000 check for a $10,000 bill, ABC could instead send two separate $10,000 checks for the same invoice. 1-2-3 would deposit one of the $10,000 checks and return the other by mail. When 1-2-3 returns the duplicate check, ABC's owner does not void it and delete it from the books, but instead endorses it over to themselves and deposits it into their personal account. Again, the owner has successfully decreased ABC's assets (in this case by $10,000) while simultaneously increasing their personal net worth without leaving an obvious record in the company's checkbook.

In addition to schemes like the ones listed above, it is also possible to use these types of techniques to defraud customers and business partners. Individuals selling items on eBay or Craigslist are typical victims. They agree to sell an item for a specified amount, but the check or money order that arrives in the mail is for considerably more. The "purchaser" tells the seller to simply deposit the money and return the extra funds. Unfortunately, the check or money order is forged and will eventually be returned by the bank—usually after the seller has sent a check refunding the difference between the payment and the purchase price.

If you do not have access to the company's books, fraud like this can be almost impossible to detect. If you suspect this type of activity is going on, it may be worthwhile to have a forensic auditor or bookkeeper examine the company's accounts payable records. Just keep in mind that consulting an expert can be extremely expensive and the amount of the fraud needs to justify that type of investigation expense.

Invest

In addition to giving your money to someone else who will safeguard it, you can also give it to someone so they can use it. When we do so, we typically expect to receive more in return than we contribute. But sometimes an owner will transfer funds to a business for purposes other than simply earning a profit.

TRANSFER TO THE SUBJECT BUSINESS

Many business owners will have their business buy assets for their personal use or will transfer assets from their personal ownership to that of their business. By transferring ownership of property to their company, a business owner can keep it from being accessed to pay personal debts or calculate personal obligations (such as child support or alimony). Many business owners attempt to run as much of their personal finances as possible through their business in the belief that doing so eliminates or minimizes their taxable personal income. Old habits can be hard to break, and a business owner may continue these practices even though it increases the firm's liability and makes the owner's personal property vulnerable to satisfying the company's debts.

TRANSFER TO A RELATED BUSINESS

Common ownership and common control are just two of the underlying reasons why two businesses might be affiliates of one another. One company owning another clearly indicates a relationship between them, but what if both are stand-alone companies? Shared owners, officers, directors, partners, managers, employees, industry, business locations, equipment, and other resources may indicate two businesses are not actually independent of one another. Other indications include "less than arm's length" transactions such as interest-free loans; below-market rent for premises, vehicles, or equipment; and commingled bank accounts, inventories, or other assets.

Transferring assets from a potentially liable company to a seemingly unrelated firm is one possible technique to shelter those assets. In order to determine if payments from one firm to another indicate an affiliation between them, you will want to consider normal industry practices for that particular business. What is the going rate for those types of supplies? How much do those services usually cost? Do other companies in that industry usually have transactions like that? And the definitive question: would the subject business make the same deal with a company they had never worked with before? If not, then you may want to reconsider the validity of the "transfer" or "payment."

Finally, don't overlook a company's management history as a source of relevant information. If common officers and directors indicate affiliation between two firms, it makes sense to check with the Secretary of State (or equivalent office) to verify who those officers and directors are. The lack of common management isn't necessarily conclusive; they may simply be covering their tracks. It may be worthwhile to check the companies' historical records (maybe as much as five years back) to see if ownership, management, or corporate control has recently changed.

TRANSFER TO AN UNRELATED BUSINESS

If a subject is sufficiently concerned about protecting their assets, it may become necessary to transfer those assets to a completely unrelated business. This can be a risky move: if the recipient is truly an unrelated entity, then the subject doesn't have any control over those assets. If the subject can still exercise control over the asset after transfer, then it is more likely that the two businesses are actually affiliates of one another and are not independent.

An illegitimate transfer to a completely independent firm can be extremely difficult to prove. However, it is probably safe to assume that a subject isn't going to make this type of transfer unless they trust the recipient. Therefore it may be worthwhile to look for a personal relationship between the owners, officers, or managers of the two companies. They may be family members, lifelong friends, or trusted business associates.

TRANSFER TO AN ILLICIT BUSINESS

Depending on what type of investigations you usually perform, you may not tend to think of this option. Many legitimate business owners are also involved in illicit business activities. Whether it's selling things that "fell off the truck," manufacturing illegal drugs, or providing "companionship" on an hourly basis, legal businesses are frequently used to launder money and otherwise cover for illegal activities. If your review of a company's books and tax returns doesn't reveal the source of funds used to support an owner's extravagant lifestyle, there may an off-the-books affiliate involved in less seemly business activities. In the alternative, a business trying to minimize its financial exposure might try moving funds from the legal portion of the business to the illicit one where they are less likely to be detected.

Spend

The next thing you can do with money is use it for your own purposes. The first and most obvious place to look is the subject's lifestyle. Where do they live? What kind of car do they drive? Someone who reports a monthly gross income of $2,000 shouldn't be able to afford to live in a million-dollar house or drive a brand new Mercedes even if both are leased or inherited. And who takes care of that big house with the beautiful yard—the subject? Not usually: housekeepers, gardeners, and nannies all cost money. Other luxuries that should be red flags include weekly manicures and spa treatments, gym memberships, country club memberships, car detailing, season tickets, exotic vacations, and designer clothing.

LIVING EXPENSES WITH LONG-TERM VALUE

We all spend money on things that have long-term value. Homes, cars, boats, aircraft, art, and jewelry are just some of the assets we spend money on. When we spend money on items with long-term value, there tends to be a clear record of it. There are deeds for real estate, titles for vehicles, and insurance policies for jewelry and other valuables. While some personal property can be difficult to value, the Internet can be a good place to start looking. Many high-end assets may also have owner or serial number registrations.

Don't overlook intangible assets. Patents and royalty agreements are two common types of intangible assets that can have significant value. A free Internet search can reveal if someone currently holds a patent or trademark, and tax returns should show whether a subject is receiving royalty payments from patents, trademarks, copyrighted material, or other intangible assets (such as oil and mineral rights).

LIVING EXPENSES WITH SHORT-TERM VALUE

Some items we purchase have value but only for a short time. Designer clothes, fashionable handbags, and electronic equipment are examples of things we spend money on, but which become obsolete relatively quickly. While these types of items may have a significant purchase price, their value depreciates very quickly.

LIVING EXPENSES WITHOUT THIRD-PARTY VALUE

Some things we spend money on have no value to anyone except ourselves. Costs for vacations, gym memberships, personal services (such as weekly manicures or trips to a spa), and entertainment expenses (including restaurant meals) can be substantial. However, these types of expenses rarely leave any significant evidence. Gambling expenses fall into this category, as do illegal activities such as use of illicit drugs or "escort" services. A subject's inability to document how they manage to spend large amounts of money with nothing to show for it may indicate significant expenditures on these types of activities.

LIVING EXPENSES WITH UNKNOWN VALUE

Sometimes it's difficult to assess an item's true value with a high degree of reliability. One-of-a-kind items and items with high demand but low supply can be notoriously challenging. If the waiting list is longer than a year, you can probably assume the item or membership is an asset worth including in your analysis. If it's longer than five years, it's probably worth a significant amount. Country club memberships, marina slips, and yacht club memberships can be excellent examples of situations where the expense may be disproportionately low to the asset's true value, but where that true value is difficult to determine.

LIVING EXPENSES FOR MAINTENANCE EXPENSES

Roofs wear out, gardens need tending, and boats need painting. Your mortgage company requires you to maintain insurance on your house. Vehicles, whether expensive or cheap, require constant maintenance. We all spend money on maintaining our real and personal property. If a subject is reporting maintenance expenses out of line with the value of the asset, further investigation is probably warranted. That goes for expenses that are both disproportionately high and those that are disproportionately low. ("You only paid $500 for homeowner's insurance last year, but your house is worth $2 million? Who paid the rest of the premium?")

CHARITABLE DONATIONS

While many charitable donations are religious in nature, many others are not. Donations to education, cultural, and artistic organizations can not only be a legitimate charitable expense, they may provide some other type of tangible benefit to the donor. If a subject gives substantial amounts to secular charities, it may be worth checking to make sure the amount they are reporting is the actual "charitable" portion of their contribution.[1]

Knowing what religion someone practices can also give you a clue about where they spend their money. Many religious denominations (including Judaism, Islam, Latter Day Saints, Seventh Day Adventists, and some large evangelical churches) have a very strong tradition of mandatory or quasi-mandatory religious and charitable giving. A tithe for Christians is typically 10 percent of annual gross income; the tzedakah for Jews is usually calculated at 10 percent of net income; and the zakat on wealth for Muslims is 2.5 percent of assets held during the lunar year.

If you have access to personal tax returns, you may want to compare the amount of charitable donations against the amount of reported income (although some business owners will report charitable donations on their company's tax returns). If someone reports gross income of $250,000 and charitable donations of $125,000, you might want to look more closely at what they're really bringing home in income. While it is possible that a subject could give half their income to charity, it isn't very likely. Some people who wouldn't hesitate to cheat on their taxes (or to give you false information about their income and assets) would never consider cheating when it comes to their religious obligations. Charitable donations that are significantly disproportionate to the subject's culture should raise red flags; when I see them, I assume they are inaccurate until proven otherwise.

Hoard

Finally, if you don't want to give money or other assets to someone else, you can always keep it for yourself.

CASH AND OTHER ASSETS HIDDEN AT HOME

This also includes cash equivalents, such as traveler's checks or bearer bonds. Cash and its equivalents have a significant advantage over other assets: they are the definitive "liquid" asset and can be spent on anything with little or no effort. Antiques, art, and collectibles such as coins, stamps, or baseball cards typically have a ready market and are easy to convert to cash if necessary. However, while storing assets at home keeps them firmly under your control, it also subjects them to possible theft, fire, or other damage. Hoarding cash does leave indirect evidence such as withdrawal slips and other bank records.

While hoarding cash does not leave a direct record, hoarding other assets sometimes does. Check homeowner's and other insurance policies for art and antiques. A check to an appraiser may indicate ownership of a valuable asset you might not otherwise find out about. Is that really the "kid's pony" out in the barn, or a descendent of Man O' War?

---

1   For example, in 2009 a $600 donation to the Oregon Shakespeare Festival gave $193 of benefits to the donor including free tickets, souvenir programs, and a year's subscription to the festival's magazine. That means only $407 was actually tax-deductible as a charitable donation.

CASH AND OTHER ASSETS STORED AWAY

Hoarding cash, cash equivalents, and other assets has another significant disadvantage: it takes up lots of space. Contrary to what you see in the movies and on television, cash is heavy and bulky. Want that $2 million ransom in unmarked, non-sequential $20 bills? Better start working out now—it'll weigh more than 200 lb.[2] Art, antiques, collectibles, and precious metals all take up space, so a subject may not have enough room at home to properly store everything. Storing those assets in a locked storage facility or safe-deposit box keeps them out of sight, but also typically leaves records such as the rental agreement and monthly or annual rental fees.

TRANSFER OF ASSET TO FAMILY MEMBER OR TRUSTED FRIEND

This is a favorite technique for hiding assets. Transferring assets to the names of children, parents, siblings, cousins, or close friends can be extremely effective. While transfers of real estate and titled personal property (like vehicles, boats, and airplanes) are the easiest to find, transfers of stock and cash equivalents are documented somewhere.

Asking a subject for documentary proof related to a transfer can be very effective. If a subject says they gave $25,000 to his or her child, you can ask to see the applicable "gift tax return" documentation. Either they'll give you the appropriate document or they won't. If they do, now you have clear documentation of the transfer and the subject's true financial situation. If they don't provide the documents, you can argue that the transfer was not legitimate. ("Well, Your Honor, if they had actually given this money to their child, they would have been legally required to file this document. Since they didn't file the document, I have to assume that they didn't really transfer the money.") If they claim the amount was below the reportable threshold, ask for other supporting documentation like canceled checks or deposit slips.

TRANSFER TO TRUST

Trusts are a common method for protecting assets from creditors and taxes. There are many perfectly legitimate reasons to create a trust. But trusts can also be used to hide assets from legitimate claims. It may also be hard to detect an illegitimate trust because there are frequently no requirements to file a trust agreement or otherwise make it a public document. While some trust agreements might be recorded, you shouldn't be surprised if you can't find any written record of who created a trust, who the beneficiaries of that trust are, or what the trustee is or is not allowed to do.

In some states, like California, New York, Pennsylvania, and Florida, trusts (especially Living Trusts) are extremely common in estate planning. In other states, trusts are much less common. If your investigation reveals the use of a trust, knowing about applicable state laws can give you a clue about whether the trust is legitimate or being used to try and illicitly hide assets.

---

2   Based on estimates from US military cash shipments to Iraq, a pallet of $100 bills approximately 4′ × 4′ × 5′ would total somewhere around $64 million and weigh approximately 1,500 lb, or approximately 254 lb for $2 million in $20 bills. In 2006, the website Fivecentnickel.com estimated one million dollars in $20 bills would weigh approximately 106 lb (*http://www.fivecentnickel.com/2006/02/07/how-much-does-a-million-dollars-weigh/*).

Regardless of whether a trust is legitimate or not, there should always be documentation of assets transferred to the trust. Just like when a subject transfers ownership of an asset from themselves to a family member, they have to sign a deed transferring their ownership interest in the property from themselves to the trust (even if they are both the trustor and the trust beneficiary). While you should look for property that is owned by the subject as well as property that is owned by family members or a trust, it's frequently easiest to look for documentation of the *transfer* of property from the subject to the trust. In other words, look for footprints instead of Bigfoot.

Commonly Overlooked Assets

In addition to the assets we all own and deal with on a daily basis, there are some assets that are easy to overlook. Here are some assets that you might come across, whether owned by a business or its owner.

TIMESHARES

Some folks may consider a timeshare to be more of a liability than an asset, but vacation homes, campground memberships, resort accommodations, even yacht and airplane ownership can be acquired through a timeshare arrangement. Some timeshare ownership interests can be extremely valuable, especially in desirable locations during popular times (such as the weeks around July 4th). Financial records should indicate both the amount of maintenance and related fees being paid to maintain the timeshare, as well as other benefits received by the owner. Pay special attention to the possibility of income received from renting out the timeshare to another person, or other benefits (such as frequent flyer miles or alternative vacation packages) received in exchange for not using the timeshare during the designated period. For subjects who are trying to sell their timeshare, there are many services who will advertise the unit for sale. However, many of these services charge very high fees—sometimes even higher than the final sales amount of the timeshare. If a subject claims to have taken a loss on a timeshare sale, make sure you get documentation to support that loss.

SECURITY DEPOSITS

These can be substantial, especially for a business location. If a company does not own their business location, they probably paid a substantial security deposit when they signed their lease. Large equipment, personal residences, luxury vehicles, and other valuable property that is rented or leased may also have a corresponding deposit. At the very least, you should ask the question and get a clear statement on the record as to whether a security deposit exists and, if so, how much it is.

FREQUENT FLYER MILES

Accumulated miles are probably not worth very much, especially when spread out over multiple airlines. However, if the miles accrue to a company instead of an individual employee, there may be thousands of dollars worth of travel for you to consider as an additional asset of the business.

"POTENTIAL" ASSETS

For both individuals and businesses, check to see if they are listed as the plaintiff in a lawsuit or if they are a member of a class with a pending action against a major defendant. Although there is no guarantee the asset will have any value, it is still worth considering. Other "potential" assets include rebates and refunds, life estates, interests in insurance policies, and the future value of crops or livestock. Any asset that might not have a current value, but which might have significant value in the future, should be considered when evaluating a subject's assets even if you ultimately do not assign any worth to that potential asset.

Other "Dirty Tricks"

Although not technically methods for hiding assets, other techniques can be used to minimize the appearance of wealth and net worth. These "dirty tricks" include methods for moving money, making it seem to disappear, or making it seem to fail to appear. Some of these methods include the following.

DELAYED PAYMENTS

Recurrent payments typically happen about the same time each month or year. When attempting to minimize their apparent wealth, subjects may attempt to delay these payments beyond the reporting period. By delaying their receipt of income, bonuses, rental payments, royalty payments, dividends, or stock options, a subject can make their financial situation appear less stable than it actually is.

DELAYED SALES AND CONTRACTS

When faced with an impending financial investigation, some subjects may attempt to delay a significant sale or executing a profitable long-term contract. Transactions of this nature are extremely valuable and should be reflected as an asset in a business valuation. By delaying a sale or execution of a contract, a firm can minimize its apparent long-term value.

FRAUDULENT PAYMENTS

Another attempt to minimize the appearance of net worth can be made through the use of fraudulent payments. These so-called "payments" typically take the form of checks written to nonexistent employees, nonexistent suppliers, or real people for nonexistent debts. They show up as a debit on an individual's or firm's books, but are not legitimate deductions. Since no money actually changes hands, it's not really a hidden asset, but it operates the same way—hiding in plain sight.

Legitimate expenses always have a paper trail of some sort. Legitimate employees have timecards, file taxes, and have worker's compensation coverage. Legitimate suppliers provide invoices and bills of lading. Legitimate debts have loan documents and canceled checks, wire transfer receipts, or electronic funds transfer tracking numbers. If you suspect a reported payment or debt is not real, ask for the appropriate documentation to support the expenditure.

UNDERVALUING ASSETS

Because they have technically been disclosed, a purposefully undervalued asset is not a "hidden asset." The true value of tangible assets can frequently be established through independent third-party sources. However an undervalued intangible asset can be more difficult to estimate. It is relatively easy to undervalue patents, trademarks, franchise agreements, goodwill, intellectual property, and rights to oil, gas, and minerals. If you believe you are dealing with a case of an undervalued asset, especially an intangible asset, it might be worthwhile to consult or hire an expert.

Sometimes a tangible asset's value is legitimately reduced, but the decrease in value is purposeful. The apparent value of an asset can be reduced by allowing it to be unused or fall into disrepair. If a subject owns an office building but does not try to find tenants or perform preventative maintenance, they can argue the value of the property is not as high as it might otherwise be. If your subject argues that the value of their property is reduced due to vacancies or the property's condition, you may want to consider asking for documentation showing they have tried to find tenants and improve the property's "rentability" (e.g., real estate listings, contractor's billings, and similar documents).

ASSET LIST EFFECTIVE DATES

A very simple, yet easily overlooked, technique for disguising wealth is to manipulate the effective dates of a disclosure. Just because a subject signed a financial disclosure statement last week doesn't mean that it's actually current. Always verify the effective dates of any financial disclosure documentation and make sure they are recent enough to be meaningful. Many financial disclosure documents have a space for an effective date that is different from a signature date. An effective date may be at towards the top of the document while a signature line and date may appear at the end of the document. Financial disclosure documents should never be older than the most recent fiscal year; documents that are more recent are always desirable.

ALTERED RECORDS

Finally, don't overlook the possibility that the records provided to you by the subject are not accurate. Just because the tax return you're looking at has an accounting firm's stamp and the taxpayer's signature doesn't mean it's the information that was actually provided to the IRS. Misaligned numbers, missing pages, and incomplete schedules are all clues that the document you're looking at may have been doctored. If you see something that "just doesn't look right," trust your instincts.

Remember: money *never* disappears. It may move, and it may change form, but it doesn't simply evaporate. It *always* goes somewhere and it *always* leaves a trail. Also remember that most dishonest subjects are going to try to spend as little time and money as possible in order to hide assets. If they have to spend money on a lawyer and spend lots and lots of hours transferring assets, it's very likely that there are substantial assets involved. It is a rare person who will be willing to spend $25,000 in order to hide $10,000 (although they do exist).

Doing Logical Things with Money

One last thing to keep in mind is that most of us tend to spend our money in logical ways—at least in ways that seem logical to us. Once we find something we like, it's natural to spend more money on things that are related. Thinking about assets and how they relate to one another can be a good way for investigators to find new leads and identify assets that have not been disclosed. If the subject has a canal-front home with a huge dock, it's logical they might own a boat also. If the subject and their family always have their vacation at the same resort the same week every year, it makes sense to look to see if they own a timeshare nearby. While there may not be concealed assets associated with every activity, it is usually worth a quick check just to make sure.

Case in Point

When you have access to a subject's tax returns, you can find a wealth of information and potential red flags. During one investigation, I reviewed the tax returns of a business owner whose family was very active in their church. The tax returns showed income of just over $250,000 and charitable contributions of $116,000. While the subject's church did have a policy of requiring members to tithe, a charitable donation of more than 45 percent of the subject's gross income was far beyond what their faith and church leaders expected from even the most devout members of the congregation.

The proportion of income to charitable giving may have been the first red flag, but the subject's reaction to my request for additional information was an even bigger warning sign. Instead of providing receipts or other documentation to support the charitable donation deductions as listed on their tax return, the subject instead first challenged my authority to request the information and then tried to convince the head of my agency not to pursue further verification of the information they had provided. All of those red flags made me suspect something else was going on with this particular subject.

Eventually, I changed jobs and someone else handled the subject's appeal of my determination—and apparently the subject won. I don't know if that is because they eventually provided the documentation to prove the legitimacy of the claimed deductions or whether they simply exerted sufficient political pressure to convince a decision maker to overlook some of the applicable regulations in their case. Either way it is a good reminder that sometimes, despite your best efforts, you can't always get the resolution that seems fair or proper. Losing may not be any fun, but it's a part of life when you're an investigator.

5 *Legal Structures*

The next logical issue to address is what type of business entity you are investigating. There are four types of business structures you are most likely to encounter: corporations, partnerships, limited liability companies, and sole proprietorships. You may also see references to entities that are not actually businesses, but which might still play a role in concealing assets.

Corporations

A corporation is "an organization formed with state governmental approval to act as an artificial person to carry on business" (Law.com 2009). That means a corporation can do almost anything a person can do, including sue, be sued, and sign a contract. The key reason a business incorporates is to protect the owner's assets from being accessed to pay company debts. Fewer people would start businesses if their home, car, and retirement savings could be seized to pay the debts of their failed company or obligations arising from defective products.

As explained in more detail in Chapter 6, corporations file "Articles of Incorporation" with the appropriate agency in their home state to establish a new entity, and annual reports every year thereafter. A corporation should also have "Bylaws" which explain how the company is going to be governed, corporate minutes memorializing the events at official corporate meetings, and corporate resolutions authorizing the corporate officers or directors to take specific actions. Bylaws, minutes, and resolutions are not usually filed with the state agency and are only available from the firm itself.

Some corporations sell stock in their companies on the open market: a stock exchange. In the United States, the New York Stock Exchange (NYSE) and the National Association of Securities Dealers Automated Quotations (NASDAQ) are the two major stock exchanges. In order to sell stock on an exchange, a company must meet very strict reporting requirements. Companies that sell their stock to the general public are referred to as "publicly-traded" companies. Corporations that do not sell stock to the public are not subject to the same reporting requirements and are referred to as "privately-held" companies. There are four types of corporation that you might run across: C corporations, S corporations, QSubs, and PSs.

C CORPORATIONS VERSUS S CORPORATIONS

As far as you are usually concerned, in financial investigations a corporation is a corporation is a corporation. It makes very little difference to you whether a firm is an C corporation or an S corporation (usually referred to as a "corp"). The only time you are probably going to care which type of corporation you have is either (1) when something doesn't match, or (2) when you're reviewing the corporation's tax returns.

"C" and "S" corporations are designations that tell you how the company is taxed by the IRS (and possibly a state taxing authority, depending on the applicable state laws). S corps must meet strict requirements about the number of shareholders, the citizenship of those shareholders, and the classes of stock made available by the company. As of 2009, an S corp could not have more than 100 shareholders, none of whom may be a nonresident alien (IRS 2009).

Two companies could be otherwise identical as far as the number and identity of shareholders and availability of stock, but one could be an C corp and one an S corp. The difference between an C corp and an S corp is who pays the taxes on money earned by the firm: an C corp pays taxes directly on its income while a S corp does not. An S corp is what is known as a "pass-through" entity. That means the corporation itself does not pay taxes directly, but instead its shareholders are responsible for paying their proportional share of the company's tax obligation based on how much stock they own. This eliminates a significant disadvantage of an C corp—double taxation. Double taxation means that taxes are paid twice on the same money, once by the corporation on its income, and a second time by the shareholder on the income they receive from the corporation (IRS 2009). But eliminating the second round of taxation comes at a price: an S corp shareholder might need to pay a significant tax bill on behalf of the firm even if they didn't receive any cash from the company. S corps will always be privately-held corporations, while C corps may be either privately-held or publicly-traded.

QSUBS

The term "QSub" is shorthand for "qualifying subsidiary." A QSub is just another normal type of corporation that has some special tax considerations. A QSub is a corporation that is 100 percent owned by an S corp. As far as the IRS is concerned, a QSub is considered to be the same corporation as its parent "and all of the subsidiary's assets, liabilities, and items of income, deduction, and credit are treated as those of the parent" (IRS 2008). It is very unlikely that you will see a QSub since they have only existed since 1996 and, in my experience, are relatively uncommon (California FTB 2000). However, if you are looking at tax returns or other financial records and don't understand why a business doesn't appear to be paying any taxes, it might be a QSub. If you do come across one and have questions, consulting a tax attorney or accountant is likely to be helpful.

PS

A "PS" corporation is short for "Professional Services" corporation. This type of business is, by definition, a company that provides some sort of professional service to its customers. PSs are common for attorneys, doctors, dentists, accountants, and sometimes architects and engineers—people whose businesses involve providing services that require a special professional license. Again, for purposes of a financial investigation this is just another corporation. There may be some special limits on professional liability but those probably won't enter into most financial investigations.

Regardless of which type of corporation it is, it's very likely that you won't be able to access the owner's personal assets to pay company obligations (at least not without some very fancy lawyering). This rule may not apply if you can demonstrate that the corporation itself is a sham or in some other way is not legitimate. More on this topic is provided later in these materials under the "Piercing the Corporate Veil" section.

Partnerships

Another common business structure is the partnership. Partnerships don't have the same protection for the owner's assets that a corporation has, but they can offer substantial tax benefits to some firms. Like an S corp, partnerships don't pay taxes directly but instead pay taxes on their income through their owners/partners. There are two basic types of partnerships: general partnerships (sometimes designated "GP" or "a partnership") and limited partnerships (designated "LP" or "a limited partnership").

General partnerships are created by an agreement of at least two partners. While that agreement should be in writing, don't be surprised if it isn't (especially in very small companies). In a general partnership, authority to manage the company and liability for the company's obligations rests with each of the general partners. If the partners so choose, they can elect a "Managing Partner" who is responsible for managing the company's day-to-day operations. Even if an owner leaves the partnership, they are still "individually liable for debts incurred while partner participated in the firm" (Moye 2005: 45).

A limited partnership is similar to a general partnership, but it provides some liability protection for some partners. A limited partnership must have at least one general partner and one limited partner, and the agreement between the partners must be in writing in accordance with statutes of the LP's home state. The general partners are responsible for the day-to-day operations of the firm, just like in a general partnership. However, the limited partners do not participate regularly in the firm and their risk is limited to the amount they have invested in the company. That means that being a limited partner in an LP is very similar to owning stock in a corporation. In a financial investigation, that means the general partners' personal assets might be far more vulnerable than those of the limited partners. That could give the general partners more incentive to conceal assets than it does the limited partners.

Limited Liability Companies

Limited liability companies (LLCs) and their relatives are a relatively new hybrid between corporations and partnerships. They offer the flexibility of a partnership and the asset protection of a corporation. Firms can elect to be taxed either as a partnership or as a corporation, whichever is more advantageous to them. Instead of "shareholders" or "partners," LLCs have "members." Limited Liability Partnerships (LLPs), Professional Limited Liability Companies (PLLCs), and Professional Limited Liability Partnerships (PLLPs) are all very similar to LLCs.

LLCs have only been around since the 1980s and are frequently selected as a business structure instead of an S corp. In addition to tax differences and no restrictions on who can be shareholders, LLCs can frequently operate in a less formal manner than corporations can. An LLC Agreement is similar to a corporation's Bylaws and details the appropriate limits on a member's liability and the management procedures that will be followed in the firm's operations. An LLC Agreement should also explain whether the members are responsible for the firm's operations, or whether the members will appoint "managers" to run the company.

Please note: an LLC or PLLC is *not* a corporation! LLC stands for "Limited Liability *Company*" not "Limited Liability *Corporation*." A corporation, by definition, limits the personal liability of its owners. Thus, the phrase "Limited Liability Corporation" is redundant. If you hear people use the phrase or see it in writing, it is probably safe to assume the speaker or author meant to say "Limited Liability Company."

Sole Proprietorships

Finally, a sole proprietorship is the simplest business form. Commonly referred to as "sole props," the business is the same legal entity as the owner. That means the owner's personal assets can be accessed for the company's debts because the company and the owner are one and the same. Sole props are technically owned by just one person, but occasionally you will find a sole prop owned by a married couple (especially in some community property states). When conducting a financial investigation of a sole proprietor, you need to consider *both* the business assets as well as the owner's personal assets.

Don't Let Your Eyes Deceive You

Many times the true legal structure of a business is not apparent even though it should be. The absence of "Inc." or "LLC" from the company's letterhead doesn't tell you that you are looking at a sole proprietorship. Likewise, just because a company claims to be a corporation doesn't mean their corporation is in good standing or that they've ever even filed incorporation documents. While the name of a company may be a good starting place, you should not accept its accuracy at face value. I have personally seen sole proprietorships claim to be corporations and corporations claim to be an LLC. I have seen corporations claim to be active corporations even though they filed dissolution papers with the Secretary of State's office and I've seen more corporations than I can count that were dissolved for failing to file their annual paperwork. The lesson here is to make sure you verify the actual, current legal structure of any business instead of relying on potentially misleading information like letterhead or business signs.

Other Entities

In addition to businesses, there are a number of other legal entities you may come across during a financial investigation. Sometimes you will be able to find information about these entities on the Internet, sometimes not. Although these types of entities are far less common than businesses, you should still have a basic understanding of each.

TRUSTS

Of the nonbusiness entities you might come across, a trust is probably the most common. Trusts are used to isolate control over an asset. A "trustor" is the person who sets up the trust, a "trustee" is the person who controls the trust, and the "beneficiary" is the person who receives a benefit from the trust's assets. Sometimes these may be the same person, but usually they will be different people or institutions (such as a bank trust department acting as trustee or a charity being the beneficiary).

Depending on the type of trust, the trustor, trustee, and beneficiary can be different people or might be the same person. Key words to look for are "revocable" (which means the trustor can change or undo the trust) or "irrevocable" (which means the trustor can't change or undo the trust). Depending on the state involved (and its probate laws), it might or might not be common for residents to create a "revocable Living Trust." Other common types of trusts that you might run across include special needs trusts and Crummey and life insurance trusts. There are many types of trusts, all serving different purposes. If you discover a trust is involved in the matter you are investigating, it may be necessary to consult with an attorney to help you figure out whether a trust is being used for legitimate purposes or not.

REAL ESTATE INVESTMENT TRUSTS

A Real Estate Investment Trust, also known as a REIT, isn't really a "trust" in the same way that an estate planning or life insurance trust is. REITs are businesses that are created to own and manage real estate. Structurally speaking, REITs in the United States are established and managed like corporations and can even be publicly traded companies. REITs are usually not used to protect personal assets due to strict requirements about shareholders and ownership.

ESTATES

While the word "estate" can apply to a large home and surrounding grounds, in this case the word refers to the entity that manages and distributes assets from someone who has passed away. The person in charge of an estate is usually called a "Personal Representative" or "Administrator" (which replaced the old term "Executor" and its assorted variations). Having someone's Power of Attorney is not the same thing as being their Personal Representative; Powers of Attorney are only good if someone is alive—after they die, you can only deal with their estate. An estate lasts as long as the probate is proceeding. Assets that are part of a Living Trust are not part of the probate estate.

ASSOCIATIONS AND COOPERATIVES

These organizations are formed to protect the interests of a group of similar people. Associations are typically more informal groups. They may or may not have official recognition from a government entity and are formed around a common interest. Cooperatives are typically more formal organizations. They usually offer their members benefits related to purchasing, marketing, or similar business activities. Farmers Cooperatives may be very common in some rural areas.

CORPORATION SOLE

Unless you are investigating a church or other religious organization, a "corporation sole" should be a big red flag to you. IRS Revenue Ruling 2004-27 states, "A legitimate corporation sole is designed to ensure continuity of ownership of property dedicated to the benefit of a legitimate religious organization" (IRS 2004: 626). However, some scam artists and anti-tax activists have tried to use this type of entity to avoid paying taxes. If you come across a corporation sole and you're dealing with the local archdiocese, it's probably OK. If you're dealing with a private business or an individual, you've got a problem.

FOREIGN ENTITIES

Companies and other entities based in other countries can be challenging to track down. Abbreviations like "SA," "AG," and "GmbH" denote common corporate forms in other countries. But remember that a "foreign" corporation doesn't necessarily mean a corporation from another country, but may instead mean a company that is incorporated in another state. The law in the home jurisdiction of a company will usually determine how much information is available about it.

Piercing the Corporate Veil

So why is it so important to understand a company's actual legal structure? The relationship between owners and companies is key to understanding which assets you should include in a financial investigation and analysis. Under some circumstances, it may be possible to include or seize not just a company's assets but the owner's personal assets as well. However, those circumstances are rare and challenging to execute.

This concept is known as "Piercing the Corporate Veil." Essentially, if a court permits the corporate veil to be "pierced," the corporate form is disregarded. So just like a partnership or sole proprietorship, the owner's personal assets can be accessed to pay the company's obligations.

To prevent the corporate veil from being pierced, the owners, officers, and directors of the corporation need to maintain the corporate form. They need to have official meetings with proper corporate minutes. They need to have elections, authorize actions on the corporation's behalf, and keep track of ownership with a stock register and certificates. Failure to perform these simple housekeeping tasks can result in the corporate veil being disregarded. In other words: if you don't treat it like a corporation, then your creditors might not have to either.

LLCs also have a type of corporate veil. But unlike corporations, LLCs frequently aren't required to follow all the same formalities. This means that much of the case law that has been developed over decades related to piercing the corporate veil may not be on point for matters involving LLCs. The presence or absence of fraud may be a key in whether the courts will permit an LLC's "corporate veil" to be pierced.

If you believe it is appropriate to attempt to pierce a company's liability shield, you should start by examining the company's business records. Are there corporate minutes? Is the company's management team authorized in writing? Do the owners pay personal expenses from business accounts or vice versa? Was ownership of the property in question transferred to a separate company with no other assets? Did the company take actions for no reason other than avoiding financial liability to your agency or other creditors? All of these factors can help answer the question whether a subject company is truly independent, or whether it's just a sham intended to improperly minimize financial responsibility.

Captive Insurance

One other item to look for related to legal structures is the use of "captive" insurance. Captive insurance companies are different from other insurance companies. Unlike the company that provides your homeowner's or automobile insurance policy, a captive insurer only writes policies for companies that are part of its corporate family. This can be a legitimate method for financially healthy companies to self-insure their workers' compensation and other liabilities. Instead of paying premiums to an independent third-party and making claims based on the terms of an insurance policy, all related companies can instead pay their premiums to another corporate affiliate—one that exists solely to provide insurance.

Unfortunately, captive insurance can also be used by less stable companies to make it appear their risks and other liabilities are covered by a third-party when that is not actually the case—all while simultaneously saving money on insurance premiums. It is possible for a corporate parent to create a captive insurance subsidiary by investing a significant amount of money. The investment shows up as an asset of the new insurance company. The subsidiary uses the investment to offset the liability from potential insurance claims. A significant investment from the parent company can make the subsidiary's balance sheet look great—lots of assets and minimal liabilities. But problems can arise when companies start playing accounting games. One potential problem would be if the subsidiary makes a big loan back to its corporate parent. The subsidiary's books still show sufficient assets—the problem is that those assets aren't real. If the parent invested $50 million in the insurance subsidiary, and the subsidiary then makes a loan back to the parent of $49 million, the subsidiary doesn't have enough cash assets to cover potential insurance claims. The company can write as many insurance policies as they want, but those policies are essentially worthless.

There is no quick way to tell if you're dealing with a captive insurance company or a regular insurance company. Instead, you need to do some checking. You can check to see if the company has been rated by AM Best or another rating company. Most captive insurance companies do not get an outside rating, so any company not showing up in the AM Best database may well be a captive. Checking the Vermont State database is also a good resource. More information on available web sites is included in Chapters 10 and 11.

Why It's Important

Understanding a bit about business legal structures and related entities can help you understand the documents you find on the Internet and know what documents you should find. Many times, documents you are able to access from the Secretary of State, county auditor, or the court clerk will contain information that can help guide your investigation. If you stumble across business structures, non-business entities, or other situations where you don't understand what you're looking at, consult with an attorney, an accountant, or a more experienced co-worker for help.

Case in Point

Understanding corporate structures (and the legal separation between a business and its owners) can be very important when conducting a financial investigation. Subjects are frequently too clever for their own good, as I once discovered while checking the assets of a business and its owners. The subjects had purchased a number of acres of farmland years earlier with the expectation that they might eventually develop and relocate their business to the site. They never bothered to transfer ownership of the property from themselves as a married couple to the business. After all, it was rural farmland they purchased for somewhere in the neighborhood of $10,000.

For years, that business decision made a lot of sense. By owning the property as a married couple instead of as a business, the land was insulated and protected from any claims that might be made against the subject's company. Everything was fine until the area around the property began to be developed. By the time I started my investigation, the land in question was the last remaining undeveloped land in the area, surrounded on three sides by highways and on the fourth side by light industrial warehouses. The area was now extremely popular with a new freeway entrance about to be built that would provide almost instant access. The little bit of farmland the subjects had purchased for a few thousand dollars was now worth millions—tens of millions, actually. And since they had purchased the property with no mortgage, there was no liability to offset the increase in value. Suddenly, the subjects weren't struggling small business owners—they were multi-millionaires who had failed to disclose their ownership of this particular asset. Understanding that this asset was owned personally by the subjects instead of by their business was very important to my investigation. In fact, it turned out to be the determining factor in my final determination.

6 *Legal Documents*

When trying to track hidden assets, legal documents are not only going to be your strongest evidence but can also provide clues for additional investigation. In order to determine whether your subject owns property they have failed to disclose, you will need to understand what legal documents exist and where you can find them. The explanations provided below are not intended to be a "legal" definition that an attorney or accountant might provide. Instead, the purpose of the following is to explain, in plain English, the importance of certain types of documents and how they can be useful in your financial investigation.

Corporate Documents

Documents related to the establishment and control of a business are frequently available from a number of government entities. In most states, the Secretary of State's office will keep documents related to corporations, LLCs, and some partnerships. In some states, the Secretary of State may also keep records related to business trade names, assumed business names, and tax registrations, however, in many states, these records will be maintained by a separate agency such as a licensing department, professions board, or even the state taxing authority. Some states (such as Idaho) will let you review actual corporate filings online for free, whereas other states (such as California) will let you review a summary of information but not the actual document filed by the company. There are even states (such as Texas) that will only let you search for and review documents if you pay a fee ($1 per search as of December 2009, according to the Texas Secretary of State website).

ARTICLES OF INCORPORATION

Articles of Incorporation are a relatively short document (sometimes just a single page) that sets forth the name and address of the company, who created the company, who the company's registered agent is, and some other basic information. The information required to be in the articles will be established by state law. When looking for hidden assets, checking a company's articles can give you clues as to whether the company's ownership or control has changed. For example, if a married couple claims their business only belongs to one spouse, check to see who signed the articles as the company's "incorporators." If both spouses signed, that could be evidence that they intended the company to belong to both of them. An even bigger red flag is if they claim the business only belongs to the wife but only the husband signed as an incorporator (or vice versa). That could indicate the couple has transferred ownership in order to conceal this asset.

One word of caution that bears repeating: confirm the information before drawing any conclusions. Just because someone is listed in the firm's articles as an incorporator does not mean they are currently involved in the business. In fact, it is possible an incorporator was never involved in the day-to-day operations of the subject business. Perhaps the only incorporator listed is the company's attorney—who could be the incorporator and registered agent for hundreds of unrelated businesses. Maybe the husband was the only signer because the wife was out of town and the filing had to occur before she was scheduled to return. Or perhaps the couple's lawyer drew up the documents, told them both to sign, and they simply followed instructions.

BYLAWS

Corporate Bylaws explain how a company is run: how many officers there are, how many directors are on the board, what powers are granted to officers and directors, etc. Bylaws can be very helpful in determining whether or not someone controls a business. Most corporate bylaws have fairly standard provisions, so something unusual should grab your attention. For example, if the bylaws contain a provision that says the President can only take actions authorized by the Board of Directors, the President doesn't really control the company.

Quorum provisions can also (intentionally or unintentionally) restrict or enhance someone's ability to control a company. If the bylaws establish that there will be two directors[1] and that a majority—50 percent plus one—of directors are necessary to obtain a quorum for a meeting, both directors must be present to operate the business. If there is a falling out between the two directors, one can hold the business hostage by simply not showing up for a board meeting. Quorum requirements can also give undue power to board members. Say the bylaws establish the board as having three directors and a company's 100 percent owner only controls one seat on the board. The quorum requirements would allow the two non-owner directors to hold a meeting and vote the sole owner off the company's board. They could also appoint someone else to be the firm's President, Treasurer, or other officer.

It is also possible that corporate bylaws can give undue control to a single individual in the company. A company could include a provision that both the company's President and the Treasurer must sign checks over a specified dollar amount. This sensible precaution could actually not provide as much protection as it might seem, especially if the offices of President and Treasurer are filled by the same person. If the bylaws also contain a provision that the President will act as Treasurer and the Vice President will be the Secretary, a restriction on check signing isn't really a restriction. When reviewing complicated documents like bylaws, it is important to keep in mind how different provisions interact with one another.

Unfortunately, corporate bylaws are not typically collected by state agencies; many Secretaries of State will not accept them for filing. If you want to review a company's bylaws, you will most likely have to request them from the company itself. If the company claims not to have bylaws, check your state's corporations statute for the legal requirement to possess and maintain corporate bylaws (there should be one in each state).

---

1   This is a common arrangement when a small business is owned by a married couple, a parent and a child, siblings, cousins, or close friends.

CERTIFICATE OF FORMATION

A Certificate of Formation is very similar to Articles of Incorporation although instead of establishing a corporation, it establishes a Limited Liability Company or Limited Liability Partnership. It may also be a very short document of one or two pages and contains very basic information as required by state statute. This is the document that is filed with the Secretary of State. One key item to look for on a Certificate of Formation is whether an LLC will be managed by its members or by managers.

LIMITED LIABILITY COMPANY AGREEMENT

A Limited Liability Company Agreement is similar to a corporation's bylaws, but contains information about ownership as well. This document should outline the rights and responsibilities of each of the owners (called "members" instead of "shareholders") and the company's managers. Just as with bylaws, unusual provisions should give you pause to consider why they exist and what effect they could have in the real world.

PARTNERSHIP AGREEMENT

A Partnership Agreement is similar to an LLC Agreement, except the business is either a general or a limited partnership. Typically, Secretaries of State do not collect much, if any, information about general partnerships, but may have registration requirements for limited partnerships. The partnership agreement will outline what type of partnership the company is, the rights and responsibilities of each partner, how the partnership will be managed, and how assets will be disbursed. Most states have laws mirroring the Uniform Partnership Act and Uniform Limited Partnership Act, so frequently have very similar requirements (Uniform Law Commissioners 2002a, 2002b).

ANNUAL REPORT

The Annual Report is a document filed each year with the Secretary of State's office that lists the current information about the company, such as the officers, company address, and industry or line of business. If a company fails to file the proper documents, the corporation will likely be dissolved. LLCs usually must also file annual reports.

CONSENT TO SERVE AS REGISTERED AGENT

Corporations and LLCs are required to have a "registered agent" for the company. This is a person who is responsible for receiving service of process in case the company is sued. The registered agent is frequently an officer, director, or owner of the company, but this is not a requirement. Many companies have their business lawyer act as the registered agent, and some contract with large companies to serve in this capacity. Before an individual or company can serve as a registered agent, they sign the "Consent to Serve" document to verify they accept responsibility for this role.

MINUTES

Corporate minutes document the activities that occur at company meetings. At the very least, businesses should have at least one meeting per year of their governing board (such as the Board of Directors) and at least one meeting per year of their owners (such as a shareholders' meeting). The minutes from those meetings should detail who was present for the meeting, what was discussed, and what corporate actions were taken. Corporate minutes can be very helpful in establishing whether someone really controls a company—if the "President" is never involved in the meeting, how can they run the company? The opposite is also true—if someone who is unrelated to the company shows up at every meeting, are they really "unrelated" to the firm's operations?

Unfortunately, corporate minutes are not typically collected and retained by any state agency. Like bylaws and operating agreements, minutes are documents that are supposed to be maintained and held by the firm itself. On occasion, some companies choose to post minutes of their board or shareholders' meetings so you can sometimes find these documents on the company's website, but this is rare. Otherwise, you will need to request copies directly from the company. If the company claims not to have any, check your state corporation or an LLC statute; it is likely there is a legal requirement for a business to conduct these meetings and keep appropriate records.

CONSENT IN LIEU

Sometimes companies will execute a "Consent in Lieu ..." for some other document. This is particularly common in privately-held companies that are owned and managed by families or small groups of close friends. Instead of holding an annual meeting of shareholders, the shareholders might sign a document entitled "Consent in Lieu of Annual Meeting of Shareholders." The document would lay out all the authorizations and appointments of officers needed for the business to operate for the next year. It would be signed by all the shareholders. That means you could request copies of minutes of the shareholder meetings, but instead receive documents entitled "Consent in Lieu ..." fulfilling the same business purpose.

UCC

Commonly referred to as a "UCC filing," a more accurate term would be to refer to this document by its form number UCC-1.[2] A UCC-1 form is filed to document that an item of personal property (such as a vehicle or piece of industrial equipment) is being used as collateral to secure a loan or some other type of debt. This gives other potential creditors notice so a debtor can't use the same piece of property to secure multiple loans. UCC documents are usually filed with the Secretary of State's office in the applicable state. Most jurisdictions charge a small fee to obtain copies of UCC-1 forms, but a few states allow you to search an index of filed documents for free. There are also paid services that can provide UCC filing information.

---

2   There are other types of UCC forms, but UCC-1 forms are the ones that will most likely be applicable to a financial investigation.

Real Estate Documents

When trying to locate hidden assets, real estate documents can provide a wealth of information. Even in times of economic downturn and buyer's markets, real estate is generally viewed as a good long-term investment. If you are not familiar with common real estate terms, deciphering property transfers can be extremely frustrating. Remember that when you buy a house, the seller grants you their ownership interest in the property, so they are the "grantor" and you are the "grantee." In contrast, when you get the mortgage for your new home, you grant some rights related to the property to your bank, so you are the "grantor"—even though you are not selling the property—and your bank is the "grantee." The following documents related to real estate are good to look for and examine closely when conducting a financial investigation.

PURCHASE AND SALE AGREEMENT

This is usually a pre-printed form detailing the specifics of an offer to buy a parcel of real estate. Most purchases will use standard forms available from the local Multiple Listing Service. There are standard forms for residential homes, commercial properties, and vacant land. While the standard terms on the form can be amended, this is not particularly common. Use of nonstandard forms, however, is not at all common. In my experience, real estate professionals (especially closing agents and title companies) don't like to handle purchases with custom forms; they prefer buyers and sellers to use the familiar forms and simply change specific provisions as needed. The use of nonstandard forms should get your attention. You will want to make sure there are no unusual provisions in any non-standard purchase documents. Purchase documents are not typically available over the Internet and will need to be requested from the subject.

REAL ESTATE DISCLOSURE

Many jurisdictions have standardized disclosure forms a seller completes and provides to a buyer. Usually it consists of a series of questions about the property and its history and whether specific conditions have been present—a leaking roof, cracked foundation, insect infestation and damage, etc. Information on this form can help you evaluate the relative worth of a parcel of real estate. If your subject claims the true value of their home is only half the amount you expected, a disclosure form they received from the seller (or offered a potential buyer) could help establish the accuracy of the value due to problems like a leaking underground storage tank or boundary line dispute with the neighbor. Like other purchase documents, these forms are not going to be available on the Internet and will need to be obtained directly from the subject.

WARRANTY DEEDS

Warranty Deeds are probably the most common form of deed for real estate. This document verifies (or "warranties") that the buyer is the real owner of the property. When you buy property from a stranger, you would usually expect to receive some sort of Warranty Deed. If there were a problem in the future regarding the title to the property, the seller would be responsible for fulfilling the "warranty" on the title. Warranty Deeds are filed with the applicable county recording office and should be searchable by either the name of the seller (the "grantor") or the buyer (the "grantee").

One other point about deeds: don't automatically assume something is amiss if you see the deed was executed for "ten dollars and other good and valuable consideration." In my experience, the true sales price of a parcel of property is rarely included on the deed. Just because the deed says ten dollars changed hands does not mean the property was sold for ten dollars. If you want to know how much a parcel of property sold for, check with the county tax Assessor's office and don't rely on the deed.

QUIT CLAIM DEEDS

Quit Claim Deeds are different from Warranty Deeds in that there is no guarantee on the title. Instead, a Quit Claim Deed is basically the seller saying, "Whatever title I have I give to you." Married couples frequently use Quit Claim Deeds to transfer property to one another. Quit Claim Deeds are also common in estate planning to transfer property from an individual to a trust. A business that changes corporate forms or names might also use a Quit Claim Deed to change the name of a property owner. However, use of a Quit Claim Deed between strangers is unusual and should cause you to investigate more thoroughly. Just because someone files a Quit Claim Deed doesn't actually mean they own the property. I could theoretically Quit Claim my interest in the White House or the Brooklyn Bridge to a buyer—since I don't have an interest, nothing would be transferred.

Consideration can also be exchanged for Quit Claim Deeds. Like with Warranty Deeds, you could see that a Quit Claim Deed was executed for "ten dollars and other good and valuable consideration." Quit Claim Deeds between family members may even omit the reference to any money at all—the consideration may be "for love and affection."

TRUSTEE'S DEEDS/PERSONAL REPRESENTATIVE'S DEEDS

A Trustee's Deed, Personal Representative's Deed, or Executor's Deed is a deed that is executed on behalf of an entity such as a trust or probate estate. Since a Trustee or Personal Representative frequently doesn't have personal knowledge about the validity of a title, they don't want to be held personally responsible. However, the buyer will likely want more assurance than would be provided by a Quit Claim Deed. If you buy property from a trust or estate you will likely receive something called a Trustee's Deed or Personal Representative's Deed (depending on what type of entity is selling the property). This type of deed allows the person signing to sign on behalf of the entity and not for themselves. You should never see this type of document unless a trust or probate estate is a party to the transaction.

DEED OF TRUST

A Deed of Trust and a Deed are not the same thing. Where a deed transfers title from one owner to another, a Deed of Trust is security for a loan. When you buy a parcel of real estate, the seller gives you a deed to the property. You, in turn, give a Deed of Trust to your mortgage company. Deeds of trust can be very informative in a financial investigation because you can use them to estimate the outstanding mortgage balance on a home.

LIEN

A lien is a document filed to secure payment of a debt. If a parcel of property has a valid lien filed against it, the debt will be paid from the sales proceeds if the property is sold. Tax liens are filed by government entities for back taxes. Mechanic's liens are filed by contractors and materials suppliers for construction work related to a property; if you hire a plumbing contractor and don't pay the full amount due, the contracting company will file a lien for the unpaid debt. Filing a lien does not guarantee payment; the debt will only be paid if the property is sold (and even then only if the lien is valid and perfected). Liens may also be paid off if the owner refinances the property.

When conducting financial investigations, the existence of liens can be very informative. If a parcel of real estate has a mechanic's lien filed against it, it's a safe bet the owner had some work done to the property—which may have affected the property's value. A parcel with a single mechanic's lien may be due to a dispute between contractor and property owner; the existence of multiple liens generally demonstrates significant problems with cash flow.

LIS PENDENS

A *lis pendens* is similar to a lien but is related to a lawsuit. It allows a plaintiff to secure their interest in real estate owned by the defendant by giving notice about the plaintiff's claim. While the property owner could still sell the parcel of real estate, most buyers would be hesitant to take the risk the plaintiff could win their lawsuit and most banks would be hesitant to loan money using the property as collateral since the title isn't clear. A *lis pendens* should only exist if there is a dispute about the property (and only the property the *lis pendens* is filed against, not other property owned by the same subject) or if a foreclosure is imminent. Even though it is related to a lawsuit, a copy of a *lis pendens* should be available from the county recorder's office, not the county court (assuming they are separate entities in the applicable jurisdiction).

LEASE

Most of us are familiar with the concept of a lease. In fact, most of us have signed a lease agreement at least once or twice. When a subject rents an apartment, house, business location, vehicle, or equipment, they should sign an agreement outlining the rights and responsibilities of both parties. A lease is generally a longer term agreement that locks in a specific rental amount for a specific period of time. On rare occasions, the parties may file a copy of a lease at the county auditor's office. Unfortunately, this doesn't happen very often. If you need to obtain a copy of a lease, you will probably have to do so directly from one of the parties to the agreement.

Estate Planning Documents

The jurisdiction where your subject resides (that is, their legal residence—not just where they spend most of their time) can greatly affect the subject's estate plan. What is perfectly normal in one state may be unnecessary in another. Just because the talking head on television says, "everyone should have this document" doesn't mean that's actually true. The following types of documents may be helpful when conducting a financial investigation.

WILL

A Will explains what you want to have happen to your property after you die. It has no effect until that time. After a person dies, their original will should be recorded with the local court that handles probates. Copies are not typically going to be available online, but can be obtained from the applicable court. Wills can help establish familial relationships as well as property ownership.

When you're dealing with wills and probate, it is extremely important to understand what is common in the area. In some jurisdictions, Living Trusts are the norm. Residents may have something called a "pour-over Will" transferring ownership from a deceased person's estate to their trust. In states like California where probate fees are based on the value of a person's estate, the use of this type of estate planning arrangement is widespread. In other states, like Washington, probate fees are not based on the value of the estate and there is little advantage to avoiding probate by using a Living Trust.

TESTAMENTARY TRUST

A Testamentary Trust is a trust that is established because of the terms of a deceased person's Will. There is likely not a separate trust agreement. Instead, if you want to know the provisions of the trust, you need to obtain a copy of the probated Will. You should be able to get a copy for a nominal fee from the applicable court clerk's office.

LIVING TRUST (REVOCABLE OR IRREVOCABLE)

Living Trusts are a very fashionable alternative to writing a Will. They basically do the same thing as a Will: they transfer ownership of property from someone who has died to their heirs. However, a Living Trust accomplishes this very differently than a Will. Instead of going through probate with a court supervising the activities and making sure everyone gets what they are supposed to, a Living Trust is administered privately. There is no court file to request unless there is a lawsuit related to the trust administration. There may not be any public record of how a Living Trust was administered other than deeds and other property records showing a transfer of ownership.

(DURABLE) POWER OF ATTORNEY

If you want someone to be able to do or sign something on your behalf, you can give them the necessary authority by signing a Power of Attorney. This gives the "attorney-in-fact" (the person acting on your behalf) the legal authority to do whatever you authorize in the document. Some Powers of Attorney are for very limited purposes (such as for health care decisions) and some are far more wide reaching. If you come across a Power of Attorney during your investigation, check to see whether it is a "Durable" Power of Attorney. If so, it means the Power of Attorney will still be good even if the grantor is no longer competent (such as they develop dementia or have a stroke or other brain injury and can no longer make decisions for themselves). A Power of Attorney, even a durable one, ends when the grantor dies. After that, you can only deal with their estate.

LIVING WILL

A Living Will is not the same as a Will nor is it a Living Trust. Instead, this document outlines a person's wishes regarding life support measures. It can also be called an "Advance Directive" or "Health Care Directive." A Living Will is not helpful during financial investigations, but it is important to make sure a subject doesn't supply this document when you've requested a copy of a Will or Living Trust.

PRE-/POST-NUPTIAL AGREEMENT

Many of us are familiar, at least in principle, with Pre-Nuptial Agreements. These are agreements that a couple signs before they get married addressing issues such as ownership of property, allocation of debts, and spousal support (alimony) in case of divorce. A Post-Nuptial Agreement is the same type of agreement, but is signed after the wedding instead of before. These documents will not typically be available through a public record unless the couple has filed for divorce and entered a copy of the agreement into evidence in the dissolution proceeding.

Other Miscellaneous Documents

BIRTH/DEATH CERTIFICATE

Birth and death certificates are typically not available online and must be requested from the subject directly. While most states restrict access to birth certificates to relatives, some states do not—anyone can purchase a birth certificate if they have the necessary information (Brown 2000: 9). Death certificates are not always restricted to family members. If you can legally obtain a copy of a birth certificate directly from the applicable Department of Vital Statistics, you should have an excellent reason for doing so instead of obtaining the document from the subject themselves. Older birth certificates, death certificates, and baptismal/confirmation records can sometimes be obtained for free from genealogy websites.

CERTIFICATE OF NATURALIZATION

This is the form a naturalized US citizen is issued when they become a citizen. It contains a photo, a registration number, and information about when citizenship was obtained. The original of this form is number I-550; if a naturalized citizen needs a replacement certificate, it is form number I-570. A naturalization certificate is different from a Certificate of Citizenship (form I-560). Citizenship certificates are issued to US citizens born abroad, not to foreign nationals who become US citizens (North Dakota 2004).

"GREEN CARD"

Although Americans still commonly refer to this document as a "green card," a "Permanent Resident Card" is no longer green. It is an identification card that looks like most other forms of ID. It will contain a subject's photo and other identifying information. Any permanent resident should be able to produce this document just as they can produce their driver's license or other forms of identification, but it is not available for free on the Internet. This document may also be referred to by its form number, I-151.

MARRIAGE CERTIFICATE

Marriage certificates are filed in the county where the marriage took place and are usually available from the county recorder's office. However, because of privacy concerns, many counties have stopped making marriage licenses and certificates available from online searches. If that is the case in your jurisdiction, the summary information may still be available online, including the date of the application or certificate and the names of the bride and groom. This information can help narrow your search and, if you need to obtain a copy of the application or certificate itself, you can request it by its recording number. Marriage certificates can be helpful to establish the true date of a marriage or simply to establish that a subject is, in fact, married. They can also be useful to establish familial relationships (by tracing maiden names) and other personal relationships (by examining the names of the witnesses).

DD-214

A DD-214 is the document that is issued to former members of the United States military when they are discharged from service. This document will not only verify dates and branch of military service, but will also verify whether a subject received an honorable discharge or some other type of discharge. Access to this document may be limited because it contains the subject's Social Security Number, but they are frequently filed with the local county recorder's office. If you have collected a DD-214, either from the county or directly from the subject, make sure you note whether the subject's Social Security Number and other legally protected information has been redacted and make sure it is marked to prevent unauthorized disclosure.

RELEASE

A release can apply to a number of legal situations, but usually means exactly what it says: someone is released from an obligation of some sort. If you find a release, look for the document that is being released. In order to have a "release of lien," there must be a lien to release. There should also be some reason the lien or other obligation was released, such a payment of the amount owed or some sort of settlement for a lesser amount.

Other Documents

The list above is not completely comprehensive—there are other types of documents you may discover during your investigation, however, the ones listed here are a good start and will be the ones you are most likely to discover, especially from Internet-based sources. If you find other documents that seem like they might be applicable, but you don't know what they are or why someone would create them, consult with an attorney, accountant, or more experienced co-worker to find out more information.

Case in Point

Sometimes when verifying information with recorded documents, you find things you didn't even know you were looking for. My favorite example is a case I investigated that seemed fairly routine at first. The subject had provided the requested documentation, but things just seemed a bit off. The subject lived in another state, so I decided to check the address they had listed as their home address. It was an address on a major thoroughfare and caused me to assume it was actually the subject's business address instead.

When I typed the address into the search box at the county Assessor's office, I got a very odd result. The search told me it was a municipal property. Public property? How could that be? So I typed the address into a mapping website and found what the address belonged to: a major international airport. While the subject did have a business relationship with that particular airport, they had reported this as their home address. The phrase, "All hail Jay! All hail Jay!" (from the movie "*Men in Black II*") became a running joke in the office—we imagined the subject living in a storage locker at the airport (Sonnenfeld 2002).

Additional checks on the county Assessor's website finally located the owner's home address. I never received a clear explanation from the subject why they reported this as their home address. But given the subject's behavior during the case, I suspect they were just careless. The subject assumed it didn't really matter what address they provided and that no one was going to check. That carelessness led to hundreds of hours of unnecessary work that could have been avoided if the subject had simply followed instructions.

CHAPTER **7** *Starting the Search*

So now you're ready to start your investigation. Just log on to Google and go for it, right? Not quite. Instead, the first step in your investigation should be organizing the information you have and starting to identify the information you still need. This extra work at the beginning may take a few minutes but will help save unnecessary work later in your investigation.

Preparing Your Investigation

One preliminary step I recommend is starting four lists: one for follow-up questions, one for verification, one for investigation, and one for important names. Depending on your personal preferences, these could be four different sheets of paper with handwritten notes, a single sheet of paper with four columns of handwritten notes, a word processing document with separate sheets of paper, or maybe a spreadsheet workbook with four columns or worksheet tabs. If your computer setup has multiple monitors, keeping your lists in your word processing or spreadsheet program might be the most efficient. However, if you have just a single monitor it may be easier to keep handwritten notes so you can refer to your lists while still looking at information on your computer screen.

Your list of follow-up questions will be questions you need to ask the subject or other interested party. Application questions that have been skipped, missing supporting documents, or questions that need more explanation are good examples of follow-up questions you need to ask. Depending on the results of your investigation, you may want to ask follow-up questions about specific information you discover or about results that don't make sense to you.

The second list you will want to keep is of information that needs verification. If your job entails reviewing routine information, you may even want to develop a checklist for the information you need to verify on a regular basis. Any information related to the subject or the purpose of your investigation might require verification, so don't limit yourself to verifying only the most important facts. Is the company really a business? Does the tax parcel number provided match up with the subject's address? Is the subject's professional license active or has it been suspended for misconduct? What is the current value of the subject's luxury car? Even information that seems tangential may lead you to crucial information later in your investigation. Remember, when subjects lie about the small things, they are frequently lying about the big issues as well.

The third list you need to keep is of information that needs investigation. This is the list where you will want to keep track of related businesses and people, red flags you discover during your review, and other information that needs more research. Information on this list might include a history of ownership of a parcel of real estate, other property or vehicles not included on a list of assets, or the corporate history of a subject company. Anything you come across that raises a red flag should go on this list.

After you have your first three lists ready to go, look at the information you already have. Depending on the nature of your investigation, you could have a comprehensive application with boxes of supporting documentation or maybe you're starting with nothing more than an anonymous phone tip. Whatever you have, make sure it is organized and as complete as possible.

Next, you'll want to assemble some basic information about your subject, any associated businesses, and any related entities. Record this information on your fourth and final list. For an individual, knowing their complete name is vital. Make sure you know the proper spelling, any spelling variations, previous names, suffixes, and nicknames. Every name and spelling you come across should go on your names list. For businesses and other entities, you'll also want to know the names of all officers, directors, managers, trustees, and other responsible individuals. For all investigations, you'll want current and previous street addresses, current and previous mailing addresses (which may or may not be different from street addresses), and current and previous telephone numbers (including fax and cell numbers). If you have a legitimate reason for obtaining it, a Social Security Number can be helpful—but keep in mind the ethical issues related to this type of sensitive information. Names of current spouses, former spouses, current and former girl/boyfriends, children, parents, cousins, former business partners, and other known associates can also come in handy, especially when looking for transferred assets. One approach I sometimes use is to ask myself whom I might trust with an asset I was trying to hide. Family and friends are always at the top of that list. For each of these names, give them a separate line on the page with enough room to note their relationship to your investigation and any other relevant information.

OPTIONAL BUT HELPFUL INFORMATION

While not absolutely necessary, there is other information that can be helpful in an investigation. If you have access to any of the following, make sure to include them in your lists so they aren't overlooked.

Signature

A handwriting or signature sample can be extremely useful for determining whether the document you're looking at applies to the subject or someone else who happens to have the same name (which is a very common occurrence). For example, if you believe you have located a parcel of real property that the subject didn't disclose, look at the Deed of Trust. If the signature the not the same, then you have probably found property owned by someone who happens to have the same name as your subject.

Previous connections

Previous employers, customers, and clients can be both interesting sources of information as well as good identifiers (again for distinguishing the subject from someone else with the same name).

Hobbies

The subject's hobbies, social activities (both industry-specific and not), religious affiliation and activities, hometown, schools attended, and any previous military experience can also be helpful information. In addition to distinguishing different people with the same name, this type of information can help you determine if a subject is underreporting their income or assets. Specialized hobbies, mandatory religious obligations, and attendance at conferences and other meetings can all be very expensive; a subject's participation in these activities should correspond with their reported financial situation.

Tax returns

Tax returns and supporting schedules can contain a wealth of information, especially when you are looking for assets that have not otherwise been disclosed. With regard to personal tax returns, other key things to look out for include deductions for mortgage interest, profits or losses from business ownership, self-employment tax, and other deductions. Does everything match and does it all make sense?

Other business records

Business records can provide clues that warrant further investigation. What sort of inventory should the company have, especially if they are in a service industry? Who are the listed owners? How many shareholders are reported and how much of the company does each own? Does that information match other information you have about the company? Does the company identify any parents or subsidiaries? Are the firm's retained earnings increasing or decreasing? Is the amount of depreciation listed in line with the amount of real and personal property they're reporting? Anything that doesn't match or seems out of place may warrant additional verification and investigation.

Insurance policies

If you have access, another great place for information is insurance policies. If a subject's home is worth $500,000, they shouldn't be reporting personal property of $10,000. Depending on your insurance company, your personal property is probably valued somewhere around 60–80 percent of the total value of your home (70 percent is a common figure). Is what they're telling you the same as what they're telling their insurance company? If not, why not?

Planning Your Investigation

While optional, I strongly recommend beginning your investigation by writing an investigation plan. If the nature of your investigation is more routine and doesn't tend to vary, an investigation plan may not be particularly helpful and using the four forms listed above may be enough. However, for complex, nonroutine, or potentially controversial investigations, an investigation plan may prove invaluable by helping guide your investigation and providing you with some protection in case you are accused of an improper or negligent investigation.

What exactly is an investigation plan? It is a summary of not only what you need to investigate but also how and where you are going to do so. The four lists explained above are a big component in your investigation plan with each being an important section. By preparing the four lists, you've finished half your investigation plan without even trying. The remaining half of your plan explains the purpose of your investigation, the various websites and other resources you are going to access, whether personal visits or interviews will be needed (and if so, with whom and for what purpose), any specialized assistance you think you will need, and any other information related to your investigation. Most importantly, your investigation plan should include an explanation of how and when you accomplished each step in the plan. That means your investigation plan is not something that is prepared once and never referred to again. Your plan is a "living" document that grows, adapts, and changes to meet your needs throughout the investigation.

If your agency does not already have a standardized form for an investigation plan, refer to the boilerplate provided in Appendix C. Feel free to adapt and customize the form to meet your individual needs.

How Should I Start Looking on the Internet?

Searching the Internet is as much an art as it is a science. That means you need to think about not only what you are looking for, but also how that information could be mistakenly entered. Typos happen; that's just an unpleasant fact. The trick is finding a balance between focusing your search so you don't find too much extraneous information and expanding your search to find relevant information that might be mislabeled or misspelled.

When using a search engine or searching a database or for an individual, you'll want to search under their current name, previous name(s), and nicknames. For many names, you'll also want to run searches for common spelling variations (e.g., Mary Anne, Mary Ann, MaryAnne, MaryAnn, Maryanne, Maryann, Marianne, Mariann, Marian, and Marion). You should also search using both the "Given name, Surname" and "Surname, Given name" formats. Depending on the structure of the database you're searching and the personal preferences of the subject, you might also want to search using the initial instead of the full given name. If you know the subject's middle name, you should also search using the "Middle name Surname" format and, if the last name is not too common, using the "M. Surname" (middle initial) format. Varying the name order is especially important when running searches for non-English names, especially Asian names and other cultures where the family/surname comes before the individual's given name. Also remember to check common nicknames and shorter versions of the subject's name, even if the subject doesn't typically use those shorter names. (I never cease to be amazed by the number of people who are introduced to me as "Kimberly" and immediately respond, "Nice to meet you, Kim.") If you are searching using an initial, make sure to search for initials for both the name as well as the nickname if they are different: "R" for Robert and "B" for Bob.

Searching for business names can be a bit more challenging. Starting your search with the company's true legal business name is a great place to start. Keep in mind that some databases are sensitive to the use of punctuation—"ABC Company, Inc." may not be the same as "A.B.C. Company, Inc." which may be different from "A.B.C. Company Inc." Not every database will make these distinctions, so it is important to make sure you know what type of database you are working with. It is also important to search for multiple variations of a company name in case the information you're working with is incorrect or incomplete. Just because your subject company reports their name as "ABC Company, Inc." doesn't necessarily mean they didn't tell your Secretary of State or state taxing authority their name is "A.B.C. Company, Inc." Take the time to search under each variation.

When searching for businesses, it's important to expand your search parameters more than you might when searching for an individual. While you should start by searching for a business under its real name, you should always follow up with any trade names the company either currently uses or has used in the past. Other variations should include searching for company names excluding any "Inc." or "LLC," searching for company names excluding any odd words, and searching for a company by the owner's surname and a one-word description of the company's industry. In some cases, searching for the names of competing companies or searching by an industry in a given city may produce results if other searches aren't generating leads.

One final note about business names: I have found that business owners who establish multiple companies have a tendency to be fairly unoriginal in naming those companies. They seem to pick names that are directly related to themselves or some aspect of their business. Are there two owners of the company? Don't be surprised if they set up a company that combines their two names. Variations on pet's names, children's names, parent's names, family names, hometowns, physical locations, and personal experiences all provide inspiration for company names. When company owners find a name they like, they may simply give subsequent companies the same name with a "I," "II," or "III" at the end.

Performing the Investigation

One important aspect of conducting an investigation—especially one using Internet resources—is to document your findings. Internet pages can change at a moment's notice. If there is a potential you will rely on Internet-based information to make a decision or substantiate an allegation, you must have a hard copy of the information. Do not assume the same information will be there tomorrow. Make sure you print out any important information and set up your Internet browser so that it automatically includes the date, time, and web address of the page in question. When dealing with extremely long documents when only a small portion is relevant, print out both the first page of the document, the relevant portion, and any other information documenting the source or author.

Where Should I Start Looking on the Internet?

There's no single place to look or single procedure to follow when trying to track down hidden assets. The purpose of this book is to discuss a methodology for conducting a financial investigation, not merely to provide a specific procedure to follow step-by-step. Keeping up with what's available on the Internet is a full-time job and none of us has the time to dedicate to keeping current with every possible resource. The web resources highlighted here are not the only ones in existence. There will undoubtedly be more resources available tomorrow than there are today. The goal of this book is to give you a taste of what's out there, how you can go about finding it, and how to use it once you do find it. Even routine investigations that cover the same basic information every time don't follow the same procedure every time. However, it is a good idea to follow a standard procedure at the beginning of each search. This minimizes the possibility that you will forget something. Follow a standard procedure for the basics, then customize your search based on what you find.

STARTING YOUR SEARCH: HOME PAGES AND GOOGLE

After you've organized your investigation, the next step would be checking the sites listed that are applicable to your investigation. The first place on the Internet you should visit when conducting an investigation is any website related to your subject. While many individuals don't have personal web pages, most businesses do. These pages can provide a wealth of information, including the names of owners, officers, managers, and key employees, as well as relationships with other companies and the company's history. Each of these pieces of information can be important to your investigation. And although an individual may not have a website, they may have a blog ("web log"), MySpace, Facebook, or Twitter page that can provide interesting and helpful information.

After reviewing an individual's or company's web pages, it's logical to see what other web pages are readily available. Now is the time for at least one search engine. While Google may be the first name that jumps to mind, there are many other options available. Start with the one you are most comfortable with, be it Google, Bing, Ask.com, Quintura, or one of the others. Make sure you follow-up on the various search possibilities mentioned above (Given name Surname; Surname, Given name; etc.). If you find too many results, limit your search by placing quotation marks around your search terms—such as "Given name Surname"—to restrict your search to results that are more likely to be applicable. You can also try adding terms you know might show up on a web page along with your search term; good choices might include the name of a city or the industry or profession of your subject. If your search does not return enough useful results, try another search engine. Each has strengths and weaknesses, and sometimes one will work better than another will. Specific information about many different search engines is available in the next chapter.

STATE BUSINESS AND PROFESSIONS SOURCES

The next source of information to investigate comes from your investigation plan: your list of information to be verified. This most likely means starting with government databases to verify licenses, permits, business registrations, and similar information. Is it required that you start with this type of website? Of course not, you can start anywhere you please. However, starting your investigation with simple and routine matters helps set the tone for the rest of your investigation. If a subject has misrepresented their business or lied about having a professional license, it's best to know that before you delve deeper into your research.

The government databases you access for this initial round of review should probably start with the applicable Secretary of States' offices—both your state and the company's home state if different. Look for a "Corporations" division or something with a similar name (even if you're looking for an LLC). Although not all types of businesses are required to register with the Secretary of State, it is still good practice to run a routine check. Just because a company claims they are a sole proprietor or general partnership does not mean that information is actually correct. In most states, it takes just a few seconds to double check and make sure the company's representations about their legal structure are accurate.

Some states may allow you to directly access copies of corporate filings, but others just provide summary information. At the very least, you should be able to learn a company's legal structure, who its officers or managers are, where it is located, and who its registered agent is. Some Secretary of State websites—Georgia is an excellent example—have extensive search capabilities; you can search not only by company name and registered agent name, but also by the names of corporate officers. This capability can prove extremely helpful if you are trying to find names of related individuals as well as other companies a subject might own or control. In many investigations I have conducted, I found multiple companies owned and controlled by a relatively static group of people. Members of an extended family or a group of trusted friends will typically involve each other when they open a second, third, or fourth company. If you can search by officer or manager name, you can find other businesses that may not have been previously disclosed. Even if your subject is not listed as an owner or officer, finding other companies that are owned or controlled by their friends or family members can provide you with insight about business transactions between your subject or their company and the businesses owned by friends and relatives.

If the Secretary of State search does not have an option for searching by officer, there may be another agency in that jurisdiction which does. Washington State is a good example of this: although you cannot search the Secretary of State's online database by owner or officer name, you can search the Department of Licensing's business database using those fields. If the jurisdiction where you're searching does not provide either option online, try calling the agency and asking if they can perform the search for you.

Be aware that many companies use a professional firm, attorney, or accountant as their registered agent, so you cannot assume the registered agent has any control over a company's day-to-day operations. However, if your subject is both the registered agent and an officer or director of the company, then that is a good indication they are involved in the firm's operations. In addition, if a subject company has retained the services of an attorney or accountant to act as their registered agent, they may have done the same for other affiliated companies. While you cannot assume that every company with the same registered agent is connected to one another, a search for all the companies with the same agent can provide you with a list for further investigation.

For searches that allow you access to copies of filed documents, this is a good time to review those routine filings. Articles of Incorporation, Certificates of Formation, and Annual Reports (as applicable) should be at the top of your list. Who were the incorporators? Who are the current officers or managers? Has the business changed location? Each of these items could prove useful later in your investigation, so it is worth taking a few minutes early in the process to collect the relevant information.

If you are dealing with a company that was formed in another state, you should always make sure you compare the information available from both your state and the company's home state. The registered agent should be different in each state, because a registered agent must be based in the state where they serve. However, the officers and directors (for a corporation) or the members and managers (for an LLC) should be the same in both states. If they are not, this is a red flag that needs additional follow-up. You may be looking at two companies with the same name instead of two registrations for the same business.

Some states have a separate state agency that handles assumed business names and related filings, but others make it available from the same website. If the Secretary of State's office handles these filings—as they do in Oregon—make sure you verify this information at the same time. Knowing a company's trade or "doing business as" (or "DBA") name is crucial to any financial investigation. If a company has different trade and legal names, many of the records you are looking for may be listed under the trade name instead of the legal name.

Some jurisdictions also maintain a separate listing for business licenses and tax registrations. While you may not find much tax information available online, you can sometimes find a taxpayer identification number. Independently, this information may not be particularly helpful. However, taxpayer identification numbers are similar to Social Security Numbers in that a company should not have more than one in any jurisdiction, and the same entity should have the same number. If a subject company claims that "Joe's Lawnmower Shop" and "1-2-3 Legal Services, Inc." are separate companies, yet they share the same taxpayer ID number for either the state or federal taxing authority, that would be an indication the taxing authority thinks the two companies are not separate.

Another search that you may be able to perform at the Secretary of State's website is a search for UCC filings. In many jurisdictions, there is a fee for searching and obtaining copies of UCC documents. However, some jurisdictions will allow you to perform a search for free even though you will need to pay to obtain the relevant documents. If you can search for free, or if you have reason to believe a UCC document should be on file for your subject, run a check for all the relevant names.

After you have examined the available business records, the next step is to review any other licenses or permits that may be connected to your subject. Some types of companies are required by law to have specific licenses held either by the company itself or by an owner, officer, or other key manager. Knowing about these types of licenses can help you discover an ownership interest in another business or another owner or manager that you previously weren't aware of. This review may include checking professional licenses and registrations (such as for doctors, lawyers, or accountants) and other occupational licenses and registrations (such as for construction contractors, collection agencies, or notaries public). You may be surprised at the number of professions that require licensing, so it is a good idea to check with a jurisdiction's business or professions regulating body to find out which are subject to registration requirements and which are not.

Checking the status of professional licenses and registrations can provide you with additional insight into a subject. Obviously, if a firm is required to have a license but has allowed it to expire, it may not be legal for that business to operate. Businesses that maintain a license but work outside the scope of their authority (such as a licensed plumber performing electrical work) may play fast and loose with other legal requirements. The presence of an unused license may also provide insight about a subject or a related company. Licenses and professional registrations typically require effort to maintain: fees must be paid, continuing education credits must be reported, and forms must be completed and returned to the licensing entity. When a subject maintains an active license, yet purports to not use that license, it is worth investigating why the license is still active. Sometimes, it makes sense for a subject to maintain a license because they would have to do extensive work if they allowed the license to lapse and changed their mind in the future. A good example would be a law license: no one wants to have to take the bar exam over again. Even if an attorney chooses not to practice law, it is likely worthwhile for them to maintain an active law license in case they ever want to practice in the future. Other licenses, however, do not make sense to maintain if they are not being used. A Notary Public registration or a Food Handler's Permit are examples of registrations that may not make sense to maintain if they are not being used. If allowed to lapse, they are relatively easy to regain.

Professional licensing can also affect how a business operates on a day-to-day basis and who in the company actually exerts control. Many types of professions require someone in the company to take ultimate responsibility for overseeing the firm's operations—such as a professional engineer signing and stamping plans prepared by an engineering firm's employees or a master electrician overseeing the work performed by an electrical contracting firm. Even if that person is not an owner of the company, they may ultimately control the firm's operations. If you are investigating a company that has some sort of a requirement for an ultimate authority, make sure you take this opportunity to establish whom that person is and what their ownership interest is in the company. If that person does not have an ownership interest in the company, it is important to understand why the owner gives that employee control over the company's operations.

Another resource that may be available through a state government website is information about political contributions. Some jurisdictions require all political donations to be disclosed using the donor's name, address, and employer. Some subjects may list an alternative name for their employer, which can give you more search terms. Remember that subjects will often donate to both sides in a political contest, so don't assume donations tell you about the subject's personal beliefs. The point of looking up political contributions is not to figure out whether the subject is a conservative or liberal, Democrat or Republican. The point of your investigation is to find hidden assets; that means a subject's political contributions should be in line with their alleged net worth and income. A subject claiming they can't afford to pay a $25,000 fine or $2,500 per month in child support shouldn't be able to afford to donate $250,000 to the political cause of their choice. If you choose to access information about political contributions, make sure you stay firmly on the side of the financial aspect of the donation—the name listed, the address provided, employer name, and the amount donated. The recipient of the donation is likely irrelevant to your investigation and may not even be relevant to your final report. Keep in mind that any use of political contribution information could lead to allegations of unfair treatment, so the information you gain needs to outweigh any potential conflict it causes. This may be a bigger issue in some jurisdictions than in others. In states or locales well-known for colorful politics, it might be wise to avoid the issue of political contributions all together.

If you are a brand-new investigator, or if you are investigating a subject in an unfamiliar jurisdiction, you may not know where else to look. In cases like this, it can be very helpful to look for information about starting a new business. Most states make it relatively easy to find information about how to start a new business and what requirements you need to comply with in order to operate legally. If you don't know what state agencies regulate or oversee your subject and their business, pretend you are establishing a new business in the same line of work. What steps would you have to follow in order to create and operate your new business? Those steps are the same steps your subject should have followed. The agencies that would oversee your new business are the same ones you should check to find out about your subject.

Finally, the jurisdiction you're searching in may have specific websites that are only applicable to that particular locale. If you are working in the state where you live, think about things that are unique to your state: special licensing requirements, special taxes, special permits, etc. If any of those exist, there may be a database you can search. If you are unfamiliar with the jurisdiction or are otherwise unsure of what options are available, go to the main state government website and look for a link to a list of all government agencies and offices. From that list of agencies, look for anything that looks like it might be applicable to your investigation.

COUNTY SOURCES: PROPERTY RECORDS AND COURT FILINGS

Many of the most helpful financial records can be found at your local county offices—or if you're lucky, on the county's website. While smaller, less populous, and less affluent counties may not have made records available online, many counties will allow you to obtain at least an index of documents from their website. In many jurisdictions you can search for free, but in other jurisdictions you may have to pay a commercial indexing service to obtain the records.

Court records, both at the state and federal level, can be helpful as well. State courts are frequently administered on a county basis (or a group of counties that make up a circuit court), so the records should be available at that local level. While the specifics of divorce and other family-related cases may be restricted, criminal and most other civil (noncriminal) cases should be available for review. Local, county, and state courts that provide online searches typically make case dockets or summaries available. You should be able to learn the type of lawsuit, who the parties were, and the final outcome. It is not common for local, county, or state courts to make actual documents—such as motions, affidavits, or judgments—available online. Even though decisions for cases in local and county courts are not typically available from the court's website, decisions in cases that are particularly noteworthy or controversial might be published on a website by one of the parties to the lawsuit. As electronic filing of legal documents becomes more common, it is more likely lawsuit documents will eventually be routinely available online. Until then, you should plan on visiting the county courthouse or requesting specific records by mail if you actually want copies of relevant documents.

Some court resources are available online, especially decisions in cases that have been appealed. State court appeal decisions are usually reported in the official state reporter, a reporter covering numerous states, or both. Federal court cases are the published in a similar manner: initial decisions are not typically going to be available on-line, but decisions of appeals are available from a variety of web sites. Bankruptcy Court filings can also provide a great deal of information. More information on accessing court documents can be found in Chapter 10.

FEDERAL RESOURCES

Most of the time, the government records that you can access over the Internet are going to be from state and local websites, though on some occasions you may get lucky and find federal resources as well. Depending on the type of investigations you typically conduct and the industry your subject is in, you may also want to try checking some federal databases as well.

Industry-specific registrations and certifications aren't always going to be helpful and don't apply to most businesses. However, when they do apply you may find interesting information about ownership, control, and assets. Certifications through the Small Business Administration's 8(a) Program or US Department of Transportation's Disadvantaged Business Enterprise Program can be good resources for information. Both of these programs are for businesses owned and controlled by minorities and other people who have encountered systemic discrimination. The application process for both these programs can be long and arduous, depending on the type of business and the certification being applied for. Businesses with one or both of these certifications typically try to participate in public works projects, public contracting, or other public jobs. These certifications are similar to, but are not the same thing, as private-sector certification as a minority-owned, woman-owned business, or veteran-owned business.

Public comments, like the proposed regulations they cover, are public records. Many federal agencies make public comments filed with their office available through a searchable database at *www.regulations.gov*. If you don't find what you're looking for there, check the website of the specific agency. State agencies may or may not make copies of public comments available online. Public comments can sometimes help you better understand your subject—who they are as a person and how they see the world. Public comments can also sometimes help you identify connections between subjects and companies. If you find your subject has submitted a public comment on a proposed new federal regulation, take a look at other comments submitted about the same proposal. You may be surprised to find identical or nearly identical comments from multiple commentators. It is not uncommon for industry advocacy groups to supply form letters for their members to submit. Multiple subsidiaries in the same corporate family may have their attorney draft a single set of comments that each corporate sibling submits independently. If you find your subject has submitted public comments that are identical or very similar to other comments submitted by other companies, you should try to establish the source of the comments and whether there is an undisclosed relationship between the commentators.

Patents and trademarks are potentially valuable assets, especially in the technology and telecommunications industries. The federal patent and trademark database is searchable for free either directly from the US Patent and Trademark Office's website or from Google's patent search. I actually find Google's site more user-friendly, but both sites contain the same information.

Other federal agencies also provide extensive public information over the Internet. The US Environmental Protection Agency provides numerous searchable databases for some types of businesses. Information about hazardous waste sites, toxic chemicals released, and dangerous chemicals used can be obtained directly from the EPA as well as from many state environmental agencies. Even in you are not specifically interested in a company's environmental obligations or violations, they tend to carry very high price tags. A company that is obligated to perform a multi-million dollar environmental cleanup may not have funds available to fulfill the obligations you are investigating.

Stumbling Across Other Sites

In addition to the sites listed here, there are two other categories of websites you may want to check during your investigation. The first of these categories is websites that are specific to your industry or regulations. Maybe your investigation requires a fingerprint check, so you routinely check AFIS (the Automated Fingerprint Identification System). Or maybe your state requires businesses to obtain a unique registration to conduct business, so you need to verify that registration in all your investigations. Whatever the underlying reason, make sure you always check any websites that apply to your work even if there is no mention of them in this book.

The other type of website not mentioned here that you may want to check during your investigation is websites that don't exist today. Keep your eyes open for news articles, links, and other mentions that may give you clues about new websites. Web portals like Yahoo! and AOL can give you helpful tips about new websites that may be applicable to your investigation work.

Case in Point

Sometimes you need to do more than simply rely on the documents you obtain from the subject, receive from a complainant, or find on the Internet yourself. Sometimes visiting a business location can provide a wealth of information that you might not be able to obtain in any other way. For example, during a routine investigation, I once decided to stop by a business I was investigating. At the time, I had some suspicions about whether the business was legitimate. That day, I happened to be attending an unrelated meeting at the university just up the street from this company's storefront location, so I decided I'd stop by on my way home and introduce myself to the owner. I hoped to get a better feel for who this person was and whether the company's application was genuine.

After my meeting was over, I got in the car and drove up the street towards the business. As I was looking for the address, I found a car dealership with a similar address adjacent to a lot that was vacant except for cars for sale. The street number of the building on the other side of the vacant lot was too high, but the street number of the car dealership office was too low. I couldn't understand why I couldn't find the store and instead chalked it up to a typo.

When I returned to my office, I double-checked the address and found that there was no "typo." I had been in exactly the right place. It turned out the address the applicant provided as being the company's store was, in fact, the street address of the vacant lot. There was no store selling products to the public. The company was actually a sham—an attempt by the applicant owner to get a government contract through fraudulent means. Once I discovered this deception, the rest of the pieces fell into place. The company did not end up getting a government contract.

8 *Real Estate Records*

Real estate documents—especially deeds and Deeds of Trust—are probably the best resource when looking for hidden assets. All ownership transfers leave a trail, irrespective of whether the transfer was for legitimate reasons. Reviewing real estate documents can help you establish when a subject has attempted to hide assets in someone else's name.

Accessing Land Records

The first county resource I usually access is the county auditor's office, sometimes referred to as the "recorder's office." This is where you can look for real property records (like deeds and liens), marriage records, and powers of attorney. Due to privacy concerns, many county auditors do not make all documents available online, or they limit those available online to documents that are unlikely to contain information such as a Social Security Number or other personal information.

Recorded property documents are the best way to track and establish ownership of real estate. If you want to find out how many parcels of real estate someone owns, you could simply call up the county Tax Assessor's office and ask. But if your subject has hidden assets in someone else's name, you won't find them using this method. Instead of looking for property owned by your subject, try running a search for property records listing your subject's name irrespective of whether they are listed as an owner. Deeds and Deeds of Trust are the most helpful documents because they clearly show an ownership interest in a parcel of real estate. If you are lucky, the documents you find may reference a tax parcel number—this is golden. It will save you considerable time and effort if you know the parcel number. Unfortunately, recorded documents frequently do not contain a tax parcel number and instead only list the property's legal description. Although more cumbersome this is still a good way to identify parcels of property. There may also be an abbreviated form of the legal description including three or four references: Section, Township, Range, and Quarter. These four numbers are not sufficient to locate the exact property, but will get you in the right neighborhood. You may find a street address listed on the document; this can also be helpful, but don't assume the mailing address listed on the document is the same as the subject property's address. Street addresses can also be less helpful when they refer to a portion of a bigger property, such as a single condominium in a large complex. I have also found that the common street address used by the post office is not always the street address according to the county; occasionally, the street number will be the same but the name of the road will be different.

Make a list of every deed that lists your subject, both as grantee or grantor. Your list should contain the recording number of the source document, the type of source document (e.g., a Statutory Warranty Deed, a Quit Claim Deed, etc.), the buyer's name, the seller's name, the date of acquisition, the parcel's identifier (tax parcel number, abbreviated legal description, and/or street address—whichever one you know), and a column to mark which entries need additional follow-up and why. Keep track of each parcel of real estate you find because you will eventually want to confirm current ownership for each of these parcels, even if it appears your subject no longer owns the property.

Repeat the steps above for each subject and related party. This is especially important if the names of related parties appear on the documents you've found. Any deeds from your subject to a company they own, a member of their family, or a close friend deserves a closer look. If you are checking for properties in more than one county, separate lists for each jurisdiction will probably be helpful.

After you have completed compiling your list of properties, the next step is to verify the current ownership and value of each property. The easiest way to accomplish this is to visit the website of the county Assessor's office. The assessor can tell you who is listed as the taxpayer for each parcel and the current assessed value of each property. Although the taxpayer isn't necessarily the owner, it's a safe bet that any taxpayer has some connection to the property. (Would you pay the real estate taxes on a property you didn't own or occupy without a really good reason?)

If you were lucky enough to find deeds referencing a tax parcel number or street address, enter that information into the applicable search box and see what comes up. At the very least, you should be able to find out the name of the taxpayer, the amount of annual taxes on the property, a payment history, and most importantly, the assessed value of the property. It's important to know how assessed value and market value compare in that jurisdiction; it's generally safe to assume that assessed value is less than the true market value of a property. I have seen cases where the assessed value was 20–50 percent lower than the actual market value of the property in question. If you don't know how market and assessed values compare in the jurisdiction you're searching, try comparing the assessed values against market values of nearby properties. Checking real estate ads and then comparing the sales price against the assessed values can give you an idea of how close assessed values are to the true market value. Some assessors may give you information other than just taxpayer name, taxes assessed, and property value. Sometimes the information you can obtain from the county Assessor may include specific information about the property such as the type of building, year built, and any building permits issued. This information can also be helpful because it can help you establish or verify the purported value. If your subject claims the property is worthless, they shouldn't have recently obtained building permits on the site. Even in the slowest market, a property should probably not rent for less than its annual property taxes.

If the county you are searching in provides the option to get property information from a map, this can also be helpful. If you don't have the option to find property information from a map, simply write down the tax parcel numbers or street addresses of nearby properties and look them up separately. Check the properties adjacent to, or nearby your subject's property, including properties across the street and behind the property—you may find properties owned by the subject's companies or related individuals that you didn't know to check.

One additional note: it is important not to restrict your search to just the county you know is applicable. County size varies from region to region. The states of Washington and Missouri are about the same geographic size, but Missouri has almost three times as many counties as Washington—115 versus 39. Just because a subject lives or works in a particular county does not mean they don't own property in other counties. It is worthwhile to check a reasonable radius around the subject's home or workplace, depending on social norms in the area. A 60–100 mile radius might not be unreasonable, especially in rural areas where residents are accustomed to driving long distances. If the subject lives near a common recreational area, you may also want to check for cabins or campsites even if they fall outside your predetermined search radius.

The overriding lesson with real estate is not to look for ownership of assets, look for transfers of assets and follow that up with verification of ownership. If your subject has surreptitiously transferred the title to one or more parcels of real estate, the only way to prove that is to establish the subject's ownership and that the subsequent transfer was not legitimate. Again, don't look for Bigfoot—look for footprints instead.

Establishing a Reasonable Value

The first place I usually check when trying to establish the value of a parcel of real estate is the county Tax Assessor's office. While the assessor won't report the current fair market value of a property, you can use the assessed value to estimate the fair market value (as discussed above). The accuracy of the assessed value when compared to the fair market value is going to vary from county to county and year to year. Usually, the assessed value will be lower than the fair market value and may reflect a true market price minus an estimate for real estate closing fees and agent commissions that would be paid at the time of a sale. When real estate values in an area drop quickly and significantly, the assessed value may be too high until the next round of assessments is performed.

The next website to visit when estimating a value for real estate is Zillow. This website uses some proprietary algorithms to estimate a fair market value for residential property based on recent comparable sales. Zillow isn't perfect, but can give you an excellent ballpark for confirming or refuting an alleged value. If your subject reports their home is worth $100,000 but Zillow reports a value of $1 million, you know you're onto something. Zillow's main limitation is that it only applies to residential property, not commercial real estate.

Real estate comparables are a good way to estimate the value of a parcel of real property. Although Zillow might be your first and best resource, don't overlook other sites as well. The multiple listing service in your jurisdiction should be accessible through any one of a number of real estate agencies, covering both commercial and residential properties.

Falling Real Estate Values

Depending on economic conditions at the time, it is possible the subject is underwater on their mortgage. An "underwater" mortgage is one where the borrower owes more on the property than the property is currently worth. During the last recession, this became a significant problem for many homeowners when the housing bubble burst. Using Internet-based tools is probably the best way to confirm or refute the existence of an underwater mortgage. The Internet is dynamic and up-to-date. Information that helps you determine value and debt can change on a daily basis. Sometimes the only place to find current data is on the Internet (on sites such as Zillow).

In my experience, underwater mortgages are a relatively uncommon occurrence in normal economic times. If a subject claims to be underwater on their mortgage, do not simply assume this is correct. Depending on the market, the type of property, and how long the subject has owned the property, their claims of being underwater may or may not be overstated. Even in cases where a subject is underwater on their mortgage, this fact does not in and of itself demonstrate a lack of financial stability. Unless the subject is actively trying to sell the property, the fact they owe more on the mortgage than the market will currently support may not be relevant.

Underwater mortgages are only a significant concern if the subject is behind on their mortgage payments or is required to sell the property (say because of a divorce or need to move to a new city). If you are looking at a subject's bigger-picture financial situation, underwater mortgages can be challenging to account for if the rules are not black and white. Say you're investigating whether the subject has a net worth of less than $1 million. Perhaps before the real estate market collapsed, their real estate holdings were worth far more than the subject owed on the mortgages, so their net worth far exceeded $1 million. Now, even though they are not in any immediate financial difficultly and are up-to-date on all their payments, their underwater mortgages bring their net worth below $1 million. If that is all you look at—whether the total is above or below $1 million—then the subject may get a benefit from an economic downturn. However, if you are trying to determine whether the subject can afford to pay a fine, the fact that they owe more on their mortgage than the property is worth is less important.

Real estate generally increases in value over time. I would not assume the value of the subject's property will continue to fall in the future; in fact, I would assume just the opposite. Look at the information you have collected thus far: deeds, Deeds of Trust, tax assessed value, estimated fair market value, and real estate comparables. None of these documents or pieces of information stands on their own; they all need to be combined to give you a complete picture.

"Is That Really What They're Paying?"

Using the Internet can be a good way to verify expense and income amounts reported by your subject. Sometimes you can use the Internet to verify actual amounts, other times you can use it to verify whether the amounts reported are reasonable for the situation. For income related to real estate, you should compare the subject's reported income against other similar rents in the area. Be sure to consider not only total rent but also rent per square foot. To verify market rental rates in the area, look for similar rental listings on craigslist, websites for local real estate agencies, Zillow, and the classified section of the local newspaper. Another good source, surprisingly, is Google. While many landlords simply post a sign in the window of a rental property, your subject may have advertised. If they did, or if they contract with a property management company, it is very possible there was an online advertisement for the property. By Googling the property address, you should be able to find links to any previous advertisements, including the requested rental amount. (If you get a result, make sure you select the "cached" version of the ad, so you can see what it originally said. If the property is no longer for rent, there won't be a current version of the ad to access.) If the subject has a basement apartment they rent out to local college students, compare their monthly income against other basement apartments in the area. If similar apartments rent for $1–2 per square foot per month, but the subject reports a rental income equal to $0.25 per square foot, you may be justified in asking for verification that the space is really only worth $0.25 per square foot.

Remember that there are many possible reasons that a subject may report a seemingly low rental income. Maybe the subject doesn't know the apartment is worth more than they're charging. Maybe the subject has a long-term tenant and has never bothered to increase the rent. Maybe the subject is actually renting the space to a family member at a significant discount. Maybe the apartment is a dump in serious need of repair and upgrades and the subject can't find a tenant who will pay more for the space. Or maybe the subject simply isn't reporting all their income. The Internet usually can't tell you which of those answers is correct, but it can give you the information you need to determine whether to request more information from the subject.

Another comparison you can make is to look at a subject's mortgage indebtedness on the property. If the subject reports a mortgage payment of $2,000 per month, but they rent the property out for just $1,000 per month, they may be hiding rental income. It is possible the subject could have such an arrangement, but it is not common. If you see this type of rental deal, you will want to both verify the accuracy of the report and look for other explanations.

One legitimate explanation you might encounter for such a significant monthly loss is if the subject uses this rental loss to offset business income from a pass-through entity (an LLC, partnership, or an S corporation). To verify this situation, you would need to review the subject's IRS Form 1040 (their personal tax return), paying close attention to any Schedules K-1 that exist. The K-1 details the subject's proportional share of the pass-through company's taxes. As noted above, those owners must still pay their proportional share of the company's taxes. They must do so even if a pass-through entity doesn't distribute any money to those owners. That means if a company earned a substantial profit, but reinvested its earnings instead of distributing them to the owners, those owners can be stuck with a hefty tax bill on April 15th. It may make sense for a subject to take a significant loss on a personal asset—such as a rental property—in order to offset some of their tax liability from their company.

Another legitimate explanation you may encounter is if the subject was forced to move to another city (say for a job transfer or family obligations), but was unable to sell their home for a reasonable price. In this situation, many homeowners decide to rent their home out to cover some of their expenses until the market improves and they can sell the home for a fair price. A subject faced with taking a $100,000 loss on their home would actually save money by renting the home out for five years at a $1,000 per month loss—and they get a tax write-off to boot. They could logically assume that the real estate market will improve over the next 2–5 years and that they will eventually be able to sell the home for the full asking price.

Other Resources

In addition to knowing the specifics about a parcel of real estate and its estimated value, there are other websites available that can help you understand about that parcel of land and how a subject might use it. Some of the more interesting resources include the following.

SATELLITE MAPS

Google Maps, Google Earth, MapQuest, and Expedia are the most well known mapping resources that allow you to see a parcel of real estate from space. You can use these images to understand the surrounding area—whether it is rural or urban, residential or commercial. You may also be able to see items that help you understand how the property is used, such as fence lines, vegetation cover, and driveways or unofficial roads.

STREET VIEW MAPS

Street views are a relatively new feature to some mapping websites. This option compiles a series of still photographs into a single image so you can see what the site looked like from street level on the day the photos were taken. This is a very convenient option, especially when you're visiting a new city and want to know what the entrance to your hotel looks like. When conducting a financial investigation, this option can help you understand what condition a property is in and what is nearby.

SATELLITES VERSUS STREET VIEWS

In areas where a street view option is available, it may be worthwhile to carefully compare the images you see against the images provided from satellite views. The two may be significantly different and may have been taken at very different times. Look at the colors of the roofs of the building in question and those of neighboring buildings—a different color means a new roof. Are all the trees in one photo present in the other? How about sheds and other outbuildings? Maybe the buildings themselves are present in one photo but the other shows vacant land. Each of these discrepancies can assist you in understanding the value of a parcel of real estate. These discrepancies can also document whether a subject is actively maintaining or improving the property.

SCHOOL DISTRICT INFORMATION

When buying a home, one of the key considerations for many people is the quality of the local school district. Even if a buyer doesn't have children, the price they pay for a home is affected by whether the school district is well regarded. If a subject claims the value of a home is less than you believe is fair, it may be worth your time to check how the schools compare to others in the area and see if a reduction in real estate values is justified.

Case in Point

Sometimes a photograph can provide vital information and leads that you might otherwise never know to look for. During one investigation, a business owner claimed his industrial business was located at a specific address. When I pulled up a satellite photo of that address, I found that it was not in the industrial part of town, but instead was in the middle of a residential neighborhood. When I questioned how his company could maintain the large chemical tanks needed for his business, the company disclosed a second location that we had not previously known about. When I investigated the ownership of that second location, I discovered another unrelated company actually owned and operated that site. If I had not bothered to check the satellite photo, I might have missed the connection to the second company.

9 Search Engines and Web Portals

Search engines are sites that search and index the Internet so you can find what you are looking for. Google has become the best known and most popular of these sites, but there are many to choose from. Each one is unique and uses different methods for searching and cataloging the information that is available.

Different search engines not only search differently, they can display different results and display them differently as well. Most search engines allow you to do a "Boolean" search, meaning you can add words like AND, OR, and NOT (in all caps) to add or remove words to your search parameters. A search for "salt AND pepper" will give you a different result than a search for "salt OR pepper." The first will only find pages that have both the word salt and the word pepper, while the second will find pages that have either the word salt or the word pepper, but not necessarily both words. Keep in mind that not all search engines can do Boolean searches and some can only do partial Boolean searches.

If you don't find what you're looking for with one search engine, try another! Not all search engines are going to find the same websites, and not all search engines will prioritize results in the same way. The Internet changes every moment of every day. There is no way any search engine can possibly find every website in existence. Just because Google is the most popular search engine doesn't mean your search should start and end there. Here are some of the most popular and most helpful search engines (but certainly not the only ones) along with a brief explanation of why I use them.

Google: www.google.com

Regardless of how many search engines there are in the world, Google is still the 800 lb gorilla dominating all others. As of the time of writing, 10 of the current top 40 most popular websites in the world are Google sites—Google, Google India, Google China, and Google Germany are in the top 20, and Google's sites in the UK, France, Japan, Italy, Brazil, and Spain are all in the top 40 (Alexa 2009a). The only other search engines with more than one entry in the top 20 are Yahoo! and Yahoo! Japan and (although not technically the same but still deserving mention) both Windows Live and MSN also appear in the top 20 with Bing appearing at number 22 (Alexa 2009b).

As a general rule, I usually start a search by looking for someone on Google. Google automatically runs a Boolean search using the "AND" operator—which means it's going to search for web pages that contain ALL of the words you enter into the search box. For more specificity, try putting quotation marks around specific phrases. Google is helpful in that it will sometimes offer possible spelling corrections or alternate spellings, depending on your search terms. Google frequently skips searching for extremely common words, such as "and" or "or." To confirm which of your search words have been included in Google's search, look in the upper right-hand corner. Google gives you the number of search results for the words in blue; words in black were skipped. To include words that Google excludes by default, simply add a + sign immediately before the word you want to include.

You may also want to try searching nontext resources, such as Google's "Image" search. This can be extremely helpful when you are looking for a photo of your subject or something specific related to your investigation. While there is no guarantee your search results will actually be the person you are looking for, you may find links to related individuals or you may be able to confirm a link you have tentatively established through other means. You can easily switch between text results and image results. A link to image results should show up about halfway down the first page of search results from a Google web search. If you don't see a link to image results, simply click the "Image" link at the top of the screen above the search box.

One other suggestion is that if you don't find what you're looking for in your first set of search results, try changing the order of the words in the search box. You don't necessarily need to add or remove words; simply changing their order can change your search results. I find this to be especially true when I am using the image search option. A search for "New York hotels" gives you a different set of results than "hotels New York" (they are similar sets of results, but are slightly different and appear in a different display order).

WHY I USE GOOGLE

I was an early convert to Google and find it very comprehensive. If it exists, it is likely going to show up on Google. More importantly, Google's search results are less focused on social networking results and are more likely to give substantive results higher on the list. I also find the image search to be particularly helpful, especially when I'm looking for background research or other very specific information. However, it is important to keep in mind the more comprehensive Google becomes, the harder it can be to find what you're looking for. The two or three sites you are interested in might be hidden far down the results list. I still use Google as my first resource, but I find I am looking to other resources more often because I have to scroll through too many results to find what I'm looking for.

Google Books: http://books.google.com

Google Books shows screen shots of pages from thousands of books with the ability to search the text. Not every book is available nor is every page of every book included.

WHY I USE GOOGLE BOOKS

Google Books is a great option when you're trying to track down a book that isn't available at your local library or through interlibrary loan. It can also be a great resource for finding a quick quotation or citation to back up a statement in an investigation report or other document.

Google Scholar: http://scholar.google.com

Google Scholar does for journal articles what Google Books does for books. It gives quick and easy access to the full text of scholarly journal articles. The site is focused on academic and scholarly research as opposed to financial investigations, but can be an excellent resource when you're trying to find obscure information.

WHY I USE GOOGLE SCHOLAR

When you do not have subscription access to journal databases like JSTOR or EBSCOhost, Google Scholar can be a great backup. While not every article will be available through Google Scholar, you can find great journal articles without traveling to your local university library.

Google Finance: www.google.com/finance

Google's Finance page gives a quick overview of financial markets at a single glance. You can see the day's stock market performance (both US exchanges as well as foreign exchanges), currency exchange rates, financial headlines, and how various sectors of the economy are performing. You can also create portfolios of publicly-traded companies to provide easy access.

WHY I USE GOOGLE FINANCE

Google Finance does pretty much the same thing as other finance sites. The main advantage to Google's offering is that it is a simple and uncluttered interface. There aren't flashing ads and news videos taking up space on the screen. The sector summary graph is also helpful if you are interested in one particular type of company. If your job involves keeping an eye on self-insured companies or companies in a particular industry, you might want to create a portfolio of those companies so you can quickly see which ones are performing well and which ones might be headed for financial trouble.

Google Patents: www.google.com/patents

Google's Patent search is a more user-friendly version of the official US government patent search, but still provides the same information. You can search for a patent by its number, by its inventor, by key words, by classification, or even by date. This particular site only searches US patents, however. At the time of writing this book, neither foreign patents nor US trademarks are searchable at this particular site.

WHY I USE GOOGLE PATENTS

I tend to use the Google Patent site instead of the official government site because it is easier to find the document I'm looking for. Google Patents displays thumbnail images of the drawings from the patent and gives easy links to the different sections of the patent.

Google Translate: http://translate.google.com

Google's Translation page is not particularly unique, but is easy to use and provides as-you-type translation. It allows you to translate a number of different languages, including both common languages like French and Spanish and more unusual languages like Irish and Yiddish.

WHY I USE GOOGLE TRANSLATE

Obviously, any translation service is a great way to quickly remind myself how to say something in a foreign language or to find out what a document says when it's not written in English. But online translators can be helpful in financial investigations because they can help you find the names of hidden companies and assets. For example, if you find a deed showing "Siopa Gairdín na Seosamh" bought the property in question, you might think that document doesn't help you. But if you translate that name and find it's merely the name of your subject business, "Joe's Garden Store," that's a pretty good indication that your subject is trying to hide that asset by using a fraudulent transfer.

Google Maps: http://maps.google.com

Like many online mapping services, Google Maps will help you find maps for locations all over the world. You can almost always find a satellite image of your location (Area 51 may come up nice and clear, but the residence of the Vice President is blurred). Google Maps also offers street views of many locations—actual pictures of the business or property so you can see its condition and the surrounding neighborhood.

WHY I USE GOOGLE MAPS

The maps, driving directions, and satellite images available from Google Maps are not significantly different from those available from other sites. However, Google's ability to integrate web searches with map images can be helpful sometimes and seems (at least in my experience) to be slightly more comprehensive and reliable than other services. Google's street views can also be helpful, especially if you want to explore the neighborhood surrounding a business or if you want to familiarize yourself with an area before visiting.

Google Earth: http://earth.google.com (download only)

Google Earth is sort of a super-sized version of Google Maps. You can explore the world through satellite images and photos added by users. There are discussion boards and other links with Google Earth and extensive information is provided on thousands of locales all over the world.

WHY I USE GOOGLE EARTH

This is a very important point: I do not use Google Earth! At least, I don't use it at work. I do have a copy on my home computer, which I use occasionally if I'm planning a vacation or if I'm just curious about an area and its history. But I do not have a copy of this program on my computer at work and I do not use it during investigations. My employer does not have a license for the program and my agency has a strict policy against any employee downloading the program. Your employer may well have a similar policy. So before you even consider downloading Google Earth to your work computer or using it in an investigation, contact your IT department and get clearance to do so.

Bing: www.bing.com

Bing is Microsoft's newest search engine, which they promote as a "decision engine" (for more information about the development of Bing, visit www.discoverbing.com). Bing is the underlying search engine for a number of different sites, but you can access it directly as well. Microsoft's previous search engine, Windows Live, now forwards you to Bing.

Bing does have one significant advantage over Google: it has a natural language search engine built in. If you type a question into Google, it will only search for the words in your question, not the question itself. Bing uses both the words you type in as well as their context to try to find the answer to your question. Bing also offers a "More On This Page" feature that can be helpful. Simply hold your mouse over the arrow to the right of a search result and a small window will appear with more information about what you will find if you follow that link. If you are trying to comb through a large number of search results and you want to increase the likelihood of selecting a relevant result, this feature may save you considerable time. Like Google, you can instantly access a map by typing an address into the search box and, like Google, you can obtain satellite views and frequently street-level views.

WHY I USE BING

To be honest, I have not yet fallen in love with Bing and I don't use it very much. But that is not to say that you won't find Bing to be significantly better than Google or any other search engine. I definitely like the "More On This Page" feature and find it to be helpful when trying to determine which results are what I'm looking for and which aren't. Bing is also a bit fancier, visually-speaking. It uses lovely pictures as a background, as where Google defaults to a plain white screen. Although I enjoy the pictures, my personal preference is for a more streamlined interface—which may explain why I tend to use Google first and Bing second. When conducting financial investigations, I find Bing has a tendency that some other search engines do: it relies very heavily on social networking sites for information. Results from LinkedIn, Facebook, MySpace, and ZoomInfo are more likely to come up first than websites featuring substantive information. While these types of sites may be helpful, I am usually looking for different information about a subject—information that doesn't show up in Bing until the second or third page of search results.

Ask (formerly Ask Jeeves): www.ask.com

Ask.com is a natural language search engine. Although other search engines have now adopted this technology (like Bing, as explained previously), Ask.com was the first search engine I became aware of that could perform this type of search. Ask.com's biggest advantage is that it gives you suggestions for other similar questions if you don't find what you're looking for in your first set of results.

WHY I USE ASK.COM

Sometimes it's just easier to type in a question than to try to figure out which key words are going to help me find what I'm looking for. Whether I want to know the average price for a particular type of equipment in my area or whether I need to know how to perform a certain task, Ask.com can frequently find the information I need and display it at the top of the search results list.

Yahoo!: www.yahoo.com

Although Yahoo! may have started out as just another search engine, it has transformed over the years into what is now referred to as a "web portal." A portal incorporates a search feature, but also includes other options such as email, news articles, movie reviews, and discussion boards. You can customize the appearance of your Yahoo! portal to display only areas that you think are interesting. It also uses cookies to track your location and give you local news results. Yahoo! also has an instant messaging feature for chatting on-line.

WHY I USE YAHOO!

Although I don't use Yahoo! as a true web portal, I do use many of the features they offer. I frequently consult the Yahoo! Finance page for updates on financial markets and am a member of a number of Yahoo! discussion board groups. I also use a Yahoo! email address for much of my correspondence, especially between the US and Europe, because other email providers (including my ISP) tend to block many European email addresses due to high numbers of phishing and other unwanted emails. Yahoo! doesn't seem to have that problem. If you need to send or receive emails between the continents, you may want to consider setting up a free Yahoo! email account. Setting up a free email account also gives you the opportunity to establish dummy registrations and accounts using a secondary email address so you aren't bombarded with unwanted emails on your real email address. I like using Yahoo! to establish an email address because they do not require extensive personal information to sign up for an account.

Yahoo! Babel Fish Translator: http://babelfish.altavista.com

In the novel *Hitchhiker's Guide to the Galaxy* by Douglas Adams, a "babel fish" was a species that could perform instantaneous translations. Alta Vista's Babel Fish does exactly that: instantly translates web pages and other words from one language to another.

WHY I USE BABEL FISH

Babel Fish is very similar to Google's Translate but does not provide translations from as many languages. In my experience, sometimes Babel Fish provides a better translation, and sometimes Google does. It may be worthwhile to try both.

Excite: www.excite.com

Like Yahoo!, Excite is another search engine turned web portal. Its search feature is provided by InfoSpace, the same company that owns DogPile, Webcrawler, and Metacrawler—so you can expect it to return similar results. Like Yahoo!, Excite can be customized to provide user-specific content and email services.

WHY I USE EXCITE

I used to use Excite much more than I do today. Mostly, I use an Excite email address for sites that are likely to generate unwanted email (like when I purchase something online or fill out an owner registration card for a purchase). The interface is a bit more cluttered than some other portals, but all the same information and customizability is there. The sign up requirements for a new account include information that Yahoo! and some other portals don't require.

MSN: www.msn.com

If you buy a new computer running Windows, it may default to MSN when you connect to the Internet. While this default can be changed very easily, many people like the MSN interface. Like Yahoo!, Excite, AOL, and others, MSN is a portal. You can find current news headlines, links to interesting videos, and a search engine (this time provided by Bing). When it comes to searching, you should get the same results from either Bing or MSN.

WHY I USE MSN

To be honest, I don't really use MSN. That's not because there's anything bad about it, I just get the same information from other sources. If you want a dummy registration account, using MSN to get a Hotmail account is a reasonable choice. You'll have to provide the same basic information that you would provide to Yahoo! for an account there, which is less information than some other providers require.

AOL: www.aol.com

AOL was arguably the first web portal and probably even pre-dates that term. News, email, web search, and instant messaging all in one convenient place. You do not have to have AOL as your Internet service provider to access the portal page. Financial information is provided by the website dailyfinance.com and is a good mixture of company-specific financial data and economic information.

WHY I USE AOL

Again, to be honest, I don't usually use AOL, simply because I can access the same information from other websites. If you started using the Internet as an AOL customer, you're probably familiar and comfortable with the offerings and layout. If you've never used AOL, it might never occur to you to visit the site. AOL's web search is provided by Google, so you're not likely to get different search results from visiting AOL instead.

Lycos: www.lycos.com

Lycos is another search engine that's been around a long time and can provide some good search results. The most distinguishing feature of Lycos when compared to other search engines is that it gives you a thumbnail image of each website in the search results list. The image it provides may not be for the exact page you're interested in, but should be from the same website (it may show you the site's home page instead of the page you want).

WHY I USE LYCOS

I find the thumbnail images accompanying each search result are helpful. They help me remember which sites provided good information and which weren't applicable. Since I tend to remember things by how they look, a picture is definitely a good way to jog my memory and Lycos has that feature.

Quintura: www.quintura.com

Quintura takes a slightly different approach to Internet searches. Instead of simply providing a list of search results, Quintura looks for other words that appear in the results. It then suggests those words to help you refine your search. Although sites like Google and Ask.com may suggest search terms based on previous searches, Quintura suggests search terms based on your initial results.

WHY I USE QUINTURA

I like Quintura because of the ability to group results. That can be a huge advantage when searching for a subject because it can help you distinguish between different people with the same name. As where other search engines don't distinguish between me and the

"Kimberly Goetz" who is a marine biologist, Quintura does make that distinction by suggesting the search term "financial assurance" (sites that will refer to me) as well as the term "McMurdo" (sites that definitely do not refer to me). While some of the categories don't really distinguish between different people, I frequently get helpful results from this site.

DogPile: www.dogpile.com

Unlike other search engines, DogPile doesn't actually search the Internet. Instead, DogPile is a metasearch engine—it searches other search engines. The advantage to using this type of search engine is that it saves time by searching multiple search engines simultaneously.

WHY I USE DOGPILE

I usually use DogPile when I'm searching for information related to a topic as opposed to a person. I've been less than satisfied with search results related to subjects because DogPile seems to put far more emphasis on social networking results than to substantive results. If you're trying to find something obscure, like the rate a scarification machine can remove a concrete floor, DogPile might come in handy. If you're looking for an individual, you may be better off starting with one of the other search engines. However, many DogPile users are very loyal and find the results to be extremely helpful, so don't write this site off.

WebCrawler: www.webcrawler.com

WebCrawler is owned by the same company as DogPile and is also a metasearch engine (WebCrawler 2009). Like DogPile, WebCrawler searches other search engines and displays a single set of results. However, a search on DogPile will return similar but slightly different results than the same search on WebCrawler.

WHY I USE WEBCRAWLER

WebCrawler was one of the earliest search engines and still provides good data. However, I find that it has similar limitations to DogPile because it places too much emphasis on sponsored links and social networking results. My personal preference is for other sites, but many users find WebCrawler to be very helpful.

MetaCrawler: www.metacrawler.com

MetaCrawler is the third sibling to DogPile and WebCrawler and all are owned by InfoSpace (MetaCrawler 2009). It operates in basically the same way and again provides very similar results to the other two metasearch engines.

WHY I USE METACRAWLER

Usually, I don't use this site, but not for any particular reason. I'm just more likely to select DogPile or WebCrawler first. I've not found any specific advantage or disadvantage to one over the other.

WolframAlpha: www.wolframalpha.com

WolframAlpha is a relatively new web resource that provides answers to some types of questions. If you type in a mathematical formula, WolframAlpha will provide the solution. If you type in a stock ticker abbreviation, the site will automatically provide the last price and basic financial information for the company. So in addition to being a search engine, WolframAlpha could also be called an "answer" engine—it simply gives you the answer you want instead of taking you to a web site where you can find the answer.

WHY I USE WOLFRAMALPHA

WolframAlpha can be a great resource for information you might look up on Wikipedia. If you want to calculate Net Present Value, just type NPV into the search box. Unlike Wikipedia that gives you the formula to calculate NPV and an explanation of the mathematics behind the formula, WolframAlpha gives you a calculator that figures NPV for you. WolframAlpha is also the only web site I know of that will give you a clear (if somewhat facetious) answer to the search question, "What is the meaning of life?" While WolframAlpha isn't always going to be the best resource, it is a good site for straightforward questions requiring straightforward answers.

10 *Government and Law Related Websites*

Government entities frequently post information on websites either because they are required to do so by law, or because it is the most efficient way to meet their legal obligations to make the information available to citizens. Although many of the following websites are very specific to a particular type of business or a particular set of regulations, it may still be helpful to check them during an Internet-based investigation. You may not regulate a subject company's environmental obligations, but those obligations may affect the firm's creditworthiness and financial stability. You may not be concerned with a corporate parent's filings with the Securities and Exchange Commission, but their last annual report might talk about the facility you are investigating. Even if you don't check these sites during every investigation, they may still come in handy once in a while. Accessing information on government sites is usually free, but there are some exceptions. Some of the most useful sites that are applicable nationwide are detailed below.

SEC EDGAR Database: www.sec.gov/edgar/searchedgar/webusers.htm

EDGAR stands for "Electronic Data Gathering, Analysis, and Retrieval" and is the system used to electronically file and retrieve financial information on publicly-traded companies through the US Securities and Exchange Commission. If you want to find annual reports, quarterly reports, or other key financial documents for large companies that sell stock on a US exchange, this is the database. Annual reports are usually the most helpful document and are filed as a form 10-K.

Canadian Securities Administrators SEDAR Database: http://www.sedar.com/

Publicly-traded Canadian companies are required to file similar documents as their US counterparts. If you are investigating a Canadian company or a company owned by a Canadian parent, you may need to check the SEDAR database as well. Canada does impose some legal restrictions on who is allowed to access the information in their database, so make sure you carefully read the acceptance statement and make sure you are complying with all applicable restrictions before you search the database.

US Department of the Treasury: www.treasury.gov

This is the main website for the Treasury Department and has links to many related entities, including the Office of Thrift Supervision, the US Mint, and the Office of the Comptroller of the Currency. Of special importance on this site are regular fraud updates and a link to the Financial Management Service, which publishes Department Circular 570 (a list of companies that are approved to act as sureties).

Financial Crimes Enforcement Network: www.fincen.gov

FinCEN (pronounced "fin-sen") is part of the Treasury Department and works to prevent and detect financial crimes. Their website has good information about how to detect financial fraud and reports of successful fraud prosecutions. While you may not be able to access reports filed with FinCEN, you may be able to find helpful advice on their website.

Financial Accounting Standards Board: www.fasb.org

FASB (pronounced "faz-bee") is the organization that establishes and maintains accounting standards for the United States. These are the people who decide what is and is not a "Generally Accepted Accounting Principle," otherwise known as GAAP. All businesses, both publicly-traded and privately-held, must follow the standards established by FASB. Their website contains copies of standards and updates, staff opinions, and technical bulletins. It is important to note that FASB is not the same as AICPA—the American Institute of Certified Public Accountants—although the two organizations do cover many of the same issues.

Central Contractor Registration: www.ccr.gov

Businesses that do work for the federal government will likely be listed in the CCR database. You can search the database by company name, DUNS number, or even by industry. Businesses registered with this site provide owner and contact information as well as certification and registration information such as whether the business is certified by the Small Business Administration's 8(a) program.

Excluded Parties List (Disbarred Federal Contractors): www.epls.gov

What happens if a company or business owner is found to have defrauded the federal government? They get placed on the "Excluded Parties List" and cannot be awarded a federal contract or grant. This database will give you the name and contact information for the excluded party as well as a brief description of what led to their ineligibility.

Small Business Administration's Pro-Net Database: www.pro-net.sba.gov

The Small Business Administration allows companies to register their information in the Pro-Net database. You can search for companies by a variety of options including name, location, and industry. This is a good resource for confirming a company's SBA 8(a) registration, HUBZone Certification, or Small Disadvantaged Business Certification. Businesses can also list whether they are certified as a Disadvantaged Business Enterprise with the US Department of Transportation, but Pro-Net does not verify the accuracy of this information. The database reports owners' names, contact information, industries, DUNS number, and products and services offered. Only a small percentage of businesses are eligible for 8(a) certification, and only some of those choose to participate in the program. However, if you are lucky enough to be investigating a certified business or one of its owners, you may find helpful information on this website.

US Department of Transportation DBE Program Database: www.osdbu.dot.gov

Businesses involved in transportation-related construction, airport construction, or airport concessionaire activities may be certified as a "Disadvantaged Business Enterprise" by the US Department of Transportation or one of its state or local representatives. This website not only will give you access to a complete list of all certifying agencies but also to a database of all certified firms. Appeal decisions are also available on this site, which can be helpful in establishing whether a subject owns, controls, or has a financial interest in a certified (or formerly certified) company. This certification is similar to the 8(a) program and is likewise fairly unusual. However, if you do have a subject or company that is associated with the program, you may be able to find helpful information on this site.

US Federal Forms Hub: www.forms.gov

Although you will not find business-specific information on this site, you can find other very helpful information here. If you need quick access to what a form should say, check here. Forms from the Small Business Administration can be very helpful if you need to ask about the ownership or control of a business as well as the financial status of a company or individual subject.

US EPA Compliance Information: www.epa-echo.gov/echo/

The US Environmental Protection Agency maintains a public database of information related to companies that are regulated under the Clean Air Act, the Clean Water Act, and the Resource Conservation and Recovery Act (the Hazardous Waste law). Simply type in a company's name or other search criteria and you can learn what federal environmental laws apply to a location, whether there have been environmental violations at the site, and basic census information for the area surrounding the site. This information can be very helpful when you need to quantify the financial exposure of a company due to possible environmental contamination.

Vermont Directory of Captive Insurance Companies: www.vermontcaptives.info

In the United States, most captive insurance companies are based in Vermont, regardless of where the rest of their corporate family is based. To find out if an insurance company might actually be a captive insurer instead of a third-party insurer, you can check Vermont's website. The site contains general information relating to captive insurance as well as a directory of captive firms. (Note: although the web address ends in .info, the site is a government site.)

National Association of Insurance Commissioners (NAIC): www.naic.org

NAIC is the national organization for state insurance regulators. Their website contains background information about insurance and the insurance industry as well as specific information about insurance problems and links to local regulators.

Conference of State Bank Supervisors: www.csbs.org

This organization acts as an advocate for the state banking system. Particularly helpful is the directory of all state banking departments and the newsletter updates regarding regulatory changes. If you need to learn about the banking industry and how it is regulated, follow the link to the Banking 101 website.

NAICS Code Lookups: www.census.gov/eos/www/naics/

The North American Industry Classification System (NAICS) is a numbering system used to describe the industry or type of work performed by organizations in the United States, Canada, and Mexico. Many government databases will list a company's NAICS code and some databases allow you to search for a company by NAICS code. If you see documents listing a NAICS code for a subject company, you may want to check and see that it matches what you expect. For example, if the company has told you they are a property management firm (NAICS code 53131) but you find the company listed as a general contractor for residential remodeling (NAICS code 236118), you'll need to find out why there is a discrepancy. The NAICS code system has changed slightly since it was adopted in 1997. If you search for a NAICS code and find it does not currently exist, try checking the 1997 or 2002 versions of the system to see if that code has been superseded by a new code describing the same work. NAICS codes can be three, four, five, or six digits long, depending on how specific they are in describing the work performed. Most NAICS codes will be six digits long. One big red flag is if you see a NAICS code starting with the number "9" or "92." All NAICS codes starting with 92 describe activities of public-sector agencies, such as state and local governments, courts, and the military. Businesses and non-profit organizations should never have a NAICS code starting with the number nine.

SIC Code Lookups: www.osha.gov/pls/imis/sicsearch.html

The Standard Industrial Classification System was the numbering system used to describe the work of business and other organizations before the NAICS codes were adopted. The last version of the SIC code system was issued in 1987. All SIC codes are four digits, even the ones that start with "0" (the SIC code for wheat farms is "0111" instead of "111"). Larger classifications of industry groups use only the first three digits (the industry group for agricultural production is "011"). SIC codes are becoming less and less common and many databases no longer track them. However, if you are using a database that does still track SIC codes, it is a good idea to double check and make sure the code matches both the company's NAICS code as well as their business description.

US Federal Courts: www.pacer.psc.uscourts.gov

PACER is the system used to access docket information and other filings from court cases filed in the federal court system. Documents filed in Bankruptcy Court, any of the Federal District Courts, and any of the Federal Courts of Appeal will be indexed on this site. Access to this site requires a registration and there is a small per page charge (currently $0.08 per page, with a maximum of $2.40 per document), but fees will be waived for any account that accrues less than $10.00 per year in charges (PACER 2009).

Findlaw Legal Resources: www.findlaw.com

Findlaw might be considered a "legal portal," much like a web portal that provides you with options for exploring a variety of topics. Findlaw provides free access to court opinions, a discussion board for asking and answering legal questions, and general legal information. The site has a number of "Frequently Asked Questions" pages, including ones specifically for small business advice. The links to find court cases can be found by selecting the "Visit Our Professional Site" in the upper right-hand corner of the screen.

Cornell University Law School Legal Information Institute: www.law.cornell.edu

Cornell's website contains much of the same information that Findlaw contains, but in a more straightforward interface. The site contains links to court decisions, federal laws and regulations, and some limited information on common legal topics such as business law. The site also contains a legal dictionary.

LexisNexis Free Case Law: www.lexisone.com

The fully functional version of LexisNexis is a very expensive but very useful database. For those of us who don't have access to the full version, LexisNexis provides free access to court opinions through the lexisone.com website. Registration is required, but there is no cost to use the site. You can search by state or federal district or by party name, judge's name, or attorney's name (which can be very helpful if you want to know more about opposing counsel).

The 'Lectric Law Library: www.lectlaw.com

OK, admittedly this is not your typical legal website. While the site provides excellent legal information in language a layperson can understand, it does so in a PG-13 sort of way. If you're a geek who likes a bawdy joke, this site is for you. If you need to know what a legal term means, check out the 'Lectric Law Lexicon. Good articles on a variety of subjects are posted in the Reference Room and the various Topic Areas listed on the main page. If you're very easily offended, you might want to skip this site; but if you can handle late-night comedy shows, you should be fine.

Google Scholar: http://scholar.google.com

One other feature of Google's Scholar search is the ability to search legal opinions. The trick is to look at the green highlighted bar below the search box and above the search results. In the first box, select "Legal opinions and journals" from the dropdown menu. This feature is not yet comprehensive, but Google is still working to enhance the feature.

CHAPTER 11 *Commercial and Business-Related Websites*

Many helpful websites are provided by businesses or entities related to businesses. Although you can obtain extensive information from these sites, it is important to remember that for-profit companies don't tend to do things out of the goodness of their hearts. They do things because they can make money. When you obtain free information from a for-profit entity, always keep in mind that you don't get something for nothing. Many commercial and business-related sites will provide limited information at no cost. That limited information may be sufficient for your investigation purposes. If you have to register for the site in order to obtain the free information, make sure you read the site's privacy policy before doing so.

The following sites have proven helpful to me in doing financial investigations. Many require a free registration and a few use free information as a "teaser" in an attempt to get you to subscribe to a paid service. While there is nothing wrong with that approach, make sure you are fully informed about how the website acquires its information and why it provides free access—you may get challenged on the information's reliability.

Standard & Poor's: www.standardandpoors.com

Standard & Poor's rates the creditworthiness of companies and public entities offering bonds, insurance companies, and financial institutions. Bond ratings of BBB– and above are considered investment grade and those rated BB+ and below are junk grade (as in "junk bond"). The site does require a free registration to access the site's basic information. Additional information and research is available to paid subscribers through the company's "Premium Resources" offerings from RatingsDirect.

Moody's: www.moodys.com

Moody's is a competitor of Standard & Poor's and offers similar ratings information on private companies and public entities. In the Moody's numbering scheme, bond ratings of Baa3 and above are considered investment grade and those rated Ba1 and below are junk grade. The site requires a free registration to access basic ratings information and a paid subscription to obtain additional research and information.

Fitch Ratings: www.fitchratings.com

Fitch is the third major credit rating agency for corporate finance, financial institutions, and insurance companies. The Fitch credit designation system is very similar to Standard & Poor's system, with ratings of BBB– and above being investment grade and those BB+ and below being junk grade. Like its competitors, the Fitch website does require a free registration to access the site and additional services are available for paid subscribers.

A.M. Best Company: www.ambest.com

A.M. Best Company is another credit rating agency, but limits its focus mostly to insurance companies and banks. They also provide industry information on hospitals and health care companies. When investigating whether a subject's potential financial risks are properly insured, A.M. Best can help you determine whether an insurance company is a third-party insurer or a captive insurer. The site does require a free registration to access the ratings information.

Zillow: www.zillow.com

In addition to the tax assessed value and other information about residential property, Zillow offers a fairly good estimate of fair market value. The fair market value estimate is based on comparable sales in the neighborhood. Unlike other real estate value services, Zillow provides free lookups, online, instantly. Other sources may give you a more accurate number, but you have to talk with a real estate agent. Since you're not the property owner and aren't trying to find an agent to sell your house, those options aren't ideal for financial investigations.

FreeErisa: www.freeerisa.com

This website allows you to access copies of some pension plan documents filed with the IRS. This can be helpful during a financial investigation because these forms contain the company's contact information and their federal Taxpayer Identification Number. The FreeErisa website used to allow a limited number of free lookups of Taxpayer Identification Number (also known as Federal Employer Identification Numbers, or FEINs), but that information is now available on a paid subscription basis (three free searches with a trial offer). Companies that do not file the proper pension plan forms with the IRS will not be listed in FreeErisa's database. Other information is also available on a paid basis.

FINRA BrokerCheck: www.finra.org/investors/toolscalculators/brokercheck

The Financial Industry Regulatory Authority (FINRA) is a private organization that regulates stockbrokers and brokerage companies. If you want to know whether a person is properly registered with FINRA to sell securities, you can search this site for free. No registration is required.

Insurance Information Institute: www.iii.org

Although this site does not provide company-specific information, it is an excellent source of information about the insurance industry. If you need to learn about how the insurance industry works, view presentations on insurance-related topics, or find research and analysis on insurance issues, this site can be a great resource.

Investopedia: www.investopedia.com

If you need to find out what "Year Over Year" means or what a "zombie debt" is, check out Investopedia's dictionary. Other features on this site include articles on investing and financial theory as well as Frequently Asked Questions on a variety of finance topics and real estate matters.

XE Currency Trading Information: www.xe.com

This site provides excellent currency exchange rate information and an online tool to convert a specific amount of money in one currency to its corresponding amount in another currency.

Captive Insurance Information: www.captive.com

I rely on this site to find information relating to captive insurance. The site not only has extensive information and Frequently Asked Questions about operating a captive insurance company in the United States, it also has articles of interest about corporate financial regulation around the world.

Amazon: www.amazon.com

Almost everyone has heard of Amazon—but why would you use this site during a financial investigation? Two reasons come up most often: to examine a page in a book you don't have other access to, and to establish the value of specialty items. Like Google Books, some books listed for sale on Amazon will allow you to read limited pages. While Google Books is a far more reliable resource for this, it never hurts to check Amazon if the page you want isn't available in Google. More importantly, Amazon sells both new and used products and allows sellers other than itself to sell goods on its site. If you know the subject owns a collection of Lladro figurines, Amazon might be one site you want to visit to verify their value. Rare books, obscure albums, and other collectibles may be available for sale on the site and give you a chance to establish a proper value for those items.

eBay: www.eBay.com

Like Amazon, eBay has become an excellent resource for establishing an objective (if overly conservative) value for collectibles and other items. Final sales price on many items will be below market value (buyers can get great deals on eBay), but are frequently a good minimum.

Kovels: www.kovels.com

Ralph and Terry Kovel have written a number of books and have been featured on television for their antique and collectibles appraisals. Their website requires a free registration but will allow you to see a current estimated price for many items that a subject might possess.

Kelley Blue Book Price Information: www.kbb.com

Kelley Blue Book provides free access to prices for both new and used cars, customized by zip code. Even more helpful when conducting a financial investigation, Kelley also provides prices for motorcycles, jet skis, and snowmobiles. You can research new and used cars on other sites, like Edmunds.com and Cars.com, but they obtain their used car prices from Kelley Blue Book.

National Automobile Dealers Association Price Information: www.nadaguides.com

Like Kelley Blue Book, the NADA Guide provides prices for both new and used cars and trucks, motorcycles and jet skis, and snowmobiles. The site also provides estimated values for RVs and travel trailers, boats and boat trailers, and even manufactured homes (but not online). If it travels, NADA probably has a price for it.

RV Trader: www.rvtraderonline.com

RV Trader is not strictly a price guide, but allows you to search for RVs and travel trailers within a specified radius of a particular zip code. This gives you the ability to compare prices for similar RVs in a given area. You can specify brand, model, or just RV style when searching.

Timeshare Users Group: www.tug2.net

The Timeshare Users Group is a forum for timeshare owners and buyers to find more information. Especially helpful are the classified listings on the site, which you can access without registration. This can allow you to verify a subject's claim of trying to sell a timeshare or values for similar timeshares at the same complex or resort.

Salary Information: www.salary.com

When conducting financial investigations, I frequently find it helpful to verify the going salary for a particular job in a particular market. Should a receptionist really be making $50 per hour? Or is an engineer really only worth $15 per hour? Whenever I have questions like these, I refer to Salary.com. This site will allow you to pick a specific job classification (Senior Aerospace Engineer, Office Manager, or Accountant II) in a specified market and will report not only the average salary but also the range of salaries for that job in that area, including averages for benefits and bonuses. Although the site is free and registration is not required, you do need to sit through advertisements instead (you can click a link to skip the ads).

Facebook: www.facebook.com

Currently the second most popular website in the world (after Google), Facebook is one of a number of social networking sites (Alexa 2009a). These sites allow users to chat, post articles and links of interest, play games, and keep track of friends and family. While you can set a Facebook account to be public to anyone in the world, most users limit access to their personal information to pre-screened "friends." You can occasionally find helpful information on this and other social networking sites, but most of the time the information is either not available to the public or it is not helpful.

MySpace: www.myspace.com

Although MySpace's popularity has fallen over the years, it still remains a popular website with many users (Alexa 2009c). Unlike Facebook that defaults many privacy settings to "friends only," MySpace tends to default to "everyone"—users must take specific actions to change their account settings if they want to restrict access. That means you are far more likely to find information on someone's MySpace account than you are their Facebook account. How helpful is that information going to be? That depends on the person and the account, but it is likely to be relatively unhelpful in a financial investigation. Just because someone posts a picture of themself next to an expensive luxury car doesn't mean they own that car (or any car, for that matter). However, if you need to find a picture of a subject, MySpace may be a good source.

Twitter: www.twitter.com

Twitter is a website where subscribers can post very short messages of 140 characters or less. Although it is a very popular website, I have never used it in an investigation and do not plan to start in the future.

YouTube: www.youtube.com

YouTube is a site where users can post videos. Like Twitter, it is a very popular site. Also like Twitter, I have never used it in an investigation and do not plan to start checking it in the future. I suppose if you were looking for very specific information—a television commercial showing a subject claiming to be the owner of a business or an allegedly disabled person finishing a marathon—YouTube might come in handy. But for your average financial investigation, you shouldn't expect to find anything useful here.

LinkedIn: www.linkedin.com

LinkedIn is a social networking site for business people. It provides users an opportunity to connect with others in their field and recommend their contacts.

Classmates.com: www.classmates.com

This site allows you to find people by elementary school, secondary school, or university attended. Dates of attendance are usually provided. This site can be helpful if you need to establish a connection between two lifelong friends, especially if there are suspicious business dealings between them. This can also be a good resource for finding siblings and other family members. Because siblings tend to attend the same schools, you can search in nearby year ranges to see if you can locate other students with the same surname. If those same names show up on business or real estate documents, you may well have identified family members who could participate in hiding assets.

Military.com: www.military.com/buddy-finder

Military.com's Buddy Finder is to the armed forces what Classmates.com is to high school: a place for former colleagues to reunite, trade contact information, and coordinate reunions. Like Classmates.com, Military.com does require a free registration and sharing your contact information to search the site.

Answers.com: www.answers.com

This website provides an opportunity for users to ask questions and have other users (hopefully experts) provide answers. Like other sites that are based on user-provided content, the reliability of the information on this site varies considerably based on the subject matter. The "Reference Library" section of the site is organized by subject matter and includes sections for legal issues, business and finance issues, and technology issues (among others).

How Stuff Works: www.howstuffworks.com

This is an excellent site for providing basic information about, well, how stuff works. Whether you want to know how a nuclear power plant operates or how to set up your new television, this site can provide a basic explanation. The article entitled "How Cooking the Books Works" can help you better understand off-balance sheet accounting and the Sarbanes-Oxley Act.

Whois Lookup: whois.domaintools.com

There are a number of sites that will allow you to look up the owner or registrant of a website, but I find the site at Domain Tools to be the most helpful. In addition to telling you who registered a particular website, Domain Tools' Whois lookup will also tell you when the site was registered, when the registration expires, and some basic information about the site. Depending on who the site registrar is, the contact information may or may not be for the actual website owner. Like registered agents, the administrative and technical contacts listed on a Whois report may be a company hired to perform those services.

MapQuest: www.mapquest.com

MapQuest provides similar information to Google Maps and Expedia Maps: street maps, satellite views, and driving directions. MapQuest also offers real-time traffic flow maps in some areas as well as identifies the lowest gas prices in an area. You can set a default location, such as your home or office, to help reduce the amount of typing you need to do to get driving directions. MapQuest does offer some limited street views with their "360 View" option, but the coverage is not yet as comprehensive as Google Maps. Personally, I find MapQuest's street view option to be a little more cumbersome than Google's, but it does work very well when available. Addresses where 360 View is available are marked in orange on the MapQuest street map and should have a "Launch 360 View" option with a picture when the street map is first opened.

Expedia: www.expedia.com/maps

Like Google Maps and MapQuest, Expedia Maps will show you street maps of your location. Unlike its competitors, Expedia does not have a quick link to a satellite view nor does it offer street views like Google does. However, these options are built into Expedia's sister program Bing.com instead, so it is less important that these features are not available through Expedia. If you know where you want to go and just need driving directions, Expedia can provide all the information you need. If you want to explore an area, just type the address into Bing instead.

ZabaSearch: www.zabasearch.com

ZabaSearch has been around for a while and does, essentially, what you are doing when you conduct a search at multiple sites. ZabaSearch says it does not collect information and that it merely provides access to public records. I find the information listed in ZabaSearch to be only somewhat reliable; if a credit report or other search has a mistake in it, ZabaSearch is likely to have that same mistake because it may be using the same incorrect source information. (This is a good reminder of why you are reading this book and why you conduct your own independent investigations instead of relying on automated data.)

Pipl: www.pipl.com

Like ZabaSearch, Pipl searches public records. Unlike other sites, however, Pipl searches less common public information. A Pipl report might return voter registration data or information from court filings. Much of the information returned by Pipl may be interesting but inapplicable to your investigation.

ZoomInfo: www.zoominfo.com

ZoomInfo's search results fall somewhere between mostly professional results and mostly personal results. When searching for a person, the first set of search results you'll see are organized by profession. ZoomInfo appears to use a variety of online sources to create its listings. ZoomInfo does have a subscription option, which is available for a charge or the trial version can be acquired by providing your contacts for inclusion in their database. Personally, I would not trade contacts for a trial membership due to privacy and disclosure issues and do not recommend other public sector employees do so, either.

PeekYou: www.peekyou.com

PeekYou focuses primarily on social networking sites like MySpace and Twitter, but also provides some results you might not expect. Whether a subject's Amazon.com profile is applicable to your investigation is questionable, but PeekYou can find one if it exists. PeekYou also looks for books, patents, and blog posts during its search.

yoName: www.yoname.com

yoName is a bit like a metasearch engine for social networking sites. In addition to the typical MySpace, Facebook, Friendster, and Twitter searches, yoName also searches other sites like photo sites Flickr and Fotolog and blogging sites Vox and Blogger. While you are not likely to find helpful information on most of these sites, something may come up once in a while so keep this one on the list just in case.

craigslist: www.craigslist.org

Whether you're looking for a used car or a house to rent, craigslist can be a great resource. This bare bones site allows users to post classified ads in a variety of categories, usually for free. Searching craigslist can help confirm or refute subject's claims about trying to sell or rent an asset. Finding cached versions of craigslist ads on Google or another search engine may also help you establish whether a subject has previously attempted to sell or rent an asset and what price they asked.

Who Called Us: http://whocalled.us

Ever get a call from someone that doesn't provide any useful information on the caller ID? You may be able to track down who was calling by checking the whocalled.us website. This is particularly useful for telemarketers, but some entries on the site have also alleged fraudulent surveys and other questionable activities by callers. Depending on the nature of your investigation, you may find helpful information by searching for your subject's telephone number.

White Pages Reverse Lookup: http://www.whitepages.com/reverse-lookup

Checking a reverse lookup can sometimes provide extensive information you didn't know to look for. By searching for your subject's telephone number or address, you may find other businesses that are sharing the same site. If you already know that Joe's Garden Shop shares a common phone number with 123 Bookkeeping, fine. But if you didn't, running a reverse search can uncover connections between businesses. The White Pages reverse lookup allows you to search either by telephone number or by address.

AnyWho Reverse Lookup: www.anywho.com/rl

AnyWho's reverse lookup site is provided by AT&T. You can search by phone number, but not by address at this site. However, because many reverse lookup sites are offered on a paid basis, it is worth it to check this site. It may return a different set of search results than other reverse lookup sites and is free.

12 *Websites from Nonprofits and Other Organizations*

Nonprofits and public service organizations frequently make information available because it is their mission to do so. Sometimes these websites are supported by grant funding, corporate sponsors, or membership dues. Other times, the website is not much more than a labor of love that one person updates on a sporadic basis. It is always a good idea to double check the effective date of the information on any website, and that is even more important for non-profit websites.

One word of caution: you used to be able to rely on a website's address to tell you if it belongs to a non-profit. The ".org" domain was formerly available only to organizations not commercial enterprises, which instead received at ".com" domain name, but both .org and .com are now unrestricted and are available to anyone (ICANN 2009). The nonprofit websites I find most helpful during a financial investigation include those detailed below.

The Internet Archive: www.archive.org

The Internet Archive takes a periodic "picture" of websites. Simply type in the address of the site you're interested in into "The Way Back Machine" feature and you can look at what the website *used* to look like. While not every Internet address or page is archived, a large number of sites are included in the archive. Archived pages do not appear for six months, but may go back a number of years. I have found this site to be very helpful when the subject has made changes to their business or their website in order to hide assets or relationships. If you believe a company has changed their management for your benefit, look at whom they listed as being in charge over the last few years. If you believe two companies are connected even though they claim to be independent of each other, look at any relationships reported on the website. "Subsidiary," "in partnership with," "on behalf of," and "corporate family" are all terms that indicate a business is not independent. If those terms appeared on a company's website two years ago but are now absent, it may be worth your time to determine why—has the relationship actually changed, or is the company simply trying to make it appear the relationship has changed?

Wikipedia: www.wikipedia.org

Wikipedia is an online encyclopedia that allows users to contribute to the content. While this ability enhances the site's content, it also allows for problems such as site vandalism and misinformation. I typically refer to Wikipedia first if I'm looking for general information that isn't subject to interpretation or subtle nuances. If you're looking for the formula to calculate Net Present Value, how many DeLorean automobiles were manufactured, or the origin of the phrase "mad as a hatter," Wikipedia can be a great resource. I typically use Wikipedia for my own information; if I'm going to present the information to a decision-maker, I frequently use the references at the end of a Wikipedia entry to find a more authoritative source to cite. Letting someone else do some of the research for you is definitely OK sometimes!

Reference: www.reference.com

This all around reference site includes free access to an encyclopedia, a dictionary, and a thesaurus. Additionally, a translation feature is provided by Google Translate and a search engine feature is provided by Ask.com. The dictionary and thesaurus features search a number of online resources to provide comprehensive results and can also be accessed by typing www.dictionary.com or www.thesaurus.com into your web browser. Use of the site is free and does not require registration. The encyclopedia feature provides limited information; full information from Britannica.com is available with an annual paid subscription.

Acronym Finder: www.acronymfinder.com

Ever come across an acronym that you just couldn't make out? Using the Acronym Finder can help you translate acronym jargon into plain English. Simply type the acronym into the search box and you'll get a list of potential meanings from a variety of sources. You can restrict your search results to just specific types of meanings (such as government and military, science and technology, or business and finance).

The Free Dictionary: www.thefreedictionary.com

The Free Dictionary has a number of features that make it an excellent all round lookup too. Like Acronym Finder, The Free Dictionary also has an acronym lookup feature. However, The Free Dictionary also has built-in links to Wikipedia, The Columbia Encyclopedia, two standard dictionaries, various medical dictionaries, two legal dictionaries, a financial glossary, and an idioms search. The main sections of the website are free and do not require registration, but additional resources are available to subscribers.

Virtual Gumshoe: www.virtualgumshoe.com

This is the successor website to the former Webgator site. Originally started as an Internet resource site for investigators (hence the "web-gator" namesake), this site is full of helpful links to public records sites. This site can be especially helpful when you start to run out of ideas for further investigation. Check out the "Resources" tab and explore to see what other options you might have.

Bug Me Not: www.bugmenot.com

While not 100 percent effective, the Bug Me Not website can often allow you to bypass mandatory registration for websites. Simply type in the website address of the site requesting a registration and see if other visitors have successfully established a dummy registration for that site. Remember—many websites don't really offer their secrets for free but get something in exchange (namely, your personal information). Bug Me Not is a way to circumvent those sites. I don't always find the user names and passwords successful, and many times I don't mind giving my business contact information in exchange for access to information. However, if a site's privacy policy says they will share your information with other companies, it may be worth your while to use the Bug Me Not site and see if you can avoid having your inbox filled with unwanted emails.

Snopes: www.snopes.com

Rumors about businesses, rebates, and missing children can fill up your inbox quickly. Where can you verify or refute these claims? Snopes is a great resource. Subjects who are willing to forward a chain email in order to get a $1,000 from Microsoft, free merchandise from Nike, or a free trip to Disney World are probably vulnerable to other hoaxes as well. If your subject is someone who tends to believe these sorts of Internet scams, don't be too surprised if they make rash or inexplicable business decisions with no apparent connection to reality. And if they forward those chain emails to you, feel free to forward a link to Snopes to them (whether they choose to believe the correct answer or not is up to them).

ScamBusters: www.scambusters.org

Covering similar ground to Snopes, ScamBusters investigates and reports on urban legends, financial frauds, and consumer safety tips. Computer virus information is also available on the site. A subscription service is available but not required to access the site's information.

Guidestar: www.guidestar.org

Guidestar is an organization that publicizes information about charities. Especially useful on this website is the ability to view a nonprofit organization's IRS Form 990 and basic financial information. A premium subscription option is available, but is probably unnecessary for most financial investigators.

BBB Wise Giving Alliance: www.give.org

In addition to reporting on private businesses, the Better Business Bureau also maintains information on charitable organizations. Information on this site, including charity-specific "Wise Giving Reports" detailing fundraising and expense information, are available without registration.

Charity Navigator: www.charitynavigator.org

Charity Navigator's website contains similar information to that in BBB's Wise Giving Reports detailing administrative expenses, program expenses, and leadership salary costs. The site also provides the charity's Federal Employer Identification Number in addition to contact information and lists similar charities and organizations targeting the same audience.

Great Schools District Information: www.greatschools.org

This site offers information about specific schools and school districts and offers the ability to compare schools. There are also discussion boards for a variety of topics. Registration is available but not required for most aspects of the website. If you are trying to compare the effect of local schools on two comparable houses in different districts or the same district but feeding different schools, try the school comparison feature. This may help you substantiate or refute a subject's claims about the price difference and whether two homes are truly comparables.

School Matters District Information: www.schoolmatters.com

School Matters is a slightly more bare bones site when compared to Great Schools, but still provides access to important information. You can compare up to three schools, but you will need to know the name of the schools in order to do so (you can find the names of relevant schools on a different part of the website). No registration is required and the site does not accept user-provided content.

PSK12 School Rankings Information: www.psk12.com

Much of the information available on this site is available for free, but some is only available to paid subscribers. If you are trying to evaluate how the local schools affect real estate values, simply select the state and applicable education level under the "Standard Rankings" section. This will give you a basis for comparing schools within a school district and school districts against one another.

Town Search 1.0: http://resources.rootsweb.com/cgi-bin/ townco.cgi

If you are investigating an address in an area you aren't familiar with, you might not know which county records to check. One good way to find out is to use Town Search. Simply type in the name of the town and Town Search will tell you what county the town is in. The search results are not 100 percent reliable, but are generally pretty good. There are two situations where Town Search is not always reliable: when the address is not actually in the town (but instead is in adjacent to an unincorporated area), and when the town straddles two counties. Even in these situations, Town Search is helpful because it gives you a starting place. If you don't find the records you need, simply expand your search to the neighboring counties.

US Amateur Radio Call Sign Lookup: http://callsign.ualr.edu/ callsign.shtml

Admittedly, I have never actually used this site during a financial investigation, but it's still fun to know it exists. This site allows you to look up a ham radio call sign based on either the licensee's name or the call sign itself. This could theoretically come in handy if a subject has a personalized license plate with their call sign, which many ham radio operators do. If so, you can verify that the car really belongs to them. Or, more importantly, if they claim the vehicle does not belong to them but has their call sign on the vanity plate, you may have a legitimate argument that the car does, in fact, belong to them.

Family Watchdog Sex Offender Lookup: www.familywatchdog.us

Knowing a subject's criminal history may affect your investigation techniques and the extent that you verify information. In addition, the presence of a sex offender or halfway house in a neighborhood could affect real estate values of nearby homes. That is why on rare occasions it may be necessary to check the sex offender database. Family Watchdog allows you to search by offender name or by neighborhood. If you are trying to verify effect on property values, simply type in a zip code and see what comes up. Family Watchdog color-codes its maps to correspond to home and work locations of various types of offenses. You can also see recent address changes for offenders. No registration is required to find this information.

CriminalCheck.com: www.criminalcheck.com

CriminalCheck.com provides a similar free service as Family Watchdog. The main difference between the two sites is the interface they use; the results returned should be identical. When searching by zip code, CriminalCheck.com allows you to see a map (not color coded by offense type) and click on a result to see a quick summary of the offender's information. If you want additional information, click on the link provided and a new window will open showing the offender's photo, vital information, and offense information.

National Obituary Archive: www.nationalobituaryarchive.com

Confirming when someone passed away or finding the names of heirs and other family members can sometimes be helpful during a financial investigation. While there is no single repository for all obituaries and death notices in the country, the National Obituary Archive is one site that may be helpful. Obituaries are contributed by participating funeral homes.

Legacy Obituary Search: www.legacy.com/NS

Unlike the National Obituary Archive, where listings are submitted for inclusion, the Legacy Obituary Search examines all obituaries and death notices in participating newspapers. If you are looking for a notice from a major metropolitan area, you are likely to find a result if the death happened in the last ten years or so. Death results from the 1990s and earlier are less reliable—many of them are not in digital form and cannot be located in an electronic search. However, the Legacy site simultaneously searches Legacy's copy of the Social Security Death Index, so you may be able to find at least a date and location of death.

Social Security Death Index: http://ssdi.rootsweb.ancestry.com

After a US citizen dies, their name and Social Security Number (among other information) is entered into the Social Security Death Index. A number of genealogy websites allow you to search their version of the index for free. The Social Security Administration does not make this information available directly to the public, but instead provides it to these online services. If you suspect you have been provided a false Social Security Number, this is a good resource to check. If a Social Security Number appears in the database, it should no longer be in use.

13 *Additional Websites and Resources*

There are a number of other websites and types of website you will find helpful during an Internet-based investigation. These include sites for state and local government as well as sites of local interest. While the information provided in this chapter is not comprehensive, it is a good start for you to start building your own list of sites applicable to your unique type of work.

State Government Sites

Some state websites are fabulous while others leave a lot to be desired. Many states have implemented a portal approach to their websites. As an experienced computer user, I found most of these portal sites to be difficult to use and locate information. The search features were also very hit or miss—some took me to exactly what I wanted, others didn't give me anything relevant in the first five pages of search results. The lesson here is that if you can't find something you need, keep poking around on the website.

Another important item to keep in mind is that not every state organizes its agencies the way you might expect. For example, in most states the Secretary of State handles corporate and UCC filings. But this is not so everywhere. Some states call their Secretary of State something else, and some states (like Arizona) have a Secretary of State but another entity handles corporation filings. In some areas (like New York City and Boston), a local entity keeps track of property filings like deeds instead of the county government being responsible for that task. In other areas (like Alaska and Louisiana), the county might handle those activities but is not called a county.

The websites below reference the main website for each state and have been confirmed as of January 2010. Also listed is a website for the state agency responsible for corporate filings (usually the Secretary of State, but not always). The third entry for each state is a website for the main state agency handling professional licenses and business registrations, if there is one (many states simply refer you to the applicable licensing entity instead of a single overarching agency). The final website listed for each state is the agency handling tax filings for business entities in the state. Finally, each state's three largest counties and cities are listed. Information on the largest counties (which occasionally includes a city) is taken from the US Census Bureau 2008 population estimates at *http://factfinder.census. gov/home/en/official_estimates_2008.html*. Information on largest cities in each state taken from GeoNames geographical database, available at *www.geonames.org*.

STATE OF ALABAMA

Main state government website: *www.alabama.gov*

Secretary of State website: *http://sos.alabama.gov*

Business and professions agency website: multiple, depending on license type

Other helpful sites: *www.revenue.alabama.gov*

Most populous counties: Jefferson County, Mobile County, Madison County

Most populous cities: Birmingham, Montgomery, Mobile

STATE OF ALASKA

Main state government website: *www.alaska.gov*

Division of Corporations website: *www.commerce.state.ak.us/occ*

Business and professions agency website: *www.commerce.state.ak.us/occ*

Department of Revenue: *www.revenue.state.ak.us*

Most populous boroughs: Anchorage Municipality, Fairbanks North Star Borough, Matanuska-Susitna Borough

Most populous cities: Anchorage, Juneau, Fairbanks

STATE OF ARIZONA

Main state government website: *www.az.gov*

Corporations Commission website: *www.azcc.gov/divisions/corporations*

On-line licensing search: *http://az.gov/app/license/index.xhtml*

Department of Revenue: *www.azdor.gov*

Most populous counties: Maricopa County, Pima County, Pinal County

Most populous cities: Phoenix, Tucson, Mesa

STATE OF ARKANSAS

Main state government website: *www.arkansas.gov*

Secretary of State website: *www.sos.arkansas.gov*

Business and professions agency website: multiple, depending on license type

Department of Finance and Administration: *www.dfa.arkansas.gov*

Most populous counties: Pulaski County, Benton County, Washington County

Most populous cities: Little Rock, Fort Smith, Fayettville

STATE OF CALIFORNIA

Main state government website: *www.ca.gov*

Secretary of State website: *www.sos.ca.gov*

Business and professions agency website: *www.dca.ca.gov*

Tax Service Center: *www.taxes.ca.gov*

Most populous counties: Los Angeles County, Orange County, San Diego County

Most populous cities: Los Angeles, San Diego, San Jose

STATE OF COLORADO

Main state government website: *www.colorado.gov*

Secretary of State website: *www.sos.state.co.us*

Business and professions agency website: *www.dora.state.co.us*

State Department of Revenue: *www.colorado.gov/revenue/tax*

Most populous counties: Denver County, El Paso County, Arapahoe County

Most populous cities: Denver, Colorado Springs, Aurora

STATE OF CONNECTICUT

Main state government website: *www.ct.gov*

Secretary of State website: *www.concord-sots.ct.gov*

Business and professions agency website: *www.ct-clic.com*

Department of Revenue Services: *www.ct.gov/drs*

Most populous counties: Fairfield County, Hartford County, New Haven County

Most populous cities: Bridgeport, New Haven, Hartford

STATE OF DELAWARE

Main state government website: *www.delaware.gov*

Division of Corporations website: *http://corp.delaware.gov*

Business and professions agency website: *http://dpr.delaware.gov*

Division of Revenue website: *http://revenue.delaware.gov*

Most populous counties: New Castle County, Sussex County, Kent County

Most populous cities: Wilmington, Dover, Newark

STATE OF FLORIDA

Main state government website: *www.myflorida.com*

Secretary of State website: *www.dos.state.fl.us*

Business and professions agency website: *www.myfloridalicense.com/dbpr*

Department of Revenue: *http://dor.myflorida.com/dor*

Most populous counties: Miami-Dade County, Broward County, Palm Beach County

Most populous cities: Jacksonville, Miami, Tampa

STATE OF GEORGIA

Main state government website: *www.georgia.gov*

Secretary of State website: *www.sos.georgia.gov*

Business and professions agency website: *http://sos.georgia.gov/plb*

Department of Revenue: *https://etax.dor.wa.gov*

Most populous counties: Fulton County, Gwinnett County, DeKalb County

Most populous cities: Atlanta, Columbus, Savannah

STATE OF HAWAII

Main state government website: *www.ehawaii.gov*

Business Registration Division website: *http://hawaii.gov/dcca/breg*

Business and professions agency website: *http://hawaii.gov/dcca/pvl*

Department of Taxation: *http://hawaii.gov/tax*

Most populous counties: Honolulu County, Hawaii County, Maui County

Most populous cities: Honolulu, Hilo, Kailua

STATE OF IDAHO

Main state government website: *www.accessidaho.org*

Secretary of State website: *www.sos.idaho.gov*

Business and professions agency website: *http://idaho.gov/business/licensing.html*

Tax Commission: *http://tax.idaho.gov*

Most populous counties: Ada County, Canyon County, Kootenai County

Most populous cities: Boise, Nampa, Idaho Falls

STATE OF ILLINOIS

Main state government website: *www.illinois.gov*

Secretary of State website: *www.cyberdriveillinois.com*

Business and professions agency website: *www.idfpr.com*

Department of Revenue: *http://tax.illinois.gov*

Most populous counties: Cook County, DuPage County, Lake County

Most populous cities: Chicago, Aurora, Rockford

STATE OF INDIANA

Main state government website: *www.in.gov*

Secretary of State website: *www.in.gov/sos*

Business and professions agency website: *www.in.gov/core/2647.htm*

Department of Revenue: *www.in.gov/dor*

Most populous counties: Marion County, Lake County, Allen County

Most populous cities: Indianapolis, Fort Wayne, Evansville

STATE OF IOWA

Main state government website: *www.iowa.gov*

Secretary of State website: *www.sos.state.ia.us*

Business and professions agency website: *https://eservices.iowa.gov/licensediniowa/*

Department of Revenue: *www.iowa.gov/tax*

Most populous counties: Polk County, Linn County, Scott County

Most populous cities: Des Moines, Cedar Rapids, Davenport

STATE OF KANSAS

Main state government website: *www.kansas.gov*

Secretary of State website: *www.kssos.org*

Business and professions agency website: multiple, depending on license type

Department of Revenue: *www.ksrevenue.org*

Most populous counties: Johnson County, Sedgwick County, Shawnee County

Most populous cities: Wichita, Overland Park, Kansas City

COMMONWEALTH OF KENTUCKY

Main state government website: *http://kentucky.gov*

Secretary of State website: *www.sos.ky.gov*

Business and professions agency website: *www.dop.ky.gov/*

Department of Revenue: *www.revenue.ky.gov*

Most populous counties: Jefferson County, Fayette County, Kenton County

Most populous cities: Lexington-Fayette, Louisville, Lexington

STATE OF LOUISIANA

Main state government website: *www.louisiana.gov*

Secretary of State website: *www.sos.louisiana.gov*

Business and professions agency website: multiple, depending on license type

Department of Revenue: *www.revenue.louisiana.gov*

Most populous parishes: Jefferson Parish, East Baton Rouge Parish, Orleans Parish

Most populous cities: New Orleans, Baton Rouge, Shreveport

STATE OF MAINE

Main state government website: *www.maine.gov*

Secretary of State website: *www.maine.gov/sos*

Business and professions agency website: *www.maine.gov/pfr*

Revenue Services: *www.maine.gov/revenue*

Most populous counties: Cumberland County, York County, Penobscot County

Most populous cities: Portland, Lewiston, Bangor

STATE OF MARYLAND

Main state government website: *www.maryland.gov*

Department of Assessments and Taxation: *www.dat.state.md.us*

Most populous counties: Montgomery County, Prince George's County, Baltimore County

Most populous cities: Baltimore, Columbia, Silver Spring

COMMONWEALTH OF MASSACHUSETTS

Main state government website: *www.mass.gov*

Secretary of the Commonwealth website: *www.sec.state.ma.us*

Business and professions agency website: *http://license.reg.state.ma.us*

Department of Revenue: *www.dor.state.ma.us*

Most populous counties: Middlesex County, Worcester County, Essex County

Most populous cities: Boston, South Boston, Worcester

STATE OF MICHIGAN

Main state government website: *www.michigan.gov*

Secretary of State website: *www.michigan.gov/sos*

Business and professions agency website: *www.michigan.gov/dleg*

Department of Treasury: *www.michigan/gov/treasury*

Most populous counties: Wayne County, Oakland County, Macomb County

Most populous cities: Detroit, Grand Rapids, Warren

STATE OF MINNESOTA

Main state government website: *www.state.mn.us*

Secretary of State website: *www.sos.state.mn.us*

Business and professions agency website: *www.license.mn.gov*

Department of Revenue: *www.taxes.state.mn.us*

Most populous counties: Hennepin County, Ramsey County, Dakota County

Most populous cities: Minneapolis, Saint Paul, Rochester

STATE OF MISSISSIPPI

Main state government website: *www.mississippi.gov*

Secretary of State website: *www.sos.state.ms.us*

Business and professions agency website: multiple, depending on license type

Tax Commission: *www.mstc.state.ms.us*

Most populous counties: Hinds County, Harrison County, DeSoto County

Most populous cities: Jackson, West Gulfport, Gulfport

STATE OF MISSOURI

Main state government website: *www.mo.gov*

Secretary of State website: *www.sos.mo.gov*

Business and professions agency website: *www.difp.mo.gov*

Department of Revenue: *www.dor.mo.gov*

Most populous counties: St. Louis County, Jackson County, St. Louis City

Most populous cities: North Kansas City, Kansas City, Saint Louis

STATE OF MONTANA

Main state government website: *www.mt.gov*

Secretary of State website: *www.sos.mt.gov*

Business and professions agency website: *www.dli.mt.gov*

Department of Revenue: *www.mt.gov/revenue*

Most populous counties: Yellowstone County, Missoula County, Gallatin County

Most populous cities: Billings, Missoula, Great Falls

STATE OF NEBRASKA

Main state government website: *www.nebraska.gov*

Secretary of State website: *www.sos.state.ne.us*

Business and professions agency website: multiple, depending on license type

Department of Revenue: *www.revenue.ne.gov*

Most populous counties: Douglas County, Lancaster County, Sarpy County

Most populous cities: Omaha, Lincoln, Bellevue

STATE OF NEVADA

Main state government website: *www.nv.gov*

Secretary of State website: *www.nvsos.gov*

Business and professions agency website: multiple, depending on license type

Department of Taxation: *www.tax.state.nv.us*

Most populous counties: Clark County, Washoe County, Carson City

Most populous cities: Las Vegas, Henderson, Paradise

STATE OF NEW HAMPSHIRE

Main state government website: *www.nh.gov*

Secretary of State website: *www.sos.nh.gov*

Business and professions agency website: multiple, depending on license type

Department of Revenue Administration: *www.nh.gov/revenue*

Most populous counties: Hillsborough County, Rockingham County, Merrimack County

Most populous cities: Manchester, Nashua, East Concord

STATE OF NEW JERSEY

Main state government website: *www.state.nj.us*

Department of the Treasury Division of Revenue: *www.nj.gov/treasury/revenue*

Business and professions agency website: *www.state.nj.us/njbusiness/licenses*

Most populous counties: Bergen County, Middlesex County, Essex County

Most populous cities: Newark, Jersey City, Paterson

STATE OF NEW MEXICO

Main state government website: *www.newmexico.gov*

Public Regulation Commission website: *www.nmprc.state.nm.us*

Business and professions agency website: multiple, depending on license type

Taxation and Revenue: *www.tax.state.nm.us*

Most populous counties: Bernalillo County, Dona Ana County, Santa Fe County

Most populous cities: Albuquerque, Las Cruces, Santa Fe

STATE OF NEW YORK

Main state government website: *www.state.ny.us*

Secretary of State website: *www.dos.state.ny.us*

Business and professions agency website: multiple, depending on license type

Department of Taxation and Finance: *www.tax.state.ny.us*

Most populous counties: Kings County, Queens County, New York County

Most populous cities: New York City, Brooklyn, Buffalo

STATE OF NORTH CAROLINA

Main state government website: *www.nc.gov*

Secretary of State website: *www.secstate.state.nc.us*

Business and professions agency website: multiple, depending on license type

Department of Revenue: *www.dornc.com*

Most populous counties: Mecklenburg County, Wake County, Guilford County

Most populous cities: Charlotte, West Raleigh, Raleigh

STATE OF NORTH DAKOTA

Main state government website: *www.nd.gov*

Secretary of State website: *www.nd.gov/sos*

Business and professions agency website: *www.nd.gov/sos/businessserv/*

Office of State Tax Commissioner: *www.nd.gov./tax*

Most populous counties: Cass County, Burleigh County, Grand Forks County

Most populous cities: Fargo, Bismarck, Grand Forks

STATE OF OHIO

Main state government website: *www.ohio.gov*

Secretary of State website: *www.sos.state.oh.us*

Business and professions agency website: *http://business.ohio.gov/licensing*

Department of Taxation: *www.tax.ohio.gov*

Most populous counties: Cuyahoga County, Franklin County, Hamilton County

Most populous cities: Columbus, Cleveland, Toledo

STATE OF OKLAHOMA

Main state government website: *www.ok.gov*

Secretary of State website: *www.sos.state.ok.us*

Business and professions agency website: *www.ok.gov/about/license_renewal.html*

Tax Commission: *www.tax.ok.gov*

Most populous counties: Oklahoma County, Tulsa County, Cleveland County

Most populous cities: Oklahoma City, Tulsa, Norman

STATE OF OREGON

Main state government website: *www.oregon.gov*

Secretary of State website: *www.sos.state.or.us*

Business and professions agency website: *http://licenseinfo.oregon.gov*

Department of Revenue: *www.oregon.gov/DOR*

Most populous counties: Multnomah County, Washington County, Clackamas County

Most populous cities: Portland, Salem, Eugene

COMMONWEALTH OF PENNSYLVANIA

Main state government website: *www.state.pa.us*

Department of State website: *www.dos.state.pa.us*

Business and professions agency website: *www.dos.state.pa.us/bpoa*

Department of Revenue: *www.revenue.state.pa.us*

Most populous counties: Philadelphia County, Allegheny County, Montgomery County

Most populous cities: Philadelphia, Pittsburgh, Allentown

STATE OF RHODE ISLAND

Main state government website: *www.ri.gov*

Secretary of State website: *www.sos.ri.gov*

Business and professions agency website: *www.ri.gov/Licensing*

Division of Taxation: *www.tax.state.ri.us*

Most populous counties: Providence County, Kent County, Washington County

Most populous cities: Providence, Warwick, Cranston

STATE OF SOUTH CAROLINA

Main state government website: *www.sc.gov*

Secretary of State website: *www.scsos.com*

Business and professions agency website: *www.llr.state.sc.us*

Department of Revenue: *www.sctax.org*

Most populous counties: Greenville County, Richland County, Charleston County

Most populous cities: Columbia, Charleston, North Charleston

STATE OF SOUTH DAKOTA

Main state government website: *www.sd.gov*

Secretary of State website: *www.sdsos.gov*

Business and professions agency website: *http://dol.sd.gov/lmic/career_licensing_agencies.aspx*

Department of Revenue and Regulation: *www.state.sd.us/drr2*

Most populous counties: Minnehaha County, Pennington County, Lincoln County

Most populous cities: Sioux Falls, Rapid City, Aberdeen

STATE OF TENNESSEE

Main state government website: *www.tennessee.gov*

Secretary of State website: *www.tn.gov/sos*

Business and professions agency website: *www.tennessee.gov/commerce*

Department of Revenue: *www.state.tn.us/revenue*

Most populous counties: Shelby County, Davidson County, Knox County

Most populous cities: Memphis, New South Memphis, Nashville

STATE OF TEXAS

Main state government website: *www.texasonline.com*

Secretary of State website: *www.sos.state.tx.us*

Business and professions agency website: *www.license.state.tx.us*

Comptroller of Public Accounts: *www.cpa.state.tx.us*

Most populous counties: Harris County, Dallas County, Tarrant County

Most populous cities: Houston, San Antonio, Dallas

STATE OF UTAH

Main state government website: *www.utah.gov*

Division of Corporations and Commercial Code website: *http://corporations. utah.gov*

Business and professions agency website: *www.dopl.utah.gov*

Tax Commission: *www.tax.utah.gov*

Most populous counties: Salt Lake County, Utah County, Davis County

Most populous cities: Salt Lake City, West Valley City, Provo

STATE OF VERMONT

Main state government website: *http://vermont.gov*

Secretary of State website: *www.sec.state.vt.us*

Business and professions agency website: multiple, depending on license type

Department of Taxes: *www.state.vt.us/tax*

Most populous counties: Chittenden County, Rutland County, Washington County

Most populous cities: Burlington, Essex Junction, Bennington

COMMONWEALTH OF VIRGINIA

Main state government website: *www.virginia.gov*

Secretary of the Commonwealth website: *www.commonwealth.virginia.gov*

Business and professions agency website: *www.dpor.virginia.gov*

Department of Taxation: *www.tax.virginia.gov*

Most populous counties: Fairfax County, Virginia Beach City, Prince William County

Most populous cities: Virginia Beach, Norfolk, Chesapeake

STATE OF WASHINGTON

Main state government website: *www.wa.gov*

Secretary of State website: *www.secstate.wa.gov*

Business and professions agency website: *www.dol.wa.gov*

Department of Revenue: *www.dor.wa.gov*

Most populous counties: King County, Pierce County, Snohomish County

Most populous cities: Seattle, Spokane, Tacoma

STATE OF WEST VIRGINIA

Main state government website: *www.wv.gov*

Secretary of State website: *www.sos.wv.gov*

Business and professions agency website: multiple, depending on license type

State Tax Department: *www.wvtax.gov*

Most populous counties: Kanawha County, Berkeley County, Cabell County

Most populous cities: Charleston, Huntington, Parkersburg

STATE OF WISCONSIN

Main state government website: *www.wisconsin.gov*

Department of Financial Institutions website: *www.wdfi.org*

Business and professions agency website: *ww2.wisconsin.gov/state/license*

Department of Revenue: *www.revenue.wi.gov*

Most populous counties: Milwaukee County, Dane County, Waukesha County

Most populous cities: Milwaukee, Madison, Green Bay

STATE OF WYOMING

Main state government website: *www.wyoming.gov*

Secretary of State website: *http://soswy.state.wy.us*

Business and professions agency website: *www.wyomingbusiness.org*

Department of Revenue: *http://revenue.state.wy.us*

Most populous counties: Laramie County, Natrona County, Campbell County

Most populous cities: Cheyenne, Casper, Laramie

District of Columbia

WASHINGTON DC

Main government website: *www.dc.gov*

US Territories

AMERICAN SAMOA

Main government website: *www.government.as*

FEDERATED STATES OF MICRONESIA

Main government website: *www.fsmgov.org*

GUAM

Main government website: *www.guam.gov*

MIDWAY ISLANDS

Main government website: *http://midway.fws.gov*

PUERTO RICO

Main government website: *www.gobierno.pr*

If you want more state website links, one additional site I recommend is www.govengine. com. It is a great resource for quickly finding links to state government and other information from all over the United States. Put it at the top of your bookmarks list for quick and easy reference.

Associated Major Metropolitan Areas and 50 Largest US Counties

More than 91 million people live in the 50 most populous counties in the United States, so the odds are good that you will need to access information in one of them. These 50 counties are listed below in alphabetical order by state along with the county government's main website address. A major metropolitan area in each county is provided to help you locate it on a map:

Maricopa County, Arizona (Phoenix): *www.maricopa.gov*

Pima County, Arizona (Tucson): *www.pima.gov*

Alameda County, California (Oakland): *www.acgov.org*

Contra Costa County, California (El Cerrito/Martinez): *www.co.contra-costa.ca.us*

Fresno County, California (Fresno): *www.co.fresno.ca.us*

Los Angeles County, California (Los Angeles): *www.lacounty.gov*

Orange County, California (Santa Ana/Anaheim/Irvine): *www.egov.ocgov.com*

Riverside County, California (Riverside): *www.countyofriverside.us*

Sacramento County, California (Sacramento): *www.saccounty.net*

San Bernardino County, California (San Bernardino): *www.sbcounty.gov*

San Diego County, California (San Diego): *www.sdcounty.ca.gov*

Santa Clara County, California (San Jose): *www.sccgov.org*

Broward County, Florida (Fort Lauderdale): *www.broward.org*

Hillsborough County, Florida (Tampa): *www.hillsboroughcounty.org*

Miami-Dade County, Florida (Miami): *www.miamidade.gov*

Orange County, Florida (Orlando): *www.orangecountyfl.net*

Palm Beach County, Florida (West Palm Beach): *www.pbcgov.com*

Pinellas County, Florida (Clearwater): *www.pinellascounty.org*

Fulton County Georgia (Atlanta): *www.fultoncountyga.gov*

Cook County, Illinois (Chicago): *www.co.cook.il.us*

DuPage County, Illinois (Chicago/Wheaton): *www.co.dupage.il.us*

Montgomery County, Maryland (Silver Spring/Bethesda/Rockville): *www.montgomerycountymd.gov*

Middlesex County, Massachusetts (Cambridge/Lowell): county government abolished July 11, 1997 (Galvin 2009)

Oakland County, Michigan (Pontiac): *www.oakgov.com*

Wayne County, Michigan (Detroit): *www.waynecounty.com*

Hennepin County, Minnesota (Minneapolis): *www.co.hennepin.mn.us*

St. Louis County, Missouri (St. Louis/Clayton): *www.co.st-louis.mo.us*

Clark County, Nevada (Las Vegas): *www.accessclarkcounty.com*

Bronx County, New York (New York City/The Bronx): see *www.nyc.gov*

Erie County, New York (Buffalo): *www.erie.gov*

Kings County, New York (New York City/Brooklyn): see *www.nyc.gov*

Nassau County, New York (Mineola/Long Island): *www.nassaucountyny.gov*

New York County, New York (New York City/Manhattan): see *www.nyc.gov*

Queens County, New York (New York City/Queens): see *www.nyc.gov*

Suffolk County, New York (Riverhead/Long Island): *www.co.suffolk.ny.us*

Westchester County, New York (White Plains): *www.westchestergov.com*

Cuyahoga County, Ohio (Cleveland): *www.cuyahogacounty.us*

Franklin County, Ohio (Columbus): *www.co.franklin.oh.us*

Allegheny County, Pennsylvania (Pittsburgh): *www.alleghenycounty.us*

Philadelphia County, Pennsylvania (Philadelphia): see *www.phila.gov*

Shelby County, Tennessee (Memphis): *www.shelbycountytn.gov*

Bexar County, Texas (San Antonio): *www.co.bexar.tx.us*

Dallas County, Texas (Dallas): *www.dallascounty.org*

Harris County, Texas (Houston): *www.co.harris.tx.us*

Tarrant County, Texas (Fort Worth): *www.tarrantcounty.com*

Travis County, Texas (Austin): *www.co.travis.tx.us*

Salt Lake County, Utah (Salt Lake City): *www.co.slc.ut.us*

Fairfax County, Virginia (Fairfax): *www.fairfaxcounty.gov*

King County, Washington (Seattle): *www.kingcounty.gov*

Milwaukee County, Wisconsin (Milwaukee): *www.milwaukeecounty.org*

Other Helpful Sites and Searches

There are a number of other sites that are simply too numerous to mention here. However, here is some additional information and resources you may find helpful during your investigations:

LOCAL NEWSPAPERS

Newspapers have lots of interesting information, most of which is searchable. Can you search for news using Google? Sure, but not every newspaper is listed there. If you don't find what you're looking for, try checking the local newspapers' search features and see if you develop any leads that way.

PRIVATE MAILBOX SEARCHES

When two people or businesses share the same physical location or mailing address it is a good indication that there's a relationship between the two. So if you're trying to disguise that relationship, you might want to set up a separate address. A PO Box is easy enough to set up for receiving mail, but a physical address can be more challenging. Sometimes people use private mailbox addresses to disguise the fact that they are not providing a real street address. "123 Main Street, Suite 200" certainly looks like the address for an office building, but it might actually be mailbox 200 at the local "Mailboxes, Etc." store. A website search can help you find some of those fake street addresses. Either try a reverse directory or try Google. If multiple businesses come up at the same address, look for a mailbox business, copy center, or similar type of company at that street address.

TELEPHONE DIRECTORIES

Don't overlook the phone book. There's lots of good stuff there. You can not only search white and yellow pages, but reverse directories as well. Want to know whom that phone number really belongs to, type it in the search box and see what comes up. Remember, people put listings in the phone book (and especially ads in the Yellow Pages) to help customers find them. That means those listings can help you find them also.

14 *Requesting Additional Information and Understanding What You Receive*

When conducting investigations, I always try to keep two statements in mind: Ockham's Razor and Hanlon's Razor. Ockham's Razor is the better known of the two and can be summarized as "The simplest explanation is usually correct." Hanlon's Razor is less well known but is even more important when conducting financial investigations: "Never attribute to malice that which can be adequately explained by stupidity." It is simply a fact that subjects do strange things. They make bad decisions. They make ill-informed choices. And sometimes they do things that seem to make absolutely no sense.

Whether you've obtained documents from paid database sources, from free Internet sources, or by contacting government agencies directly, your work is not yet done. Each of those documents needs to have context. Depending on the nature of your investigation, the easiest and most reliable way to provide useful context is frequently to contact your subject to request that information. (Obviously, you don't want to take this step if your subject does not know you are checking on them, so timing is crucial.) You will eventually need to find out the underlying reasoning behind the actions and documents you've discovered; this reasoning will be a key component when you make a final determination and will need to be produced in the event your decision is appealed. You may also need to be able to explain that underlying reasoning (as well as the reasons you believed or disbelieved it) if you are called to testify in court.

Why would you want to contact your subject and ask them questions? There are a number of reasons why asking for information can be the easiest and most productive course of action. First, there may be information your subject neglected to provide when originally requested (perhaps as part of an initial complaint or application). Go back and check the lists you started at the beginning of your investigation: was there anything the subject was supposed to tell you or provide but didn't? You'll want to give them another opportunity to do so, either because you're required to do so (perhaps due to a law or agency policy) or because it's a simple way to provide good public service. Even if you're not under any legal obligation to give the subject a second chance, you may have a judge or other decision maker eventually ask you why you didn't. While "I wasn't obligated to do so" is an accurate response, it probably won't enhance the judge's opinion of you. Avoiding that unpleasant conversation can easily be avoided with a phone call, email, or letter.

Another reason to request additional information is to provide context for what you've found in your investigation. Just because your subject transferred ownership of a parcel of real estate to their child or sibling doesn't mean they did so for nefarious purposes. If the subject's corporate documents say something odd—find out why. There may be a completely legitimate, totally logical reason behind their actions. There may also be a completely legitimate, totally *illogical* reason their corporate documents say something odd. If so, you need to find out that reason as well. It is possible the subject's former neighbor's brother-in-law had a business years ago and got sued once because he didn't put some unusual clause in his Articles of Incorporation (or at least that's how the story goes), so your subject made sure they took steps to prevent that from happening to them. Or maybe they received a chain email instructing them they could get rid of all their debt by simply marking the check "paid in full" and they tried to convince the company's debtors to go along. The accuracy of the subject's belief is not the most relevant factor here; the sincerity of the belief is more important.

In some cases, contacting the subject to request information may actually be required by law. In 2007, the Navy's Inspector General's office's *Investigations Guide* advised:

> The Privacy Act requires you to "collect information to the greatest extent practicable directly from the subject when the information may result in adverse determinations about an individual's rights, benefits, and privileges under Federal Programs (US Navy 2007: 3–5).

While this particular law may not apply to you or your investigations, there may be a similar law or regulation in your jurisdiction that has the same effect. There may also be an agency policy or procedure that requires you to take similar actions.

Finally, asking the subject to explain their documents or their actions puts them on the record. It locks them into a position that will be difficult to change at a later date. If the subject gives you an explanation that demonstrates they've done something wrong, you can use that answer to justify your determination or impeach their credibility. If they try to change that answer later, you can use their changed position against them as well.

Asking the Tough Questions

While each case and each subject is different, my experience has been that it is generally most effective to call a subject on the carpet by demonstrating what you already know and then asking very specific questions. Many analysts and investigators disagree with this position, preferring instead to maximize the amount of information that is characterized as "enforcement sensitive" and which is not revealed to the subject. However, I have found that I obtain more information from a subject when I confront them with what I already know, even if I have not found everything they are hiding. Your decision whether to reveal or conceal your knowledge should be determined by your agency's policy, your personal preferences, and the specifics of the investigation. Revealing what you already know does eliminate the possibility of having the Perry Mason-like "gotcha" moment; but in the real world, "gotcha" moments don't really happen. Even when you think you're about to have one, there's likely a simple and sufficiently plausible explanation for what you think you've found.

If you do decide to send a request for additional information, you may be surprised at how effective a pointedly worded letter can be. While communicating in writing does not allow you the same opportunity to bond and build rapport with a subject that a personal interview might provide, it does provide you the opportunity to ask a subject to admit or deny (on the record) the facts you already know to be true. When confronted with their apparent deception, subjects who have negligently or knowingly hidden an asset may feel compelled to rectify their mistake; those who intentionally concealed the asset may instead create an elaborate excuse that can later be used to impeach their credibility. If the subject refuses to provide any information at all, that's fine, too. The lack of a response means you can legitimately argue that you gave the subject an opportunity to correct any erroneous information, but they failed to do so. Therefore, you must assume the information is accurate. Either way, you fulfilled your due process obligations and demonstrated your fairness and good faith to the trier of fact. Most important, sending a request for additional information could cause you to learn something that changes your mind—and you will learn that information with adequate time for research and reflection instead of being put on the spot during the middle of a hearing. Personally, I am happy to forego the possibility of having a gotcha moment in front of a judge for the guarantee that I'm not the one being surprised by information.

If you decide to request additional information from the subject, your request should be unambiguous, comprehensive, and extremely clear. Consider including a regulatory basis for your question (just once if there are multiple questions related to the same legal requirement), the fact supporting your question, and then the question itself. For example, if you discover the subject owns a parcel of real estate but didn't disclose it, your letter to them might include the following request:

You submitted a Personal Financial Statement dated January 1, 2010 in support of your application. This form included instructions for you to include every parcel of real estate you currently own as well as any accompanying mortgage indebtedness. Your January 2010 Personal Financial Statement did not disclose that you own real estate located at 2000 Lakeridge Drive in Seattle, Washington (King County Tax Parcel No. 46830001501). Within 30 days of the date of this letter, please provide a written explanation why this asset was not included on your Personal Financial Statement. Your explanation should specifically include, but not be limited to:

- *the current fair market value of this property and the current fair market value of your ownership interest in this property;*
- *the current mortgage indebtedness on the property (if any);*
- *the names and addresses of any lien holders on the property; and*
- *the names and addresses of any co-owners of the property and their applicable ownership interest.*

Please provide written documentation to support your explanation. If you have recently sold this parcel of real property, please provide a written explanation as to which line items on your Personal Financial Statement include the proceeds you received from the sale and provide copies of the settlement statement and related closing documents.

Phrasing your request with this much specificity achieves two goals: first, it gives the subject very little (if any) wiggle room to provide an evasive answer; second, it addresses most possible responses the subject can provide and eliminates the need for additional follow-up information requests. Including the regulatory basis for your question and the supporting facts are optional, but increase the question's specificity and help reduce the need for more follow-up requests.

Each time you need to request additional information from the subject, you delay your investigation and potentially alienate the subject by making them feel bullied. Sending multiple letters requesting information can make it seem like you're not doing your job properly, either because you are incompetent or because you are purposefully delaying your investigation. If additional follow-up requests are needed, clearly explain why you weren't able to ask the question earlier. For example:

Thank you for your response to my February 16 letter requesting additional information about the mortgage indebtedness on your vacation home. From your explanation, I understand you are requesting an offset for part of the value of this property because the home suffered significant damage during last winter's storms. In order for our office to allow an offset for the reduced value on your Personal Financial Statement, please provide copies of any damage or repair estimates you have obtained, any documentation you have received from your insurance company denying coverage for the damage, or any other documentation that shows you are personally bearing this financial loss. If you have already filed your personal taxes and deducted the loss, please include a copy of your IRS Form 1040 and any supporting schedules or attachments documenting the loss. Please note that if your insurance company has or will compensate you for your loss, we will not be able to offset the value from the storm damage. We are only able to offset actual losses, not potential ones.

A request such as this makes it clear that you didn't simply forget to ask about this issue in your first letter; you didn't know to ask about the issue until you received the subject's response to that initial request for information. It also makes it clear what documents you expect to receive to support the subject's requested offset and what you are prepared to offer in exchange. If your request is instead related to something you overlooked, it's acceptable to admit it—just apologize for your mistake. Again, these steps may not be legally mandatory but they can go a long way to easing what is frequently a strained relationship between investigator and subject.

Instead of omitting an asset from a financial statement, sometimes the subject will disclose ownership but either understate its value or overstate its mortgage indebtedness. In those cases, you might want to consider sending a letter such as:

Please provide a written explanation as to why your Personal Financial Statement dated January 1, 2010 includes an ownership interest in real property located at 1225 South Capital Way (Orange County Tax Parcel No. 09850005000) valued at $1,250,000 but a corresponding mortgage indebtedness of $2,600,000. This explanation should specifically include, but not be limited to, the names of the lenders for the appropriate mortgage indebtedness and documentation of all current amounts due.

Underreported rental income can also be a red flag that requires additional information. If you see the subject owns a parcel of property that they rent out for less than market value, you should consider asking why. (To determine market value of a rental, refer to the explanation above in Chapter 8.)

Your Internet-based investigation may have revealed a relationship between your subject and other individuals or companies—relationships that may not have been disclosed. Sending a letter requesting additional information is a good way to learn whether these relationships are routine or whether they might be the basis for illegitimate transfers of assets. For example, you may find the subject is involved with multiple companies, all of which share a common address, telephone number, and industry. If you need to establish whether these companies are independent or affiliated with one another, you could consider asking the subject to clarify the relationship:

> *Please provide a written explanation of the relationship between ABC Company, Inc. and XYZ Industries, LLC. Please specifically address whether the two companies share any owners, officers, managers, employees, facilities, equipment, bank accounts, or other business resources of any kind. Please also specifically address whether there is any financial relationship or transactions between the two companies and provide examples of contracts, leases, or other financial documentation.*

You would repeat the request for each company you've discovered that appears to be part of the same corporate structure. This type of inquiry is intended to both obtain needed information but also to get the subject to admit in writing the information you suspect to be true. You can use the answers provided to help substantiate any determination or recommendation you make.

One word of caution when requesting additional information from a subject: pay special attention to how you phrase your request. Is there any way the subject can give you incomplete information and still argue they answered the question? If so, you'll want to rephrase the question. For example, say you want to ask if the subject owns any other businesses. If you only ask, "Do you own any other businesses?" you may not get the information you're looking for. An evasive subject might argue, "My Revocable Living Trust owns another business, but I don't" or, "My husband and I own stock in our family's lumberyard, but we don't own the company" or even, "Oh, that's not a 'business.' That's just a hobby." When it is in their best interests to do so, subjects may also claim ignorance of the effect of applicable community or joint property laws. A business that is "ours" for purposes of obtaining a loan may suddenly become "his" or "hers" if it serves the subject's interests to argue separate ownership for purposes related to your investigation.

Avoiding this situation can be a challenge. You may want to break your inquiry into multiple questions or you use terms that are more inclusive in your question. That means instead of asking if the subject owns any other businesses, you might want to ask:

> *Do you or your spouse have any ownership interest in any business other than ABC Company, Inc.? Having an "ownership interest" specifically includes, but is not limited to: owning stock, holding a membership interest, or having any interest in a trust or other controlling entity.*

Being explicit in what you mean and what you are asking for is crucial to preventing evasive answers. This may mean you have to ask ten questions instead of five. However, being explicit in how you phrase the question also helps the subject: they have an easier time understanding what you want and providing the information you've requested. Think about the last time you tried to answer a question you didn't really understand; it's a frustrating experience. Save both yourself and your subject some trouble and be clear about what you want. A little extra time spent writing the letter may result in many hours saved by avoiding unnecessary appeals and complaints.

If there is any doubt about why you are asking the question, also be clear about why you want the information. The Internet can lead you to extensive amounts of completely irrelevant information. Part of your job as an investigator is to be able to distinguish between what is interesting information and what is actually relevant to your work. As stated before, just because you *can* collect the information doesn't mean you *should* collect it. The same guideline also applies to additional information requests: just because you don't understand something doesn't mean you should be asking for an explanation. If the subject could argue that your regulations don't require you to ask a particular question, consider including a brief statement about why you are asking. For example, say you're reviewing a subject's potential conflict of interest. Your letter might request more information and provide a brief explanation such as:

> *Our routine verification has revealed that your spouse was the Vice President of 1-2-3 Gaming, Inc. as of November 2009. Please explain whether your spouse is still employed by 1-2-3 Gaming, Inc. in any capacity and, if not, when they left that employment. If your spouse is no longer employed by 1-2-3 Gaming, Inc., please provide a copy of a resignation letter, termination letter, or other documentation showing when their employment ended. Please note that Appointees to the Oversight Board are not permitted to have a personal relationship with any regulated organization. The state's legal definition of "personal relationship" includes being an employee of a regulated organization or having a family member who is employed by a regulated organization.*

As you can see, adding an explanation takes only a few words, but clearly communicates that there is a legitimate basis for the question. This helps the subject understand that they are not being unfairly targeted for special scrutiny, which will minimize the chances of the subject filing a complaint with your manager, elected officials, or the media.

Deceptive Answer Warning Signs

There are a number of tell-tale signs of deceptive answers, whether those answers are provided in person or in writing. No single sign may be enough to prove the subject is lying; you may need a number of pieces of documentary evidence to disprove a subject's story. When reviewing written answers to additional information requests, some of these features may indicate a deceptive answer.

UNNECESSARILY LONG ANSWERS

A simple question usually provokes a simple response. If you've asked for verification of the date a company was founded but instead receive a four-paragraph explanation of the entire corporate history, something else may be going on. If you've received a long answer to a short question, read the answer very carefully and thoughtfully. While the subject may simply be nervous and trying to cover all their bases, they may also be hoping to distract you with how "well" they are complying with your request.

SUPPLYING IRRELEVANT OR UNREQUESTED INFORMATION

This warning sign may appear in an unnecessarily long answer or may stand on its own as well. I always become suspicious whenever a subject provides me with extensive information that I did not request, especially if that information does not appear to have anything to do with my investigation. Again, it is possible the subject has provided irrelevant information because they are nervous or because they think it will somehow improve the chances my investigation will end favorably for them. It is also possible that the irrelevant information is simply provided as filler to enhance a fictional explanation. In some ways, subjects who supply irrelevant information tend to remind me of a child who is telling a fib—the longer you allow the story to continue, the more and more details they add.

PARSING WORDS AND UNUSUAL WORD CHOICES

Deceptive subjects sometimes attempt to avoid giving you the information you really want by using different words or simply answering a different question. For example, if you've asked who the company's President is, a purposefully evasive answer might be "John Smith runs the company" or "Jane Jones is in charge." You didn't ask who "runs the company" and you didn't ask who "is in charge." You asked who the company's President is. Those two things are different. A response such as this may very well be an attempt to make it appear your question has been answered when it actually has not.

Another variation on this ploy is using vague words or exaggerations to reply to your question. Say you suspect the subject's company is really just a front for organized crime. If you've asked what industry the company is in, you could get an answer such as "manufacturing." Manufacturing what? Simply saying that a company is a "manufacturer" doesn't actually answer your question because the response is too vague. A subject's use of a term like "manufacturer" may also be an overstatement of what they really do. Do they really "manufacture" a product, or do they just put a label on an item produced by someone else?

Truthful answers don't need embellishing, don't need to be overly complex, and aren't so short they raise more questions than they answer. Subjects who are not trying to be evasive tend to use the same words you used when they answer your question. If you've asked about the company's President, you should expect to receive an answer containing the word "President." If you don't, be on the lookout for other red flags.

FAILING TO SUPPORT AN ANSWER

Our society is obsessed with documentation. As a result, it's extremely difficult to go anywhere or do anything without leaving a trail. That is just as true for businesses as it is for individuals: forms are filed, receipts are given, and records are kept. If John Smith really is the President of ABC Company, there will be records to support that fact. In addition to the corporate records the company should have on hand (such as meeting minutes), corporate documents will be on file with the Secretary of State's office and copies of the firm's contracts or leases would be able to support a subject's claim that John Smith is the company's President. Whenever a subject can answer a question but can't provide supporting documentation, I always suspect deception until proven otherwise. While it is theoretically possible the documentation does not exist, it is more likely the documentation *does* exist but shows a different answer.

Granted, a subject may lie when answering your questions. They may even create or alter documents to support that lie. This is why it is important not to rely on a single source of information. In some cases, a lie is actually more helpful than the truth. Disprove just one of a subject's lies and you create doubt on everything else they say. The overwhelming lesson here, as has been stated before, is to make inquiries *before* accusations.

Understanding the Answers

If you were careful to phrase your questions clearly and concisely, you will most likely receive clear and understandable answers. Unclear questions may result in long, rambling, unclear responses. When you evaluate a response to your inquiries, look for the warning signs noted previously. If you've asked a simple and straightforward question, such as "Who is the President of ABC Company, Inc." you should reasonably expect to receive a simple and straightforward response, such as "John Smith is the President of ABC Company, Inc."

More complicated questions and situations will undoubtedly produce more complicated responses. Using the question above about the missing real estate, here are some possible responses you could receive. If you are dealing with a subject who has made an honest mistake and neglected to include all of their property on their list of assets, your question might elicit a response such as:

> *Thank you for pointing out the error I made on my January 2010 Personal Financial Statement. You are correct that I mistakenly omitted the parcel of real estate I own on Lakeridge Drive. Please accept my apology for this oversight. A corrected Personal Financial Statement is enclosed, showing that my spouse and I jointly own 100% of the property, which currently has a fair market value of approximately $250,000. The current mortgage balance is approximately $46,750. I have included a printout from US Bank to verify the mortgage balance. There are no liens on the property. US Bank holds a Deed of Trust for the mortgage.*

However, if the information you found on the Internet or at the county auditor's office was inaccurate or incomplete, your question may elicit a very different response from the subject. Assuming your question was clear and specific, you might receive a letter or email with the following explanation:

> *My January 2010 Personal Financial Statement did not include an ownership interest in the property at 2000 Lakeridge Drive, S.W. in Seattle because I sold this property in December 2009. The majority of the proceeds from this sale were used to pay down the mortgage on my personal residence. I have enclosed a copy of the settlement statement from the sale, showing I received a net distribution of $500,000 from the sale of this property on December 20, 2009. I have also enclosed a letter from my bank showing I made a $450,000 payment on my mortgage on December 29, 2009. Finally, I have enclosed a copy of the canceled $25,000 check*

I wrote to Princeton University on December 27, 2009 for my daughter's tuition and related school expenses. The remainder of the proceeds from this sale is reflected in the "Cash Assets" entry on my January 2010 Personal Financial Statement.

Perhaps you were mistaken when you concluded the subject failed to disclose their ownership interest in the property in question. If that is the case, you could expect to receive a response such as:

My January 2010 Personal Financial Statement did disclose my ownership interest in the property at 2000 Lakeridge Drive, S.W. in Seattle. This property is included on the second line under real estate and is part of the same piece of property as 2500 Lakeridge Drive, S.W. The value of my ownership interest is as indicated on the Personal Financial Statement. None of your other requests is applicable to this parcel of property.

The biggest challenge you may have is deciphering evasive answers. I have noticed that not all evasive responses come from subjects who are attempting to provide inaccurate information. Sometimes evasive answers come from subjects who just don't "get it"—that is, they neither understand your question nor do they have a good explanation for their actions. Fortunately, these two types of responses look nothing alike. Say you have asked the subject to explain the relationship between a company they own and an allegedly independent company owned by their spouse. You think the two companies are operating as a single business and that they aren't really independent of each other. You've asked a detailed question asking for the relationship between the companies; whether they share resources such as facilities, equipment, or employees; and why the two companies are separate when they share a common industry and compete with each other. A deceptive answer might look something like this:

There is no relationship between ABC Company, Inc. and XYZ Industries, LLC. I own ABC Company and my spouse owns XYZ Industries. ABC Company is a manufacturing entity that works for Fortune 100 companies like Boeing, Microsoft, Disney, and FedEx. ABC was founded in 1989 and has steadily grown each year since then. We focus on producing top quality merchandise at affordable prices. In contrast, XYZ industries is a smaller company whose customers include state government agencies, school districts, and all four local television network affiliates. There is no reason my spouse and I would consider merging these two businesses because they have nothing to do with each other.

This response has many of the red flags mentioned above. Did you ask about customers? Did you ask when the company was founded or how profitable it is? Did you ask for a sales pitch? No—the subject has provided that information as a distraction. Mentioning the relationship with government agencies and television stations is probably also intended to distract (and perhaps intimidate) you. The response does not give any of the specific information you requested. Each of these is a good reason for suspecting an untruthful answer.

In contrast, an incorrect but well-intentioned answer to the same question might read something like:

There is no relationship between ABC Company, Inc. and XYZ Industries, LLC. I own ABC Company and my spouse owns XYZ Industries. While the two businesses do share a business location and office staff, they work on different jobs and don't contract together. Employees only work for one company at a time. When an employee works for ABC Company, they are paid by ABC. When the employee works on an XYZ Industries job, their check is issued by XYZ. My spouse and I keep our two businesses separate for tax purposes.

An answer such as this indicates the subject may actually believe their business and their spouse's business are independent companies, but no objective third-party would likely agree. The reference to "tax purposes" is another clue: subjects may use this phrase without having the slightest idea what it really means. Their attorney or their accountant or their cousin told them they need to do something "for tax purposes," so they do—even though they have no idea how their actions affect their taxes. "Liability" and "legal purposes" are similar key words that subjects may use without really understanding.

Why Bother Asking? They're Just Going To Lie …

Some investigators don't like to request additional information from a subject because they believe it gives the subject an opportunity to lie and create additional supporting documentation for the fiction they've already created. There is no doubt this is a very real possibility in any investigation, especially when there are big financial stakes. Fortunately, there are a few steps you can take to help mitigate any falsehoods the subject decides to submit.

ASK QUESTIONS FOR WHICH YOU ALREADY KNOW THE ANSWERS

This may seem like a waste of time, but it can actually provide excellent information. By asking the subject to verify information you've already obtained from a third party, you accomplish one of two goals: either you authenticate the evidence obtained from the third party, or you give the subject the opportunity to prove they are untrustworthy. If the subject confirms the information, you can use that information without fear of contradiction during later proceedings. If the subject instead contradicts the information, you can use this as a basis to impeach their credibility. After all, the Secretary of State or the county Recorder's office has no motivation to alter documents. If given a choice between believing the subject and a neutral third-party government employee, most judges are going to believe the third party.

ASK VERY SPECIFIC QUESTIONS AND REQUEST VERY SPECIFIC ANSWERS

As previously noted, phrasing your questions to avoid evasive answers is important to getting accurate answers. But asking very specific questions also helps minimize the chances that a subject will attempt to purposefully mislead you. When a subject has been less than forthright, they frequently worry about being caught. Smart subjects (and those with smart attorneys or accountants) may correctly interpret your very specific questions as a trap. They realize that you're offering them the shovel so they can dig that hole just a little deeper. As a result of seeing the trap, they may take steps to avoid it; the easiest way to avoid the trap may simply be to tell the truth. (Although I have also seen subjects decline to answer the question all together instead—something like an administrative version of "taking the Fifth.")

EXPECT SOME SILLY EXPLANATIONS

Sometimes subjects not only make bad choices, they do so for the silliest of reasons. Expect that you will occasionally see some strange answers to your questions. Depending on the nature of your investigation, sometimes those answers may not only be incomplete but may also demonstrate the subject's lack of understanding of the matter. For example, if you've asked why the company switched from being a corporation to an LLC, you might get a response that says nothing more than "tax reasons." Were there tax advantages for the company to change is legal structure? Perhaps so. But a more likely explanation is that some friend or family member told them they shouldn't be a corporation and instead should be an LLC because it would give them tax advantages. Not knowing any better, they changed their corporate form and have no idea what other legal implications that change created.

Case in Point

A number of years ago (long before the recent financial crisis), while I was investigating a subject who claimed to have a net worth of about $300,000, I was curious about a number of parcels of real estate the subject listed as assets. Each parcel was listed as commercial property with a relatively small value, at least as compared to other commercial properties in that city. The subject also reported large mortgage balances for each of the properties—up to three times the reported value.

After just a bit of digging, I was able to find the source of the each property's reported value: the Tax Assessor's office. Instead of reporting the fair market value of each property (as the subject had been instructed to do), they instead reported the smaller assessed value. A review of the comparable commercial properties for sale in the area gave me a clear idea about each property's true value. I was able to determine that each property was worth 20–25 percent more than the original mortgage amount. Based on these estimates, I calculated the subject's net worth to far exceed the amount claimed.

Based on my research, I was able to draft a clear and concise letter requesting additional information. I did not need to explain that I believed the documentation submitted by the subject was inaccurate. Instead, I simply requested that the subject explain why the mortgage balance for each property was two to three times the alleged value, which mortgage company agreed to lend the subject twice the value of each property, and documentation showing the current loan to value ratio for each mortgage.

I did not receive a written response to my information request. Instead, the day before the response was due, the subject's attorney called and informed me that his client preferred not to answer the questions and would not be supplying a response. I don't know whether it was the subject or their attorney that read between the lines and recognized the trap I had laid, but they were clever enough to avoid it.

This was a simple resolution to what could have otherwise been an extremely complex case involving untold hours of work and huge amounts spent on lawyers. The proper and legal outcome was achieved without causing unnecessary stress for me and my co-workers and pointless embarrassment for the subject. While not every investigation can be resolved by the subject withdrawing an application or complaint, this is an option that you should not overlook if it is available to you.

15 *Getting Help from the Numbers*

Have you ever noticed that it's socially acceptable to be afraid of math? Most of us don't bat an eye when someone says, "I can't do math." Actually, we all do math every day and don't even think about it—whether it's figuring how long it will take you to run an errand (speed and distance) or how much to leave as a tip in a restaurant (fractions). Sometimes, a little extra math can help guide an investigation and help you figure out whether you're looking at a typical situation or something that "just doesn't look right." Don't be afraid of math—math can be your savior!

Running some basic financial calculations can help clarify a situation or give you clues about what might be happening behind the scenes. If things seem amiss, or if you want to get a clearer picture of what's really going on with the firm, you can use a company's financial statements to get a better idea of its financial situation. Information for publicly-traded companies will be available from the Internet, but privately-held companies usually don't make that information generally available. In order to obtain financial statements for private firms, you'll need to request them directly from the company. (See Chapter 14 for advice about requesting additional information from the subject.)

Financial Documents

There are a large number of financial documents that may apply to a company you are investigating. For large companies that sell their stock on a stock exchange, these documents are readily accessible on the Internet for free. Privately-held companies do not usually make this information available and you may have to request it. (Financial statements for privately-held companies may also be protected from public disclosure under state or federal Sunshine laws, so be sure you know what rules apply.) If you do have access to these documents, it is important to understand what information each provides.

INCOME STATEMENT

This document shows how much money a company made by selling its products and services and how much it spent providing those products and services. This is the form where you will find entries for wages paid to employees, routine business expenses like advertising and postage, and quarterly or annual expenses like payroll or property taxes.

BALANCE SHEET

This document shows a company's assets, liabilities, and equity held by the owner(s). A balance sheet should always balance. A company's total assets should always be exactly the same as their total liabilities plus the owner's equity. Always. If you see a balance sheet that doesn't balance, you need to find out why.

CASH FLOW STATEMENT

This document is broken down into three categories: money related to operating activities, money related to investing activities, and money related to financing activities. This is the form where you will find adjustments to income, such as deductions for depreciation and amortization, as well as payments made to shareholders in the form of dividends or distributions.

SEC FORM 10-K

Publicly-traded companies in the United States have to file a report with the Securities and Exchange Commission (SEC) every year. This 10-K report includes a statement from the company's accounting firm, disclosures about the company's activities, and the three financial statements listed above. Frequently, publicly-traded companies may produce a slick, glossy version of their annual report and include either a copy of the 10-K or the same basic information. Copies of 10-K forms, as well as other mandatory filings, are available for free from the Securities and Exchange Commission's EDGAR website.

Financial Ratios

Financial ratios are one way to judge the overall health of a company. This is crucial information if you're thinking about investing in a business; but financial ratios are also important when conducting a financial investigation, especially when they change suddenly. Looking at a company's basic financial ratios can help you better understand how financially stable it is, how well its managers run its operations, and how good an investment it is.

Although there are many different financial ratios you can examine, the following ratios are the ones I find to be the most helpful during a financial investigation. Remember that these calculations only apply to companies instead of individuals. If your review reveals possible misconduct, you should probably consult with your agency's legal advisor. Manipulation of financial information may be a violation of both state and federal laws, so the involvement of an attorney or accountant may be a sensible precaution.

QUICK RATIO: (CURRENT ASSETS — INVENTORY) ÷ CURRENT LIABILITIES

The quick ratio looks at how much cash a company has. Another way of calculating the quick ratio is: add cash on hand plus marketable securities plus accounts receivable and divide the result by the current liabilities (Brouard 2002: 3). All of these amounts should be listed on the company's balance sheet. A healthy company will likely have a quick ratio greater than or equal to 1.0, regardless of what industry it is in. A ratio of 1.0 means that the company's cash on hand is equal to its current liabilities. A company that has a quick ratio of less than 1.0 has too many short-term liabilities compared to its short-term assets, or it has too much of its short-term assets tied up in inventory. If the economy falters or something unexpected happens, the company may not have enough cash readily available to deal with the situation.

When looking for hidden assets, a quick ratio alone probably won't help you very much. Instead, look for a change in the quick ratio over time. If a company suddenly has a lot more cash on hand, that could indicate the owner is no longer taking dividends, distributions, or draws. Is that because they have found a new source of income, say from another business? Did they have an on-going expense that ended, such as child support, alimony, or college tuition payments? A negative change in the quick ratio can likewise indicate an important change. If the company suddenly has a lot less cash on hand, that could indicate the owner is pulling money out of the business, either for their personal use or for some other business purpose. Understanding why a company's quick ratio has changed could lead your financial investigation in a new direction.

CURRENT RATIO: CURRENT ASSETS ÷ CURRENT LIABILITIES

Both these amounts are listed on the company's balance sheet. Regardless of industry, a healthy company should have a current ratio greater than or equal to 2.0—that is, the company should have at least twice as many current assets as they have liabilities that will need to be paid within one year. A company that has a current ratio of less than 2.0 may not have enough assets readily at hand to deal with unexpected economic downturns, supplier problems, or natural and man-made disasters. The difference between the current ratio and the quick ratio is that the current ratio does not separate out the company's inventory. The current ratio assumes inventory could be sold to generate cash; the quick ratio does not assume income can be generated by selling inventory and only looks at how much actual cash and other liquid assets are on hand.

When looking for hidden assets, the current ratio helps you in much the same way the quick ratio does. Looking for a change in the current ratio is key and comparing the current ratio against the quick ratio can help you better understand a company's stability and liquidity. How much money the company has tied up in inventory affects the quick ratio, but not the current ratio. So if a company is unable to sell their products and inventory starts to accumulate, the quick ratio will fall but the current ratio won't. However, if the owner takes cash out of the business, both ratios will fall. That means if a company argues they rented additional warehouse space to hold all the inventory they can't sell, then their quick ratio should reflect a change in inventory but their current ratio should be steady. If both the quick ratio and the current ratio change, that could instead indicate the owner took cash out of the business and the inventory is actually not unsellable. If that's the case, not only did the company lie about their financial situation, but there's a warehouse being rented for some reason that you probably want to investigate.

RETURN ON SALES: NET INCOME ÷ NET SALES

This number will vary depending on what industry a company is in, but a higher number usually means a more stable company, especially when compared to other firms in the same industry. This ratio tells you how efficient a company is because it tells you how much profit a company makes for every dollar it generates in sales. A company that sells many inexpensive products may have a lower return on sales than a company that sells a few very expensive products, even though the first company earns far more profit overall.

When looking for hidden assets, the return on sales ratio is most helpful when comparing companies in the same or a similar industry. If your subject company has a return on sales of 0.25 but its competitors have return on sales ratios in the neighborhood of 0.05, you'll want to figure out the reason for the discrepancy. While a snapshot of a company's return on sales can be helpful, it is probably more helpful to look at this ratio over time. A sudden change (either positive or negative) can signal other changes are going on. If a company's return on sales suddenly improves, it may be because the firm isn't reporting all their sales. If the ratio suddenly falls, it may be because the firm isn't reporting all their income.

RETURN ON ASSETS: NET INCOME ÷ TOTAL ASSETS

The return on assets ratio tells you how profitable a company is proportionate to their assets. This ratio gives you a way to compare two different companies on an "apples to apples" basis. A company that earns $5 profit per $1,000 of assets is a more efficient company than one earning $1 profit per $1,000 of assets. A company with a very high return on assets ratio may mean the company is hiding assets, thereby creating a false perception of profitability. That is, if they reported all their assets they would have earned $4 or $3 or $2 of profit per $1,000 of assets instead of the $5 profit they reported.

RETURN ON EQUITY: NET INCOME ÷ SHAREHOLDER'S EQUITY

The return on equity ratio, like return on assets, tells you how profitable a company is. In this case, the ratio tells you how profitable a company is proportionate to how much equity the shareholders have. This ratio gives you a way to compare two companies in a fair manner. A company that earns $5 profit per $50 of stock is presumably more efficient than a company that earns $1 profit per $50 of stock. Like the return on assets ratio, a very high return on equity may mean the company is hiding assets. The same theory applies to return on equity as to return on assets—the true rate of return is lower than reported if the company is hiding assets because the proportion of profit versus assets would change if the company reported all their assets. Underreporting equity is a way to artificially inflate the company's apparent rate of return.

Financial ratios aren't an answer in and of themselves, but they can help you predict what else you *should* find. For example, a firm that receives a disproportionately low return on assets may be hiding income. A firm whose quick ratio is very low probably shouldn't be paying the owner an extravagant salary. Each of these ratios can be one piece in the puzzle—eventually they help you see the bigger picture. Remember that if a firm is manipulating their financial information, it will show up in the ratios. If they're hiding cash (the top number), it will usually make the ratio look worse; if they're hiding assets (the bottom number), it will usually make the ratio look better.

Altman's Z-Score

Whenever I have the requisite information, I also determine the Altman's Z-Score for each firm I'm investigating. This score combines a number of financial ratios into a single number, which can be a helpful guide in your investigation. The Altman's Z-Score is intended to predict whether a company will enter bankruptcy in the next two years, but I think of it more as a good general guide to a company's overall financial health. If a firm's Z-Score predicts bankruptcy, you can safely assume the company is facing some tough economic times in the near future.

In order to determine the Altman's Z, you need to know a number of specific financial indicators, all of which can be found on the company's balance sheet and cash flow statement. For publicly-traded companies, this information will be available for free directly from the SEC or from any one of a number of financial websites such as Yahoo! Finance, Google Finance, or any other stock trading website. As noted previously, financial statements for privately-held firms are not generally available unless you obtain them from the company. The indicators you will need in order to calculate a company's Z-Score are detailed below.

MARKET CAPITALIZATION

This is simply the number of shares owned by stockholders multiplied by the current cost of the stock. The exact market capitalization for publicly-traded firms changes every day because the stock price varies every day. The easiest way to determine market capitalization for publicly-traded firms is by looking at their 10-K filing with the SEC—it's reported on the cover sheet. You can also calculate the market capitalization of a public company for a given day by going to a finance web site and looking up the number of stocks held and the trading price for that particular day. Market capitalization tells you how big a company is. For privately-held companies, you'll use the line on the company's balance sheet for "Stockholder Equity" instead of market capitalization.

SALES

This line item simply refers to the amount of income generated from selling products and services. It does not include income from things like interest. You can find this amount on the top line of a company's Income Statement. It may refer to "net income" or "cash received from customers" or something similar.

CURRENT ASSETS

Assets are "current" if they could be converted into cash within one year. For most companies, most of the current assets will be in cash, cash equivalents, and inventory. The total amount will be listed towards the top of the firm's balance sheet, below a list of each of the current assets.

TOTAL ASSETS

This number is different from current assets because it also includes long-term assets—those that are going to be held for longer than one year. This amount may include both "tangible" assets, like money or real estate, as well as "intangible" assets, like patent or royalty rights. The total amount will be below the list of the long-term assets.

CURRENT LIABILITIES

Like assets, liabilities are "current" if they have to be paid within one year. If an obligation will last longer than a year (like a mortgage or other large loan) only the amount to be paid within the next year is included in the line for current liabilities; the rest of the loan will be listed under the "long-term" obligations line. Current liabilities will appear on the balance sheet below the total assets line.

TOTAL LIABILITIES

This number is different from current liabilities because it also includes the company's long-term liabilities. Frequently, this line won't actually appear on a balance sheet, but you can easily figure it out. Look for the line marked "total liabilities and shareholders' equity" and subtract the amount listed on the "shareholders' equity" line. If you prefer, you can simply add together all the line items listed in the sections for "current liabilities" and "long-term liabilities." The two methods should produce identical results.

RETAINED EARNINGS

This amount represents money the company has saved—money that could have been paid out to its owners as dividends, but instead was kept in the business. That means the money is available for future expenses or emergencies. Retained earnings are listed on the company's balance sheet as one of the entries for shareholders' equity. If a company files a form 1120 or form 1120S for its tax return (meaning it files as a corporation), you also find entries for retained earnings on "Schedule L—Balance Sheets per Books."

EBIT

This stands for "Earnings Before Interest and Taxes." This number is important because it tells you how profitable a company is based just on their operations. Sometimes an otherwise profitable company loses money (or appears to lose money) after you deduct items like taxes and interest expenses. EBIT will appear on a company's income statement and might be called "operating income," "operating earnings," or maybe "operating profit." Please note that in order to calculate the Altman's Z-Score, you need to look up a company's EBIT, not their "EBITDA." EBITDA stands for "Earnings Before Interest, Taxes, Depreciation, and Amortization." In other words, EBITDA is EBIT plus depreciation expenses plus amortization expenses. The two are similar numbers, but would only be identical if a company had no depreciation or amortization. When calculating a Z-Score, make sure you use EBIT and not EBITDA.

To calculate Altman's Z, you'll need to do some basic arithmetic. The actual calculation steps are shown below.

MANUAL CALCULATION OF ALTMAN'S Z-SCORE

To determine a Z-Score for a company without using the computer, you'll need to run the following calculations (check the company's cash flow statement and balance sheet as noted above for the appropriate entries):

Step 1: Subtract current liabilities from current assets. The result is referred to as the company's "Working Capital." Hopefully, it will be a positive number but isn't always.

Step 2: Divide the company's working capital by the total assets. Call the final answer "A."

Step 3: Divide the company's retained earnings by the total assets. Call the final answer "B."

Step 4: Divide the company's EBIT by the total assets. Call the final answer "C."

Step 5: Divide the company's market capitalization by the total liabilities. If you are running the calculations for a privately-held company, use the stockholders' or shareholders' equity amount instead of market capitalization. Call the result "D."

Step 6: Divide the company's sales by its total assets. Call the result "E."

Step 7: Determine what category best describes the company: publicly-traded manufacturer, privately-held manufacturer, or non-manufacturer (either public or private).

For publicly-traded manufacturers

Step 8: Multiply each of the results you got above by the following factors and add the results together: $(1.2 \times A) + (1.4 \times B) + (3.3 \times C) + (0.6 \times D) + (0.999 \times E)$. A healthy publicly-traded manufacturer should have a result greater than 2.99. If the company's result is between 1.8 and 2.99, the company's future is unclear. If a company's Z-Score is less than 1.8, there is a high likelihood of bankruptcy within two years; companies that manage to survive without declaring bankruptcy are still likely to have a tough economic time.

For privately-held manufacturers

Step 8: Multiply each of the results you got above by the following factors and add the results together: $(0.717 \times A) + (0.847 \times B) + (3.107 \times C) + (0.420 \times D) + (0.998 \times E)$. A healthy privately-traded manufacturer should have a result greater than 2.9. If the company's result is between 1.23 and 2.9, the company's future is unclear. If a company's Z-Score is less than 1.23, there is a high likelihood of bankruptcy within two years or, at the very least, a significant challenge to the company's survival.

For nonmanufacturers (including retailers and service providers)

Step 8: Multiply each of the results you got above by the following factors and add the results together: $(6.56 \times A) + (3.26 \times B) + (6.72 \times C) + (1.05 \times D)$. Note that for service businesses, the company's sales are not included in the Z-Score calculation. A healthy nonmanufacturing company should have a result greater than 2.6; results between 1.1 and 2.6 are considered indeterminate. If a company's Z-Score is less than 1.1, there is a high likelihood of bankruptcy within two years.

For all companies

Step 9: If you have access to financial data from previous years, run the calculations based on the company's last three to five years. Is there a trend? Has the company's performance been steadily improving or declining? Has their Z-Score suddenly dropped in the last year? Any aberration or deviation from the trend may indicate other, less obvious changes have also occurred.

Step 10: If possible, compare the company's results with the Altman's Z-Scores of other companies in the same industry. If the company's score is 2.0, but all its major competitors have Z-Scores of 4.0 or 5.0, then your subject may be facing tough economic times. However, if all the company's major competitors have scores ranging from 1.9 to 2.3, then your subject company may be able to hang on with the rest of the industry.

AUTOMATED CALCULATION OF ALTMAN'S Z-SCORES

While you can run the calculations on a case-by-case basis, it's much easier to create a workbook in your spreadsheet program (like Excel or Quattro Pro). Follow these steps to create an Altman's Z workbook.

Step 1: Create a new workbook with three worksheets. Rename Sheet 1 as "Public Manufacturer;" Sheet 2 should be renamed "Private Manufacturer;" Sheet 3 should be renamed "Nonmanufacturer." To rename a sheet, simply double click on the sheet name and type a new name.

Step 2: On the Public Manufacturer Sheet, type the following in the designated cells:

Table 15.1   Sample Excel Spreadsheet for Altman's Z-Scores

	A	B	C
1	Working Capital		
2	Retained Earnings		
3	EBIT		
4	Market Capitalization		
5	Sales		
6	Total Assests		
7	Total Liabilities		
8			
9	Altman's Z-Score		
10			
11		Bankruptcy unlikely	3.0 and above
12		Grey area	1.81–2.99
13		Bankruptcy likely (1–2 years)	1.80 and below

Step 3: In cell B9, type the following formula exactly as written: =SUM(((B1/B6)*1.2)+((B2/B6)*1.4)+((B3/B6)*3.3)+((B4/B7)*0.6)+((B5/B6)*0.999))

Step 4: Copy the table (including the formula in cell B9) and paste it on the Private Manufacturer Sheet.

Step 5: Delete the contents of cell B9 and type in the following replacement formula exactly as written: =SUM(((B1/B6)*0.717)+((B2/B6)*0.847)+((B3/B6)*3.107)+((B4/B7)*0.42)+((B5/B6)*0.998))

Step 6: Making sure you are on the Private Manufacturer Sheet, delete the contents of cell C11 and replace them with "2.91 and above."

Step 7: Delete the contents of cell C12 and replace them with "1.23-2.90."

Step 8: Delete the contents of cell C13 and replace them with "1.22 and below."

Step 9: Copy the table and paste it on the Nonmanufacturer Sheet.

Step 10: Making sure you are in the Nonmanufacturer Sheet, delete row 5 (you can right click on the number 5 and select "Delete").

Step 11: In the new cell B8 (formerly cell B9, adjacent to "Altman's Z-Score" cell), type the following formula exactly as written: =SUM(((B1/B5)*6.56)+((B2/B5)*3.26)+((B3/B5)*6.72)+((B4/B6)*1.05))

Step 12: Delete the contents of cell C10 and replace them with "2.61 and above."

Step 13: Delete the contents of cell C11 and replace them with "1.11-2.6"

Step 14: Delete the contents of cell C12 and replace them with "1.10 and below."

Step 15: Save the document as a boilerplate.

To use the boilerplate, all you need to do is open the document as a copy, select the correct sheet that corresponds to the business, and type in the appropriate dollar amounts in cells B1 through B7 (or B1 through B6 for Nonmanufacturers). You may want to save a copy of the calculations in the appropriate investigation folder.

Altman's Z is not infallible, but it can help you boil down a large amount of financial information into a single, easily understood number. This number can help you decide if further investigation is warranted or whether a company's claims of financial hardship are truthful. If a subject company is trying to hide assets in order to avoid paying a fine or judgment, they may still have a high Altman's Z-Score, indicating the company may not be as destitute as claimed.

Looking at Z-Scores over time can also be enlightening. If a company's Z-Score is steadily increasing or steadily decreasing over the last five years that gives you a good indication about how the company is doing overall. However, if you see a sudden drop or spike in the company's Z-Score, that could be an indication that something else is going on. This is especially true for privately-held companies where the owner has the ability to take cash out of the business or otherwise manipulate the numbers used to calculate the score.

Vertical and Horizontal Analyses

Using vertical or horizontal analysis methods can also give you some insight into how a company operates on a day-to-day basis. Like using financial ratios, these analysis methods are most helpful to a financial investigation when you look at them over time. Dramatic changes from year to year may be indications that something else is going on.

VERTICAL ANALYSIS

Vertical analysis is a way of looking at how a company's assets and liabilities are distributed. You will need access to the firm's balance sheet to perform this analysis, but it is a quick and easy method. For each type of asset (cash and cash equivalents, inventory, and property) and each type of liability (accounts payable, notes payable, deferred expenses, and mortgages), divide the amount by the total assets or total liabilities. This tells you what percentage that particular line item represents. An easy way to remember this is to think about a column of numbers adding up to 100 percent. That's what happens in a vertical analysis—the different percentages add together to total 100 percent.

For purposes of a financial investigation, it is probably most helpful to look at these amounts over time. For example, if a subject company has tied up 40–60 percent of its total assets in inventory every year for the last five years, but that total suddenly drops to five percent during the last year, it's a safe bet something else is going on. Even if that reason turns out to be unrelated to your investigation, you should still figure out the cause for the change. It is entirely possible you will be asked by your boss or another decision maker to explain the change.

HORIZONTAL ANALYSIS

Instead of looking at the proportion of each category of assets and liabilities, a horizontal analysis looks at change within a category over a given timeframe. Calling it a "horizontal analysis" makes it sound more impressive than it really is. If your subject says their company's sales fell 36 percent last quarter that is a horizontal analysis.

When conducting a financial investigation by looking at financial ratios, Altman's Z-Scores, or distribution of assets and liabilities, you are most often going to look at the numbers using horizontal analyses. Tracking data from quarter to quarter or year to year is using a horizontal approach. You don't necessarily need to explain your analysis using a term like horizontal analysis, but you should be aware that is the type of analysis you are conducting—just in case anyone (like opposing counsel) asks you if you have done so.

Presenting the Numbers

Finally, a word of caution. Before including financial ratios and Altman's Z-Scores into your investigation report, think about your audience. If you've done the calculations, you know they're straightforward and relatively easy. Unfortunately, the decision makers reading your report may be phobic of math as well. It's entirely possible they will see your discussion of financial ratios and simply skip right over it.

To avoid this, you need to focus any discussion about financial analysis on the significance of your findings. You can't count on a decision maker understanding why a current ratio of 0.25 is cause for concern or why an Altman's Z-Score of 5.0 is reassuring. Even if your supervisor is an investigator or accountant, other decision makers without a financial background may ultimately be involved. You would not want to write a statement in your investigation report that merely said, "The subject company has a current ratio of 0.25." A sentence like this does not provide any context for your audience. Instead, try a sentence like, "The subject company's current ratio is a very low 0.25. This means they only have $1 of current assets for every $4 of current liabilities. Normally, a healthy company's current ratio should be at least 2.0." Providing this additional information puts the ratio in perspective and helps a nonfinancial decision maker understand why the information is important.

Sometimes financial ratios and analysis can help you explain why something seems amiss. Sometimes financial ratios and analysis merely help you understand that a subject company needs additional investigation. And sometimes financial ratios and analysis don't help you at all. Don't feel like to *have* to use these analysis tools, but don't be afraid to use them when they can add value to your investigation.

Case in Point

Sometimes a quick review of the numbers can help you detect that something else is going on. However, it's important to remember that a change in and of itself is not proof something illegal is occurring. In fact, a significant but negative change can actually reflect a company is doing well.

During a review of the financial statements for a company that is a subsidiary of a privately-held international company, I noticed the company's working capital dropped significantly in one short year. Instead of having a current ratio of more than 2.0, it suddenly dropped to far less than 1.0 and suddenly had negative working capital. However, all the company's other financial information (including their Altman's Z-Score) still seemed to indicate the company was healthy. What could account for this significant and sudden change?

The answer turned out to be very simple. The company had used their cash reserves to pay off a loan from the parent company early. Had the company continued to make regular payments on the loan, it would not have affected the financial ratios and I never would have noticed it. But because they decided to use their cash to eliminate a debt, it was a glaring change. The fact the company felt comfortable enough to use the cash it had on hand to retire this debt was a testament to how strongly the company believed it its future growth.

16 *Dealing with People Problems*

During the course of your investigation, you may encounter personality clashes and other barriers to your work. All financial investigations (even those conducted primarily via the Internet) may force you to deal with individuals who see the world in a very different way than you do. In fact, my experience is that I have encountered significantly more so-called "people" problems when conducting financial investigations than in my normal life. Financial investigations by their very nature address sensitive topics. When you start delving into intensely personal issues such as salaries and personal priorities, you may inadvertently bring out the worst in your subject.

I tend to group these "people" problems into three categories: cultural, psychological, and management issues. While no two investigations are the same, I have found there are some coping techniques that seem to be effective for each type of problem. Don't assume the following are rules written in stone—they aren't. They are simply some guidelines that have proven useful to me in my work.

Cultural Issues

Cultural, political, and socioeconomic differences can play a role in how a subject reacts to your work and should be mentioned in your investigation plan if they are relevant. This will allow you to think about these factors and plan for contingencies that may arise. It's not a matter of being politically correct, but of being polite. Being respectful of your subject, both as an individual and as a member of a culture can go a long way to helping you collect the information you need to make a proper determination or recommendation.

Cultural factors can also play a role in how your subject handles their finances. In many cultures, the group is considered to be more valuable than the individual. In those cases, it might be very logical to place assets in the name of numerous individuals instead of just the primary owner. Other cultures place bigger emphasis on the male providing for and leading his family. In those cases, you would likely expect to see ownership and business documents in the name of a husband and wife (or perhaps only the husband) even if the business or asset actually belongs to wife.

In some cases, cultural factors will motivate someone to try to hide assets. If a business owner employs numerous family members (or even nonrelatives whom they view as "family"), they may attempt to hide assets away in order to continue to support the family. Other times, subjects come from cultures where banks are unreliable and government agencies are not trustworthy. As a result, they may continue financial practices designed to protect what the subject has worked so hard to accumulate. Remember that not everyone comes from a place where you can trust the police—that mindset can be very difficult to overcome.

There are many examples of how you can keep cultural issues in mind when conducting an investigation. Personally, as a female I am especially cognizant of subjects who come from cultures where men and women don't touch. If I am interviewing a male subject from one of these cultures, I wait for him to offer to shake hands. If he extends his hand, I shake it; if he doesn't, I simply offer my business card instead. Other examples might be addressing a subject by their title until you are directed otherwise, irrespective of the subject's age. This can be an effective way to get cooperation from a potentially hostile subject (especially when they are younger than you are) because it demonstrates respect. In my experience, subjects who feel respected are more cooperative and less combatant than those who feel they are on the defensive. While you can't plan for every contingency ahead of time, preparing as much as possible can help minimize conflict in sensitive situations.

Psychological Issues

Throughout my career, I've had the opportunity to deal with a large variety of people. I've investigated subjects from all walks of life, from the rich and famous to impoverished refugees. During that time, I've had the good fortune to meet many interesting people. I've also dealt with a few individuals who had significant mental health issues. Whether you're dealing with subjects, witnesses, co-workers, supervisors, or just a member of the public, you may also encounter people who have mental health issues.

Hindsight can be a wonderful gift. I know now that I should have taken Psych 101 and Abnormal Psychology when I was in school. These classes would have helped my investigation skills tremendously. Since I did not take either of these courses, I have had to teach myself techniques for recognizing and dealing with mental health issues. The following is a brief explanation of some of the more challenging mental illnesses I have come across when conducting investigations and the techniques I developed for working with the individuals with those conditions. These techniques may or may not be the most effective or even recommended by experts. They are simply suggestions based on my own personal experience.

THE NARCISSIST

Everyone has some narcissistic tendencies—they're the basis for a healthy self-esteem. Unfortunately, those same tendencies can also make someone very difficult to work with. My personal experience of dealing with this type of person was extremely grueling. Some days I didn't even want to go to work because I was just fed up with the situation. I found the narcissist I had to deal with to be manipulative, vulgar, and all together unpleasant. This person was abusive, refused to take personal responsibility for their actions, and failed to meet even the most simple of obligations. Many of their reactions remind me of an abusive spouse: they believe everything is always someone else's fault, they are charming to strangers and decision makers but rude to those they perceive are below them, and they are incapable of empathy towards others.

My initial approach in dealing with this person seemed logical: I tried to do my job to my utmost ability. That was my first mistake. Then I made mistake number two: I (unknowingly) pointed out a change the narcissist had overlooked. It was all downhill from there. I was publicly yelled at, accused of lying, and even accused of sabotage. That led to mistake number three: I defended myself. Producing the documents to demonstrate I was being truthful just seemed to make the situation worse. At that point, I asked for the matter to be assigned to someone else. Unfortunately my supervisor was unable to find someone else to take my place, so I began to research techniques on how to handle the situation. If you are dealing with a true narcissist (not just someone who is arrogant or inconsiderate), you can try some of the following techniques for managing the situation—I found each of these helpful in dealing with my narcissist.

Compliment them

Appealing to a narcissist's vanity makes them feel important and makes them think you are jealous of them. They like that feeling and it reaffirms their pre-existing belief that you want to be just like them. This may especially be true for public sector employees investigating private sector companies. Your subject may view you as nothing more than a lowly civil servant who aspires to be rich and famous, just like them.

Don't express your feelings to them

Hearing "I feel …" or "I think …" irritates a narcissist. Your feelings aren't important to them. They will use those feelings against you if given the opportunity. Only use those phrases if the narcissist specifically requests that you address your feelings, but don't expect them to actually listen and don't go into detail. They're only asking for show. When dealing with a narcissistic subject, these phrases can have added significance. Using words like "feel" and "think" reaffirms the narcissist's belief that you don't really know what you're doing and that you aren't as smart as they are.

Don't correct them

A narcissist is always right. Expressions to the contrary are a personal challenge and a direct insult. If it is a vitally important issue and an error must be corrected, take the blame yourself. Give the narcissist the opportunity to instruct you about the correct answer, that way they can demonstrate their superior knowledge. The most direct I would ever be is something along the lines of, "I'm sorry—I'm just not getting it. I thought you sold that parcel of property to Mr. Smith back in 2006. What am I missing?" This technique allows the narcissist to find the mistake on their own and be the one that corrects it, thus re-asserting their belief they are smarter than the rest of us.

Let them take the credit

It is vitally important that a narcissist receive public recognition and accolades, even if they didn't contribute anything to a project's success. They must be the boss and the problem solver. No one else is capable of coming up with good ideas and achieving success because this disrupts the narcissist's position in the hierarchy. When your subject is the narcissist this can be a significant challenge because the only credit to be achieved is dependent on the outcome of your investigation.

Don't make suggestions unless "inspired" by them

Don't say, "There's something I'd like to try." Instead, try something like, "You know, something you said got me thinking ..." or "You gave me a great idea ..." Your great idea needs to start with or originate with the narcissist so they can claim credit for it. When dealing with a narcissistic subject, this will most often come into play during telephone conversations or face-to-face meetings. This can be a powerful tool if you are looking for a way to negotiate or mediate with your subject.

Remember they have a distorted sense of time

For the narcissist, time spent at work or in meetings isn't about how much you accomplish but instead is about how much attention and recognition you get for working. Missing deadlines not only gets the narcissist more attention, it puts them in a position of power— you can't finish your work or investigation until they give you the missing information. That's power. The narcissist may also send emails and voice mail messages at all hours of the night. They don't see this as evidence of poor time management, they think it makes them seem like they're working very hard. If you give a narcissistic subject a deadline, you need something to back it up. There must be a penalty for failing to cooperate, such as dismissal of their application, loss of a contracting opportunity, or imposition of a fine or other sanction. Also, don't be surprised if you receive the requested information shortly after any deadline you establish; this makes it harder for you to take punitive action against the subject. After all, they did comply with your request—so what if it's a couple of days late?

Don't expect them to show much initiative

At their core, the narcissist is lazy and doesn't particularly want to work. They want peons to do the work for them. Their job is to take the public praise and attention, not to get their hands dirty. If you have requested additional information from a narcissistic subject, don't expect them personally to gather the information for you. More than likely, they will either ask someone else (who may not have the necessary information to complete the request) to do it on their behalf, or they may simply ignore the request.

Mirror their behavior and tone

Mimicking or mirroring the narcissist's gestures, body language, and tone of voice can help break down barriers to communication. The narcissist believes everyone else is jealous of them and wants to be just like them. When you copy their behavior, you confirm what they already know is true. While this technique seems to work well in person, I have not personally noticed a difference during telephone conversations. I have also not found mimicking a narcissist's writing style to be effective, but I am not able to determine whether the technique is ineffective or whether I simply don't utilize the technique sufficiently.

Ignore their inappropriate comments

The narcissist desperately wants attention and won't hesitate to say some pretty inappropriate comments in order to get that attention. Ethnic jokes, sexual innuendo, and other indiscreet statements are probably nothing more than attempts to get attention and reaffirm their wit, sex appeal, and overall attractiveness. If the narcissistic subject perceives you as a threat, they may insult or even threaten you in order to get attention; to a narcissist, even negative attention is better than no attention at all. A narcissist also believes that insulting and threatening you in front of managers or other decision makers minimizes your importance and demonstrates how powerful the narcissist is. They have no fear of being perceived as a bully. To the contrary, in their eyes being a bully can be a good thing because bullies are powerful and get what they want—everyone wants to be like the bully. Those are good reasons for not only limiting contact with your subject but also making sure you never meet with or talk with them unless another person is present.

Remember they will be a sycophant

The narcissist will frequently attempt to mimic and flatter those in power because they think that's how you get ahead. They can be very convincing and seem very sincere, especially at the beginning. But their wanting to improve and learn is little more than a pretense. Eventually, even decision makers see through the narcissist's act. If a narcissistic subject suddenly stops fawning over your every word, they've likely decided you can't give them what they want. This change in behavior may signal other changes to look for in your investigation.

Remember they are manipulative

Even though they may actually have very low self-esteem, the narcissist thinks they're much smarter than everyone else. In their mind, that means they can manipulate all of us and we're too stupid to realize it. They also believe they're far too smart for anyone else to manipulate. That means if you suspect the subject is hiding assets, you may very well be on the right track. The narcissistic subject may feel entitled to keep their assets irrespective of the law and will be willing to take whatever steps they deem necessary to preserve those assets. If there is a privilege associated with not having an asset (e.g., a job that would be unavailable due to a conflict of interest or benefits only available to low-income residents), the Narcissist may feel entitled to both the asset and the privilege.

Narcissists and Internet investigations

If your subject is a true narcissist, an Internet-based investigation may be the most productive method available. Obtaining evidence directly from websites prevents the subject from altering or falsifying documents. Investigating on the Internet also minimizes your direct contact with the subject, thus reducing the possibility of a confrontation. On the other hand, the lack of direct communication that is inherent to an Internet-based investigation has a drawback: you have less opportunity to observe the subject and less possibility of detecting their narcissism.

If you suspect that your subject is a narcissist, talk with your supervisor as soon as possible. Out of all the personality types you may encounter, a narcissist is the most likely to object to being investigated and to complain about you and your work. There mere fact that you do not accept the subject's statements at face value may be offensive to them. A narcissistic subject may conclude the quickest and easiest way to get what they want is to complain to someone they feel can force you to capitulate. That may be your direct supervisor, the head of your agency organization, the Mayor, the Governor, or other elected official. I have noticed that some people who file these types of complaints go to the highest level they can think of even if that has nothing to do with your investigation or jurisdiction. Don't be surprised if a narcissist writes a letter of complaint to the Governor (even though you are a federal employee) or their US Representative or Senator (even though you are a state or local employee).

ATTENTION-DEFICIT HYPERACTIVITY DISORDER (ADHD)

One recent study found that 4.1 percent of the population suffered diagnosable ADHD during the 12-month period of the study (Kessler et al. 2005). While you may personally agree with the school of belief that ADHD is not a real disease (Jadad et al. 1999), I recommend treating it as a real medical condition during the course of your investigation if for no other reason than the heartache you will save yourself (remember that the American Psychiatric Association recognizes the condition). When dealing with a subject who has ADHD, your investigation can become extremely frustrating: applications are incomplete, details are missing, obviously incorrect information is submitted, and instructions are ignored. Depending on the nature of your investigation, you could find similar problems throughout numerous documents related to the subject, such as missing information on deeds, misspelled names, or documents that should exist but don't. You may also find that someone with ADHD can be a bit of a nuisance—frequently calling or emailing to find out the status of their case or complaint.

ADHD or just laziness?

One of the main problems in recognizing ADHD is the fact that it can manifest itself in apparent laziness. Did your subject quickly complete the paperwork and simply not read the instructions? Or did they work on it for an extended time and try to complete it, only to fail miserably? When conducting a financial investigation, the two situations are virtually indistinguishable. There is no reliable way to tell whether the documents you are looking at came from someone who has ADHD versus someone who was just inattentive or rushed. Likewise, there is no reliable way to determine whether your request for additional information was ignored because the subject doesn't care or because they simply found themselves overwhelmed.

ADHD and Internet investigations

If your subject does have ADHD, the Internet may be an efficient way to conduct your investigation. If you obtain documents directly from web sites or other third-party sources, you don't need to wait for the subject to stop procrastinating. You also minimize how much time and exasperation you spend assisting employees or family members who are trying to help your ADHD subject. Depending on the nature of your investigation, obtaining those documents in a timely manner may be extremely important. Even in cases where your agency or the public may not be harmed by an incomplete investigation (like an application you can simply deny for being incomplete), the subject may be harmed by an unfinished investigation. In a worst-case scenario, failing to go the extra mile with an ADHD subject could mean you are held responsible for failing to accommodate a subject's disability.

As noted above, investigating on the Internet minimizes your contact with the subject and thereby reduces reducing the possibility of a confrontation. In the case of ADHD subjects, this can be more helpful for the subject than for the investigator. Some ADHD sufferers hate confrontation; one of the reasons they procrastinate is that they simply don't want to deal with the unpleasantness. If you do have direct contact with an ADHD subject, it may be helpful if you adopt a non-confrontational attitude. While you may not get the results you would like, you also avoid setting up a future situation where the subject simply refuses to participate in your investigation.

PARANOID CHARACTERISTICS

Another potentially troublesome mental health issue is paranoid beliefs and behaviors. It should not surprise you if the subject of your investigation regards your work with suspicion—that can be a reasonable and healthy response to finding out someone is prying into your personal life and financial dealings. Suspicion alone, especially under these circumstances, does not make someone paranoid. The unfortunate combination of an investigation and a paranoid subject can make your work even more difficult. Some of the key characteristics I have observed in paranoid subjects (including those that seem to have one of the diagnosable conditions mentioned previously) include:

A tendency to hold grudges

We all make mistakes, even investigators. When we do, it's important that we acknowledge and apologize for those mistakes. Unfortunately, some subjects refuse to accept or believe an apology, even if it is heartfelt and sincere. More noticeable may be the tendency to hold grudges for the smallest of transgressions, such as forgetting to cc someone on an email or neglecting to save them a seat at a meeting. Subjects suffering from paranoia see meaning and purpose in the most insignificant behaviors.

Misconstruing events

Even more problematic is when a paranoid subject reverses or distorts the meaning of your actions. You may think you're doing good work by providing a subject with the opportunity to explain their actions before you make a decision. A paranoid subject can misunderstand that opportunity as a trap. Instead of viewing your actions as helpful, they see them as a threat. As a result, they may file complaints with your supervisor, the director of your agency, their local legislator, their Congressmen, the Mayor, the Governor, or even the media.

Overestimating their own importance

My limited experience with paranoid subjects has revealed one trend to me: those suffering from paranoia don't usually limit themselves to a single "offender." A paranoid subject may initially greet your presence or involvement in their case with overwhelming gratitude. They may initially see you as the solution to the unfair treatment they previously received. They may regale you with extensive stories about how your predecessors or other government agents were incompetent and simply refused to understand the law. Those government employees were undoubtedly dishonest and probably "on the take," too. Frequently, the paranoid subject attributes these bad behaviors to their own importance (as in, "the government wants to shut me up"). While it is possible the stories are accurate, find out more before you believe them. These types of tales are a big red flag that should alert you to the possibility your subject has paranoia issues.

Paranoia and Internet investigations

If your subject is suffering from paranoid beliefs, using the Internet to conduct your investigation has both positive and negative attributes. Researching and obtaining documents from third-party sources can be done covertly, thus minimizing the subject's exposure to your activities. That's both a good thing and a bad thing: good in that it doesn't feed the subject's mistaken beliefs, but bad in that if your investigation is ever discovered, your actions will merely reinforce the subject's paranoia.

Both your agency and your reputation can be significantly harmed by a paranoid subject. Even unfounded accusations of wrong-doing require checking. Public officials cannot simply ignore a citizen's complaint even if it is nothing more than a paranoid and delusional rant. That means you are going to have to take time out of your day to answer any accusations that may be made against you and to explain why your actions were fair and proper. When dealing with a paranoid subject, keeping proper investigation records is crucial because even more than your case is at stake: in extreme cases, your records may be required to defend your livelihood.

As previously explained, investigating on the Internet minimizes your contact with the subject, thereby reduces reducing the possibility of a confrontation. In the case of paranoid subjects, this can be more helpful for you as the investigator than it is for the subject. Whether you are talking face-to-face, speaking on the telephone, corresponding via email, or writing formal letters, each contact with a paranoid subject is a potential minefield. When dealing with a potentially paranoid individual, I usually try to conduct most communication in writing (either by letter or by email). Regardless of what form of communication you choose, if possible try to interpret your statements from the subject's perspective. Assume you are the subject and that the investigator has an ulterior motive— what does their request for additional information *really* mean? Engaging in this process before making a statement can help minimize potential misunderstandings between investigator and subject.

CONSIDERING MENTAL HEALTH ISSUES DURING FINANCIAL INVESTIGATIONS

Mental health issues can be particularly challenging because they do not manifest the same way that a physical health issue might. Instead, psychological problems manifest themselves through behavior. That can challenge our notions of ability and free will. We may want to tell someone with ADHD to stop procrastinating or the narcissist to accept responsibility when they've done something wrong. The challenge is to remember that people with these disorders cannot change their behavior any more than someone with Schizophrenia can simply stop hearing voices. Another way to think about it is to compare a mental health disability to a physical disability. Would you demand that someone in a wheelchair get up and walk? Of course not. As difficult as it may be, the same logic applies to mental health issues: you can't expect those affected to simply change their behavior any more than you can expect a paraplegic to go for a jog.

Using the disorder-specific techniques noted above can be one way to deal with these difficult situations. Working with someone who has mental health challenges is a bit like dealing with someone who has physical limitations and challenges: they may not be able to eliminate their limits but they can work around them. As an investigator, the burden falls mainly to you to figure out those work-arounds. You are the one in a position of power, so it is your responsibility to protect the vulnerable from that power. On a more practical note, your failure to accommodate any mental health issues affecting your subject may be the basis for overturning any determination you make and could also result in your agency being sued for failing to accommodate the subject's disability.

Management Issues

Having a great boss is a luxury, whether you work in the private or the public sector. A supervisor who believes their job is to run interference for you and keep unnecessary drama away can be your most important asset. We've all had to deal with bosses who didn't do that. Unfortunately, when conducting financial investigations—especially on the Internet—an unhelpful manager can be a huge barrier to success. Learning some techniques for coping with these situations can be one way to minimize their negative effects.

THE MICROMANAGER

Depending on your personality, having a micromanager as a boss can either be helpful or it can be an endlessly frustrating experience. If you are someone who knows they need help staying on task and avoiding distractions, working for a micromanager can be constructive. If you aren't good at holding yourself accountable, it can be liberating to turn that responsibility over to someone who excels at it. For most investigators I've met, working for a micromanager is nothing but frustrating. People who are attracted to this type of work tend to be independent, creative thinkers who are focused on results instead of busy-work.

My experience working for a micromanager gave me insight about both my boss and myself. After a long working relationship, I learned that micromanagers tend to be less trusting than managers who adopt other styles. They may be very trustworthy individuals who have a hard time trusting others. They may also be individuals who are more focused on data and facts. To them, the way to manage is to do "manager" type things: note when employees are late, make sure they follow proper procedures, and keep appropriate records of all management activities. To an employee, this can seem like the manager dislikes or disbelieves them; to the micromanager, it's not personal—that's just the way things are done.

If you feel constrained by the actions of a micromanager, you can try taking a proactive approach. When conducting an investigation, especially an Internet-based investigation, there are many opportunities to accommodate a micromanager. Try meeting with your supervisor and asking which activities they would like you to report about on a regular basis. If you can find out what is really important to them, you can focus your attention on those matters and let other, less important issues fall to the back burner. Is your supervisor most concerned about you being punctual? Suggest a magnetic or dry erase "In/Out" board with a space to write where you are when you are out of the office. Perhaps your supervisor is more concerned that you not waste time surfing the net when you should be working. You could offer to give a weekly summary report of how many websites you visited for each investigation. If the micromanager is most concerned with each complaint or investigation being resolved within a specified time, consider offering to create a spreadsheet file showing each assigned case, the date it was assigned, the date it must be complete, and its current status. You could email a copy of this spreadsheet to your manager each week or simply save it on a network drive that your manager can access whenever the mood strikes them.

For many micromanagers, a regular update meeting can be comforting. Regular staff meetings have their place, but a short one-on-one meeting can be much more productive. Try scheduling a standing meeting once per week or once every other week for 15 minutes or half an hour. Plan to give your supervisor a brief summary of your work since the last meeting, focusing on whatever aspects are most important to them. If they are most concerned about individual cases, give them a brief status update for each major case you are currently working on. If they are more concerned about day-to-day activities, try talking about numbers: "I processed 18 applications this week" or "I visited 72 websites while conducting the Smith investigation, and found three parcels of real estate they failed to disclose." From there you can address any questions your manager may have about specific cases or accomplishments.

One final technique for dealing with a micromanager is to help your supervisor see that you have excellent attention to detail and that your investigation is extremely organized. Appendix A has some suggestions about how to organize an investigation file. Follow that advice as closely as possible and try going the extra step: type the file folder labels, keep all the Post-its the same color and line them up perfectly, and transcribe your notes from telephone conversations instead of just writing them out by hand. You're probably already a detail-oriented person, so demonstrate it. Typewritten labels and notes are not inherently better than handwritten ones (especially if your penmanship is nice), but may psychologically seem better. Your micromanager may take comfort in the fact that you pay as much attention to the details as they do, which can help them feel more at ease.

Having a micromanager can also be a blessing, even if you don't need the added accountability. Micromanagers frequently focus on the same issues that an outsider looks at. If the Inspector General or State Auditor or some other accrediting entity came into your office tomorrow and asked you to prove your value to the taxpayers, what would they look at? Odds are they would look at the same types of issues that your micromanager focuses on: do you complete your work on time, is it thorough, do you goof off when you should be working, are you spending public resources responsibly, and are you giving the citizens of your jurisdiction a good value for their money? Having a micromanager keep an eye on these issues is good for both your agency and the folks paying the bill.

The trick to coping with a micromanager is to not take it personally (unless you're slacking on the job, in which case you *should* take it personally). The micromanager has different priorities than you have. They aren't better or worse priorities, they're simply different. Figuring out a way to respect and comply with those priorities while still meeting your own can be a significant challenge, but is entirely possible to do. If you are not naturally someone who works well with a micromanager, look for ways to embrace the challenge and find advantages from this different management style.

THE JARGON-SPEWING KNOW-NOTHING

Cartoonist Scott Adams built the Dilbert Empire in large part based on the ineptitude of Pointy-Haired Boss, the quintessential Jargon-Spewing Know-Nothing. He'll be happy to give you explicit instructions about highly technical matters, even though those instructions make absolutely no sense and have nothing to do with the assigned work. Unfortunately, some of us have the misfortune of dealing with the real world version of this type of boss. When conducting an Internet-based investigation, this type of supervisor can be an even bigger challenge than finding hidden assets. The first step in mitigating this challenge is to identify the real purpose to their involvement in your investigation: are they trying to build themselves up, or are they really trying to help? Those two situations are very different and call for different responses on your part.

The know-nothing boss who is inserting themselves into your investigation in order to make themselves feel more important may simply feel threatened by your specialized knowledge. Being an investigator takes extensive skill and expertise; your manager may not have the background necessary to perform the work you do on a daily basis. That can make your supervisor's job extremely difficult: just how do you supervise an employee when you don't really know what they do? If you are faced with this situation, you have some options. First, it may be helpful to help your manager begin to get an idea about what you do and how you do it. Give them a blank Investigation Plan, any checklists your agency has developed, and ask them to perform an investigation (a subject or company that has was previously involved in a complex investigation is a good choice). Show them the normal websites you would use, point out any red flags in the subject's documentation, and turn them loose. When they are finished, you can spend some time going over their results and helping them understand what they found and what it means. Unfortunately, there is a downside to this approach: a little knowledge can be a dangerous thing. If the manager is given a sample investigation that is too easy, they may underestimate the difficulty of what you do. The purpose of this activity is not to humiliate your boss but to inform and educate by giving them an accurate understanding of how complex a financial investigation can be.

If your supervisor doesn't want to try this technique or says they don't have enough time, suggest giving them regular status reports regarding the highlights of your investigation. You can explain which websites were the most productive and what you discovered at each. The advantage of this approach is that you limit your reporting to just your successes—you aren't wasting your manager's time reporting on efforts that didn't pan out. You can then ask your manager for other suggestions based on your success thus far. This technique can help guide your supervisor to suggestions that may actually have some relevance to your work.

Sometimes the problem is that the manager is just trying to help. Their suggestions are well-intentioned but not relevant to your work. Perhaps they used to be an investigator, but their skills are woefully out of date. Or maybe they know they don't really understand what it is you do, but they want to help anyway. This type of situation may remind you of your child or spouse asking if they can help. A similar answer might work for your boss as well. If your manager simply wants to make a contribution, give them the opportunity to do so. Is there an aspect of your investigation you haven't had time to deal with yet? Maybe your supervisor can check it out. Are you sure you've found all the names of individuals and businesses connected to your investigation? Why not ask your manager spend some quality time on Google? If they find a new lead, great. If not, they've still managed to contribute to the effort and free up some of your time.

One other variation on the know-nothing is the boss who can't seem to answer a question. If you have a manager who has extensive knowledge in a specialized area (for example, maybe they are an attorney or an accountant), that manager can be a tremendous resource—but only if you can get them to actually assist you. It can be very frustrating to ask a specific legal or technical question and get a five minute response that doesn't actually answer the question. Remember that a manager who has extensive training in another field such as law or accounting or engineering left that field for a reason. While it is possible that they left their field of study for a higher salary, that is not as common as you might think. A working attorney, accountant, engineer, or other professional is likely to earn far more than a manager at a government agency. It is very possible that the manager left their original profession either because they weren't very good at it or because they disliked their work. Both those reasons can affect the quality of help you receive when you ask a question.

If you are faced with a situation where you need to get help from a supervisor who can't seem to answer a question, you can either accept that you're not going to get an answer or you can try to break your question down into smaller, easier questions. If you're asking merely out of curiosity and your question doesn't really affect the outcome of your investigation, it may be best simply to let the matter go. However, if your question is vital to your work, start by doing some preliminary research on your own. Wikipedia or Answers.com can be a great starting place. Teach yourself some of the basics, then break your question down into multiple parts, each phrased in a simple and straightforward manner.

Say you need to know whether your subject's income is community property or not. Simply asking an attorney manager might get you a circuitous and unhelpful response. Instead, teach yourself the basics of community property and look up the community property laws in the relevant jurisdiction. Once you have a basic understanding of how the property law works, think about your question in smaller pieces. Instead of asking the manager whether you're looking at community property, think about asking a series of questions. Is income a type of property? When does property become community property? Is property automatically community property once it is acquired? Does the subject need to take an action to turn separate property into community property? What is the difference between community property and joint property? Breaking your question down into smaller, more clear-cut questions can be helpful for a manager who feels uncomfortable answering your question but doesn't want to admit it. This technique can also allow you to answer your question without forcing the manager to address a case specific issue, another possible source of discomfort. In the end, you can use the information you obtain to piece together the answer you need.

THE GLUTTON

Greed and gluttony don't apply just to Wall Street and they don't apply just to personal fortune. Sometimes you are faced with a boss that is really only interested in what they can do for themselves, their family, and their friends. That might be money in their pocket, a government contract for their brother-in-law's company, or a permit (no questions asked) for their friend from church. When your investigation and their personal interests are in conflict, doing your job gets a whole lot harder. They can refuse to allow you to travel, refuse to allow you to spend money, or even refuse to allow you to spend the time necessary to conduct a thorough investigation. How are you supposed to do your job when your boss blocks your every path? Dealing with this type of supervisor is probably the most difficult of all the types listed here. If any boss is going to ask you to disregard your official responsibilities, ignore your fiduciary duty, or even violate the law—this is the one who will. They may even feel their request is both justified and legitimate.

If your supervisor asks you to disregard your duties, the first technique you can try is education. It is possible your boss doesn't understand why their request is inappropriate. If you were asked to "take it easy" on a particular applicant or investigation, try explaining to your manager that could be problematic for both your agency and the applicant. As a public-sector employee, you have to take steps to make sure that all applicants are treated fairly. If you treat one subject more favorably than another, your agency could receive significant bad publicity, and your manager could get into trouble for not properly supervising your investigation. It is probably not advisable to point out to your manager the fact they have made an inappropriate request because they could interpret that statement as a threat. Instead, simply point out the potential problems your agency would encounter if the disparate treatment were ever discovered and emphasize the likelihood that someone will find out, including the local investigative reporter ambushing them in the parking lot after work one night.

If education doesn't work, the next approach would be to explain why you cannot accommodate the manager's request. If the possibility of a news camera in their face and a reporter asking uncomfortable questions does not persuade them to withdraw their request, try to explain why you would not feel comfortable doing what you have been asked. Maintain a calm and matter-of-fact attitude; you're not trying to make your boss feel bad, you're trying to explain a problem. Explain what law, rule, regulation, or policy prevents you from accommodating the request and why. If there is no rule or regulation that explicitly prohibits what you've been asked to do, look for a rule or regulation that is more general in its application. Your state's Administrative Procedure Act, civil rights laws, or even the state Constitution may address a subject's right to be treated fairly.

If neither of these approaches works, you may need to elevate the issue along the appropriate chain of command. If your agency has a dispute resolution policy, follow it to the letter. If there is no clear policy or chain of command, you may need to consult someone else for advice. Try talking with a trusted co-worker or another manager to see what they recommend. Your human resources department may also be able to help by explaining the applicable policies and procedures or providing mediation services. If you work for a large government body and there is a separate office that handles personnel issues for multiple agencies or departments, contact their employee assistance group.

If you are a union member, your shop steward or other union representative may also be able to provide advice and assistance. However, remember that when the union steps into the situation, they are probably not going to have the same goal as you. Your union representative is there to protect you and your job—they are not there to protect the subject of your investigation. While those two goals may frequently coincide, do not assume that they always will.

Finally, contacting the applicable whistleblower program or Inspector General's office is an option you should consider only if no other method achieves an acceptable outcome. "Acceptable" outcome is not necessarily the outcome you want and is not necessarily the outcome you think is the best—it is an outcome you can live with. Sometimes, that may be as simple as transferring the investigation to a co-worker. If the action your supervisor asks you to take violates your conscience but not the law, stepping aside may be the simplest way to resolve the dispute. If you are involuntarily reassigned and you believe your agency's actions violate the law, talking with a representative from a whistleblower program may be the moral and ethical thing to do. If you determine you are faced with one of these unfortunate and uncommon situations, you may want to use your personal resources to research how to file a complaint. The office should have a web site to give you the necessary information and it may be worth spending some of your lunch hour to talk with someone from your cell phone.

Dealing with a power-hungry or greedy boss is in some ways very similar to investigating a subject: make sure you confirm your information before making accusations. Your investigation of a subject will eventually conclude, but you have to face your boss every day. Unless you're trying to get fired, unsupported accusations of your boss having a conflict of interest or attempting to achieve some personal gain are not appropriate. Investigating your boss (whether on your own time or work time) may be tempting but is likewise inappropriate. Any investigation you conduct taints your objectivity on the matter—now you have a personal stake in the outcome, just like your boss does. Leave the investigation to someone who is not a party to the dispute, such as a representative from your human resources department. This is one situation where discretion actually is the better part of valor.

REACHING YOUR BREAKING POINT

At some point, we all reach the end of our rope. Sometimes the end comes from one unavoidable conflict, and sometimes it comes from a series of small offenses. Whether you're simply burned out or whether you just can't face working with a particular individual anymore, eventually it may be time to move on. Remember that investigative skills are sought after by many organizations. Even if you have extensive knowledge of only a small area of the law, that knowledge may eventually be transferrable to another field of work. Burned out investigators tend to do poor investigations. If you find you've reached your breaking point, it may be time to leave. Until that happens, continue to perform professional work. As satisfying as it may feel, burning your bridges doesn't help your future career. In fact, your new investigative life and your old one may overlap in ways you cannot predict. Preserving your professional reputation and integrity are vital to getting a new and better job.

Coping With People Problems

No job is perfect, and no investigation is problem-free. The key to success is to identify which situations you can handle and which you can't. There are many different psychological conditions that could affect your subject and there are many different types of bad bosses. The ones mentioned above are just some of the most problematic. Dealing with people problems is no different from dealing with technical problems: if you're in over your head, get help from an expert. If you needed help understanding a company's tax returns, you'd consult someone who knows about accounting. If you needed help understanding what happened in a lawsuit, you'd consult an attorney. The same goes for interpersonal conflicts. If you need help dealing with an unstable subject or an uncooperative boss, consult with someone who has specialized skill and training in the subject.

Case in Point

Complaints to your boss, to elected officials, and to the media are embarrassing and time consuming, even when you've done nothing wrong. The worst case I encountered was not as an investigator, but as a member of a volunteer decision-making body. As a member of the Washington State Disciplinary Board, I was responsible for reviewing accusations made against attorneys. Sometimes those accusations were well-founded, sometimes not. Frequently, they were the ranting of an incarcerated individual with mental health issues and too much time on their hands.

Although the details were less than clear, one of these individuals took matters to the extreme. His original complaint to the Bar Association against his attorney had been dismissed because the attorney had done nothing wrong (other than being unable to prevent his client from being convicted in federal court). Instead of suing his attorney for malpractice, the incarcerated individual filed a federal lawsuit against the Bar Association and the members of the Disciplinary Board. His lawsuit included substantial allegations of theft: namely, that the Bar Association and Disciplinary Board had conspired to steal his personal property, $300,000 of jewels, and $6 billion (yes, "billion" with a "b") of bearer bonds. Fortunately, the Bar Association handled the necessary legal proceedings to get the case dismissed. Had this lawsuit been related to my employment instead of my volunteer work, I could have been forced to retain an attorney on my own to handle the matter.

More disturbingly, had the matter been made public it could have been extremely embarrassing and damaging to my career and credibility. Did the plaintiff really believe that he owned $300,000 of jewels and billions of dollars' worth of bearer bonds? Probably not, but no one else did either. Instead consider if the claim had not been so outlandish on its face. What if he had accused us of taking a bribe from his attorney to dismiss his complaint? That would have been a much more believable accusation, and if made public, would have followed each of us around for the rest of our professional lives.

17 *Telling the Story*

After you have finished collecting information and exhausting the leads you were able to generate, it's time to look at what you found and put it all together into a tidy little package. What story does this information tell you? What conclusions can you draw? Is the subject being completely honest and forthright? Did they just make a mistake? Or is something else going on?

Assembling information into a simple, straightforward story is very important to any investigation. Ultimately, it is the story you tell that will determine the resolution of your case. Managers, judges, juries, and other decision makers don't usually understand the intricacies of how to conduct an investigation or how important little details can be. If they did, they'd be investigators, not decision makers. Most of them are not going to care about what you found—they are going to care about what it means. You need to draw the conclusions for decision makers instead of expecting them to fill in the answer themselves.

Presenting your findings in a clear, logical format might turn out to be much more difficult than actually finding the evidence. This is especially important when presenting a case based largely (or exclusively) on evidence from the Internet. Internet-based investigations are inherently different from more traditional investigations. In an Internet-based investigation, you usually don't obtain witness statements or affidavits. Instead, you rely on documents and information obtained from third parties. They likely have no personal knowledge about the subject, yet the information they can provide will be crucial to you in proving or disproving a subject's story.

Thinking Graphically

Putting it all together can be a bit challenging. Of course, the more complex your investigation, the more complex the story is going to become. To keep things straight, I usually start by creating a diagram of all the business and personal relationships I have documented in my investigation. Most of this time this can be accomplished with a very large white board and a variety of colors of dry erase pens. Use different colors, shapes, and line styles to indicate whether each object is a person, a company, a trust, or a piece of property, and the relationship between them. For example, you can denote a person with a circle, a business might be a square, and an asset might be a triangle. The line connecting a person to an asset might be solid, and the line connecting a person and a business in which they are an officer might be dashed. If there is more than one relationship between two objects, use multiple connecting lines—one for each type of relationship. Use arrowheads to show the direction of ownership, especially when connecting two companies (the arrow travels away from the owner to the asset or company owned or managed). The key is to keep the diagram relatively simple and, wherever possible, don't cross the lines. Your chart may end up looking something like this:

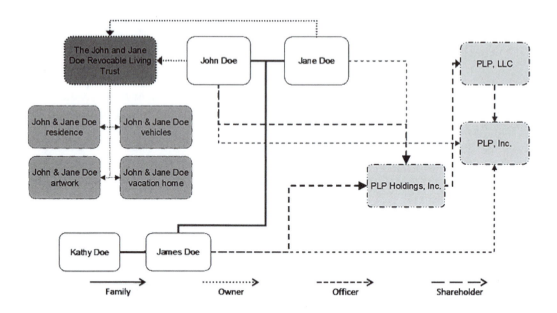

Figure 17.1 Sample Flowchart

Notice how this diagram shows not only who owns a company but who controls that company as well. If you had a more complex set of relationships to diagram, you could consider color-coding some entries: companies and assets that were properly disclosed might be green, companies and assets that were disclosed but undervalued might be yellow, and companies and assets you discovered on your own might be in red. Other color-coding notations you might want to track include the state of incorporation for various companies, companies in which the subject has an ownership interest, or assets that could be easily liquidated to generate cash. Color can be a great alternative if the connections become too complex for lines.

If you're trying to understand the relationship between a number of different businesses, you can also try graphing that information out as well. In addition to business names, you might try to include basic information to track the involvement of a particular owner or officer. You might color-code the chart to denote important information, such as companies that have ceased operations. This type of chart could end up as illustrated in Figure 17.2.

Note how the two boxes on the top right have a heavier outline that the others? That's one way you can draw attention to a particular entity. In this case, look at the dissolution dates of the companies involved. The two companies on the far right top were apparently owned by the company to their left—except the company on the left went out of business before the other two did. If you came across this type of situation, it would certainly warrant additional investigation.

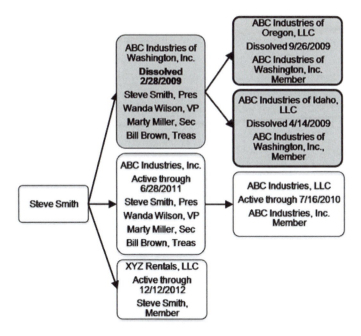

Figure 17.2 Sample Business Relationships Chart

Starting your graphing activities on a large white board is preferable because you don't always know what form the final chart will take. Don't be surprised if you need to start over (maybe more than once) before you stumble on the best layout. If you don't have access to a large white board, try sticky notes on a wall, flip charts, the organization chart option in PowerPoint, or a flowcharting program like SmartDraw. Your word processing or spreadsheet program can also work if you don't have any other options for creating a professional-looking diagram, but you'll probably want to work out the details and layout by hand and only prepare a final version using one of these methods—they're a bit more cumbersome and difficult to create exactly what you want. I have found the charting option in Word to be extremely slow (even on a very powerful computer with lots of memory). This is why I generally use PowerPoint to create a final document. However, I rarely *start* with PowerPoint—I usually only finish with it. Unless I am graphing a very clear and uncomplicated relationship, I normally work it out ahead of time with pens before making a "pretty" version using the computer.

Graphic representations should always be as simple as you can make them. Will your spreadsheet or presentation software create 3D graphs, animated charts, and cool graphic effects like drop shadows and blinking text? Of course they will. Do those options add anything valuable? Almost always, the answer is a resounding "no." Keep Albert Einstein's advice in mind: "Make everything as simple as possible, but not simpler." That goes double if you're planning to present your chart to decision makers. Fancy options tend to distract from your presentation, they don't enhance it. Also remember that options like rainbow colors are not only distracting, they are hard to read when photocopied in black and white (different colors may be indistinguishable when reproduced in grayscale). Color should have a purpose: either to distinguish different things or to make something more aesthetically pleasing. Color-coded items can (and probably should) be very different colors from each other; it's fine to use the true colors of the rainbow to represent different aspects of your investigation. Bar graphs and pie charts are different. Although many spreadsheet and charting programs may default to using all the colors of the rainbow, this can be extremely distracting to your audience. Instead, use a range of hues in a single color: light blue through to navy or a pale green through to the darkest emerald. Not only is this technique more attractive and less distracting, it also is easy to read when photocopied.

Once you have a visual representation of the story, it's time to start looking for any blanks. You'll want to make sure you highlight any holes in the story so you know what to look for next. If you are trying to prove that John Doe is secretly involved in Smith & Company, Ltd., does the diagram support that? Is there a clear path connecting the two? If not, you have more work to do. If you have established the connection between the two, is it a clear connection? If you have to make some assumptions to get there, then you have more work to do. How much work remains will depend on how many holes there are in your finished diagram. Remember that every missing link is an opportunity for the respondent to cast doubt on your conclusions.

Once your diagram is complete and the obvious holes have been filled, the next step is to examine it for any discrepancies you want to highlight. For example, you might see the arrows run the wrong way between an alleged "parent" and "subsidiary" company. Or you might notice that the subject always appoints their spouse and eldest child as Directors of the companies they own—except the one you are investigating. Make sure you highlight anything that jumps out at you as unusual: a relationship that's not normal industry practice, an unexplainable transfer, or something you can demonstrate the subject lied about. Depending on the medium you've chosen to create your diagram, you might add a sticky note to your diagram, use a different fill color or object shape, or simply circle the unusual relationship. In Figure 17.2 above, the inconsistent dates are highlighted with a different type of border—simple, yet effective. Each discrepancy you note and highlight will need a full explanation when you write up your results.

Summarizing Your Results

Summarizing the results of your investigation is really about your final determination and conclusions. In the abstract, it may seem too early in the process to reach any conclusions about the subject. In reality, by the time you reach this stage of your investigation you've known for a long time what your conclusions are going to be. Now is the time to hone those conclusions and make sure there is evidence to back up each and every one.

To determine which conclusions are worth pursuing, take a look at your diagram. What are the three things that jump out at you first? Depending on what you found, it may be fine to lump some things together (assets the subject concealed would be fine to lump together as multiple examples of a single "hidden assets" result). Try to have no more than five main results that you will detail in your final recommendation, no matter how complicated the case. If you can keep that number to three, all the better. Finding too many violations can actually be counterproductive—the real issues get lost in a sea of minor transgressions. Instead, focus on the real problems: hidden assets, undisclosed relationships, and illegal activities should be at the top of your list. Less important rules and regulations are of secondary importance.

If you're having problems identifying which problems are the most significant, ask yourself what the key program requirements are. What do you say when someone asks you about your job or the program you administer? How do you respond when someone asks you how they can participate in the program? What do you say when someone asks you how they get that particular license or registration? Whatever the key eligibility requirements you include in that "elevator speech" version of your job are probably the most important areas you should be checking for violations.

If you still believe you have more than five major conclusions, look to see if they share anything in common such as a similar underlying regulation or similar effect on your final conclusion. If so, try combining key conclusions around that common thread. If you *still* can't narrow your key conclusions down to five or fewer, it may be appropriate to use more. If you are going to use more than five key conclusions, justify the use of more by using your underlying regulatory authority. For example, you might say something like, "To pass the mandatory audit, state law requires a company prove eight things. The subject company has failed to meet their burden of proof for seven of eight items. Those seven items are: ..." Keep in mind if you do decide to focus on more than five key conclusions, you run the risk of boring your audience to such an extent that they don't really pay as much attention as you would like. It's nothing personal—there only just so much regulatory gobbledygook any of us can take. Three key conclusions is usually a safe number. Five conclusions is an upper limit. Anything more than five runs a significant risk of information overload. If you're going to take that risk, make sure the potential benefits outweigh the risks.

After you identify the three most important conclusions of your case, write each of them on the white board and make a column under each. If you used flip charts instead of a white board for your diagrams, write each conclusion on a separate sheet of paper and line them up next to each other. If you used sticky notes, write each on a regular piece of paper and tape it to the wall, leaving enough room underneath each for more sticky notes. Regardless of the method, you want to be able to clearly distinguish what your three conclusions are and have enough room to write below each one. Again, don't be distracted by the small stuff; focus exclusively on your most important conclusions. For each conclusion you've identified, figure out what evidence proves you are correct. Below each conclusion, write a brief note about which document or other piece of evidence supports or proves that conclusion. If you're using sticky notes, write each piece of evidence on a separate note and place it on the wall below the applicable conclusion. Your note can be brief, it just needs to be detailed enough for you to find and refer to it later. A note might be as simple as "1/20/2011 Smith Ltr" or "ABC Jones Deed."

After you've gone through all the various documents and pieces of evidence available, take a step back and look at your columns. Do you see three fairly even columns? Do you see one column that is very long and two columns that are short? Or is there one column that doesn't have any supporting notes? Looking at these columns gives you a sense of how much weight each conclusion has behind it. Remember that this is an indication of quantity, not quality, of evidence. One irrefutable piece of evidence may be worth more than ten documents that are open to interpretation. But quantity matters. Producing document after document after document that supports your determination is more effective than producing only a single supporting document. Judges and other decision makers are only human—we like lots of evidence, especially when there are significant consequences at stake. Using a white board or flip charts of sticky notes on a wall to outline your conclusions gives you an advantage over doing the same thing on a single sheet of paper: you instantly get a feel for how a decision maker will judge the weight of your evidence. If any conclusion needs additional support, now is the time to revisit the issue and find more evidence. If you have exhausted all possible leads and still don't have enough support for your conclusion, reconsider whether that conclusion is worth including in your final determination. Remember: one well-supported determination is better than three determinations with mediocre support.

Explaining the Discrepancies

After identifying your most important conclusions and determining which documents support each, the next step is to look for the discrepancies in your investigation. These discrepancies generally fall into two categories: discrepancies between the subject's story versus what you found, and discrepancies between contradictory documents you have discovered. Each of these discrepancies needs to be thoroughly explained either by you, by the subject, or by some sort of third-party witness or expert.

Discrepancies between the subject's claims and the evidence you've collected are the easiest to explain: you would naturally conclude that your documents are correct and the subject is being less than forthright. Unfortunately, it's rarely that easy. Your subject almost always has documents to support their version of events as well. Your task is to show why your documents and evidence are more reliable and trustworthy than the subject's documents and evidence. The most likely reason your evidence is better is that you obtained it from disinterested parties (or in the case of photos or reports based on your own personal observations). This is important because neither you nor those third parties have any personal stake in the outcome of your investigation. The subject, on the other hand, has a very personal stake in the outcome of your investigation—and that could motivate them to be less honest in their representations.

One way to validate your evidence while simultaneously discrediting the subject's documents is to explain why the two sets of documents are mutually exclusive. It may also be helpful to explain what you would have found if the subject's version were accurate. Think about that document that proves the subject was lying or hiding assets: what would it have said if the subject had been telling the truth? If you can explain that, you can help a judge or other decision maker understand the discrepancy in the evidence and why your conclusion is correct.

Frequently documents you find may contradict each other. This is to be expected, especially when the subject has actively taken steps to conceal assets or otherwise hide business relationships. These discrepancies also need to be explained so that decision makers can properly evaluate the evidence. That explanation will depend on the document; specifically, it may well depend on the source of information contained in the document. Some documents obtained from third parties are not created by those parties—the information they contain is actually provided by the subject or someone similar. Corporate filings with the Secretary of State's office are a good example. The Secretary of State's office does not create a company's annual report or Articles of Incorporation; they merely store and index those documents.

Another reason that documents you find may contradict other documents you collect might be due to inaccuracies and the part of the third party supplying the information. Just because someone puts information into a database doesn't mean that information is accurate, even if they charge for that information. If the original source data was not correct, then any resulting searches or other data will be just as incorrect.

Sometimes the discrepancy in question is hard to explain. This may be due to your lack of understanding of the situation, or it may be related to the reason for the discrepancy. Either way, you need to understand and be able to fully explain anything that "just doesn't look right." The first way to address this situation is to go back and conduct additional investigation. Is there something you missed? Is there a lead you didn't follow up on because you thought it was unimportant? Now is the time to go back and revisit those decisions and look for additional information to fill in the blanks.

If you've already followed all available leads, it may be helpful to consult with an expert. For example, if the subject changed the legal structure of their business but you can't explain why, perhaps you should talk with an attorney. Or maybe you've found an odd deduction for an unexpected expense—an accountant can help you figure out whether it's a legitimate deduction or just a way to covertly redirect money to the owner. Perhaps the subject suddenly changed all their investments from money markets to certificates of deposit; a financial planner could help you understand whether that was a wise financial decision or merely a pretext for making funds unavailable for other uses (like paying a fine). While investigators need to know at least a little bit about many different subjects, you can't know everything about every topic. Sometimes it is cost effective to consult with an expert to answer your questions quickly and accurately.

Finally, it may be appropriate for you to engage in additional analysis above and beyond what is normal for your investigations. While not required for every case, a particularly challenging or confusing investigation may benefit from doing additional research. You may want to review the subject's business records and compare them to others in the same or a similar industry. What is their typical profit margin? How much do they typically spend on materials? How much on labor? How much on overhead? If other similar businesses usually have a ten percent profit margin, but the subject business is only clearing two percent, why? Do they have a less-profitable business model? Or are they disguising profits as some sort of expense and covertly re-directing them to the owner? On occasion, you may need to do additional research such as this in order to be able to explain a discrepancy in the evidence.

The Five-Step Explanation

For each discrepancy, you need to explain its importance and consequence, and you need to do so in plain, understandable English. One way to accomplish this is to use a five-step explanation.

STEP ONE: WHAT DID YOU FIND?

A clear explanation of what you found is always important to proving your case. This can actually be more difficult than it seems. As investigators, we tend to want to explain it all and overwhelm our audience while skipping details that we assume everyone already knows. The challenge for step one is to clearly and simply explain what you found and nothing else—just the facts.

STEP TWO: WHERE OR HOW DID YOU FIND IT?

The next part of a clear explanation is where or how you found the relevant information. This part of the explanation is crucial because it is how to authenticate the information you are providing. You should always reference the most reliable source possible; an original source is always better than a secondary or tertiary source.

STEP THREE: WHAT SHOULD YOU HAVE FOUND?

Explaining what you should have found can help decision makers understand your conclusions or recommendations. Many times a decision maker doesn't have a frame of reference for understanding what it is you're talking about. This part of the explanation can be a bit more in-depth. By explaining what is normal, you provide a frame of reference for the decision maker. This is also your opportunity to explain what you should have found if the subject had been telling the truth.

STEP FOUR: WHAT DOES IT MEAN OR WHY IS IT IMPORTANT?

A lie or a misleading document usually is not the point of your investigation. The point is actually something different. A per se violation isn't necessarily important. Instead of merely explaining that you found something that violates a law or regulation, try explaining why that law or regulation exists. When decision makers understand why it's important, they may be more willing to follow your recommendation or adopt your determination. Decision makers who don't understand why a rule violation is important may choose to not impose any penalty at all.

STEP FIVE: WHAT IS THE OUTCOME?

Finally, you should carefully explain what the law, rules, regulations, policy, or other applicable governing authority tells you to do with this discovery. This can be tricky, especially if you are dealing with a judge or hearing officer who makes these decisions all the time. Some judges don't like to be told what to do, and some judges *really* don't like to be told what they "must" do. I always avoid using that phrase, regardless of whom I am addressing. This is the one situation when I find using the passive voice is always appropriate. Instead of telling a judge or your boss they are required to take a particular action, instead focus on what the applicable authority says to do. It may be appropriate for you to request a particular action by the decision maker, instead of demanding it. Your statement could be something as simple as, "Therefore, the applicant is not eligible under statute 123 and we request that you affirm the agency's denial of the subject's application."

IMPLEMENTING THE FIVE-STEP EXPLANATION

So how do you put these steps into practice? Let's say you investigated a subject who claimed to be the 100 percent owner of their business. Your investigation found the subject isn't really the company's 100 percent owner. You need to be able to provide details about what you discovered. In this case, you might explain that the company's Amended Certificate of Formation dated January 31, 2010 lists John Smith as an additional member of the company. An "Amended Certificate of Formation" is a document submitted to the Secretary of State when a company changes something about their business, like the name or the legal structure. You obtained a copy of the company's the Amended Certificate of Formation from the Idaho Secretary of State's web site on February 14, 2010 and you found this entry by typing the company's name into the appropriate box on the web site's search page. If the subject were the company's owner, their name and signature would appear on this document. Instead, the certificate is signed by someone else claiming to be a member of the company. Therefore, the only logical conclusion is that the subject is not the 100 percent owner of the company. While you were unable to verify the subject's true ownership interest in the company, you know that John Smith must own at least a small percentage of the business. Therefore, you recommend the subject's application be denied because they do not meet the criteria for this particular government program.

Putting it All Together

Telling the story can be the most time-consuming part of the process. Even if you are just doing a cursory review to determine whether you should pass the case along to an expert, take the time to sit down, analyze, thoughtfully consider the information you found. Even if you don't pursue an enforcement action or other sanctions for a subject's behavior, it is possible you may be called upon to justify your final determination. Ask yourself this question: if a reporter calls me tomorrow and asks why I set the penalty or fine at the amount I did, what am I going to need to tell them? What if the call comes from a legislator's office? If the call comes from the Inspector General's office, what will they want to know? If the company sues my agency because of my actions, what will I tell the judge and jury? Your story needs to address all these various pieces of information.

In preparation for telling the story, start with your diagram, your key conclusions, and the list of documents supporting your conclusions. Find each of those documents and make sure it has some sort of label. (Appendix A has suggestions for organizing and labeling investigation files and documents.) Create a pile for each of your conclusions and place the applicable documents in their respective pile. If a document applies to more than one conclusion, either copy the first page of the document and place the copy in each applicable pile, or write yourself a note and place the note in all the applicable piles (e.g., "7/12/2006 letter to John Smith—2nd paragraph on page 3.") Once again, look for holes in your argument. Have you come to a conclusion, but there's no document to back it up? If so, you need to either find a document that proves your point, or you'll need to change your conclusion.

For documents that are helpful but don't address one of your key conclusions, mark each one with a large sticky note and write a brief explanation of what conclusion the document supports. For example, say your regulations require the subject to have a specific educational experience but the subject doesn't have the right degree. You might label the subject's resume with a sticky note saying, "Subject doesn't have mandatory PhD in ethnomusicology per regulation XYZ123—has AA in History of Rock and Roll instead." Not having the proper educational background may be the least of the subject's problems; you may have six other, far more important reasons to deny their application or permit. In this case, the document and applicable regulation deserve a brief mention but not much else. You can organize documents in this category either by some arbitrary category (e.g., document date or author's name, etc.) or by what lesser conclusion they support (e.g., documents that demonstrate wrong education background, documents showing participating of family members in the company despite subject's denial).

After your charts, conclusions, and supporting documents are assembled and organized, it's time to start telling your story. The best way to do this is in an investigation report. If your agency or organization has a standard report form, you should use it. If there is no template for you to use, look at the example provided in Appendix C and customize it to meet your individual needs. After completing some basic information (file name, date, investigator's name, etc.), there are some key sections you should include:

BACKGROUND

A "Background" section in your investigation report can help establish the basis for your investigation and provide a bridge connecting the applicable rules or regulations to your conclusions. For example, you could use this section to explain that on August 27, 2009 the subject submitted an application for a permit under state law 9-876-5. Along with the permit application form, the subject provided copies of various supporting documents, including the last three years of corporate tax returns and copies of the company's Articles of Incorporation and Bylaws.

DOCUMENTS AND EVIDENCE OBTAINED

This section of your investigation report lists each document or piece of evidence you obtained, where you obtained it, and when you found/obtained it. This section of the report is not for explaining your conclusions or which documents support those conclusions. This part of your report is simply to document that you did a thorough job and considered all the various documents you were able to obtain. It is best to organize this list in alphabetical order because that is how most readers will best understand the list. A decision maker may wonder if you considered a particular document, but is not likely to wonder which documents you received on a particular date or from a particular source. Also, organizing documents by name instead of by date or source gives you a quick way to see if a single document has been obtained from more than one source (e.g., a copy of the Articles of Incorporation from the subject as well as a copy from the Secretary of State).

SPECIFIC FINDINGS

This is the section of your report where you explain your key conclusions and the evidence that supports them. Start with the most important conclusion: you are going to write a sentence or two (one paragraph at most) explaining what your conclusion is and why it is important. Next, go through each document that supports your conclusion and explain why it proves what you say it does. Finally, go through the five-step explanation for each piece of the evidence that contradicts your conclusion and explain why that evidence cannot be relied upon. You may want to finish by reiterating your conclusion and the consequence of that conclusion, but you can do that at the end all together if you prefer.

After you have written up each of your key conclusions, you may want to include a section for additional findings. This is where you can point out all the other violations or problems or fibs the subject told but which didn't rise to the level of the key conclusions. For each, you can shorten the above procedure and merely explain what the document is and what conclusion you drew from it. If you include a section like this, it is best to organize the documents by what they prove, keeping documents supporting similar conclusions together. You can also include specific findings for documents that didn't affect your decision either positively or negatively, such as a document that proves something that is not required by the applicable law or regulation. If you did not draw any conclusion at all from a particular document or piece of evidence, you can omit it from this section and only include it in the documents section above.

NEXT STEPS

Depending on the nature of your investigation, it may be appropriate to include a section explaining the next steps that should be taken. If your determination is final and no further actions are needed, you can simply include a statement that your report and decision are final and no additional steps are required unless the decision is appealed. If your determination is only a recommendation for others to consider, you may want to include a brief statement about who the applicable decision makers are and the time frame for them to consider an outcome. If there are statutory or regulatory deadlines, hearing dates, or other mandatory time limits, make sure to include them here.

Presenting the Final Story

From my perspective, the key difference between an adequate investigation report and a great investigation report is how the final story plays out in the mind of the audience. Does it read like the latest crime thriller? Or does it read like stereo instructions? If your report reads like the latter, you need to revisit it. Just because your report contains all the right information doesn't mean you've done your job. Your job isn't just to put facts on the page; your job is to uncover the facts, make a determination, and back up that determination in a convincing way. That means you need to be writing something far closer to the crime novel than the stereo instructions. Realistically, it will probably end up falling somewhere in-between the two.

Just how are you supposed to make an investigation report fun reading? OK, maybe "fun reading" is a bit of an overstatement, but the point is still valid. One way to make your investigation report easier to read is to be diligent about writing in plain English (or whatever language you're writing in). As much as possible, try to avoid writing in legalese or bureaucratese. Try to be conversational and avoid using words that are unnecessarily long and cumbersome. Try "use" instead of "utilize" or "employ" and "stop" instead of "cease" or "terminate."

One other technique you can use to make your reports easier to read is to highlight the bad stuff the subject did (if anything). That's the interesting part! Finding out the subject did everything they were supposed to do and that they weren't really hiding assets just doesn't make for compelling reading. Of course, not every report is going to be a page turner. If there aren't any juicy details to include, your report can be a lot shorter and simpler. Writing reports explaining misconduct is the bigger challenge. Make sure you include all the relevant details when writing up your results; sometimes they're the best part. When you have an investigation that is extremely important with egregious violations, try to make reading the report a pleasant experience for your boss, a judge, or another decision maker.

Finally, for all investigation reports make sure you take the time to double check that you've included all the relevant information, that the evidence really supports your conclusions, and that you've given proper consideration to all the evidence in the subject's favor. It may take you longer to write up your final report than it took you to conduct your investigation. It would be a waste of time to spend hours investigating a subject only to make a determination not well supported by the evidence and fail to explain why the other evidence in the case doesn't outweigh the document you relied on. Don't blow your case by being rushed and failing to write a well-reasoned and well-supported final investigation report. To verify you've covered all your bases and haven't missed any important details, you may want to have one of your co-workers read your draft report. Make sure you choose someone who is unfamiliar with the specifics of your investigation. If you've omitted key details or have failed to establish a clear link between the subject and hidden assets, it will be more apparent to them than it is to you.

Case in Point

Looking for the holes in your investigation and presentation can be as difficult as proofreading a long document you've been writing for hours. While it's easy to accidentally skip over important information, it's even easier to overlook holes you might never consider your opponent will attempt to exploit. As an example, I once handled a case where an owner no longer ran the company, but was sufficiently mentally foggy that he didn't realize his employees were running the business on his behalf. The company's tax returns showed the owner only worked part-time and the company's receptionist said the owner worked from 10:00 am to 2:00 pm each day. However, the owner claimed he worked full-time. During a hearing on the matter, the owner's attorney demanded that I prove a 40-hour work week was "full-time." In preparing the case for hearing, I never considered the company might argue about what "full-time" employment actually meant. Fortunately, the hearing panel didn't require me to produce evidence that a 40-hour work week was the standard definition of "full-time" in the United States. However, without the receptionist's testimony and the company's tax returns both showing the owner was a part-time employee, the outcome could have been much different.

The lesson here is to not take anything for granted, not even things you absolutely know to be true. "The Subject drives an expensive car." Really? How much does a Porsche or Mercedes-Benz cost these days? Find out and have evidence ready to go to back up your statement in case you are challenged. You need to be sufficiently prepared to offer a response such as, "Well, according to the manufacturer's website, a vehicle similar to the Subject's costs approximately $70,000 new and is estimated to cost approximately $2,750 per year in insurance and approximately $250 per year in licensing fees. Those expenses are being paid by someone; either by the Subject or someone is paying them on the Subject's behalf." In situations like this, clear, specific information is the most persuasive and can help highlight the silliness of the challenge.

18 *Final Thoughts and Considerations*

Now that you've managed to wade through all this information, you may be wondering what the most important "takeaways" are. Remembering the reason for your investigation is important. Government should always to continue to strive to increase efficiency, and investigating cases on the Internet for free (instead of paying for expensive databases) is no exception. Each of us needs to remember that we don't just work for the government or a particular agency, we work for the taxpayers—and that includes ourselves. So here are some final thoughts for you to consider.

Keep research and investigation costs in mind. While you may be able to track down some information for free, it might be easier and quicker to pay a service to provide that information. Benjamin Franklin noted, "Time is money." Remember that your time is expensive, too! Sometimes, it is also more effective to pay to have someone else conduct all or part of an investigation. If there is important information you need that you do not have access to, a paid service may be a good solution. However, remember that just because someone offers a service in exchange for a fee, that doesn't necessarily mean the service is legal or ethical. Paying someone else to do what you're not allowed to do is not an acceptable option.

It is a good idea to keep track of the costs related to your investigation activities as well as additional funds identified and increases in recoveries. These figures can be excellent performance measures that can demonstrate the value of your work. At the very least, try to keep track of the hours you spend conducting your investigation. Even if it is not required by your employer, it will help in future workforce planning and may be the basis for recovering some of your salary, benefits, and other costs.

Don't let someone (including your boss) push you outside your comfort zone. You may have an area of expertise, but that doesn't mean you will feel comfortable doing work that is only indirectly related to that expertise. If you feel that you're getting in over your head, say so and bring in an expert. It may take more time and money to do so, but you'll get a better result in the end. The last thing you want to do is blow a case because you didn't know how to avoid it. That means it is important to be able to admit when you don't know something. Don't guess. Guessing gets you into trouble. If you don't know the answer, say so. You can always follow it up with an, "...but I'll find out." No reasonable person expects you to know everything about every possible topic you might come across. If you don't know an answer, be willing to learn.

Do not, under any circumstances, use unethical or illegal methods for obtaining information! There are no exceptions to this rule. It is not appropriate under any circumstances and is justification for your case to be tossed out.

It is frequently easier to find evidence of a transfer of an asset than to find evidence of ownership of the asset. It bears repeating yet again—don't look for Bigfoot, look for footprints.

A sudden change in a company's or individual's financial health, either positive or negative, is a clue something else is going on. You may not have enough information to be able to determine what is actually going on, but you should be able to identify the change in circumstances. Sudden changes rarely happen. When they do happen, they're not always related to something illicit. Maybe there was a coup or natural disaster in the country that is a major supplier of a company's raw materials. Maybe the company's long-time manager passed away unexpectedly. Or maybe there isn't really a big change and someone's cooking the books. Either way, that sudden change should cause you to look much closer than you otherwise might.

Does everything match? If not, why not? Be able to explain the reason. If you can't explain the reason, check with an expert, a more experienced investigator, or your supervisor. Not knowing an answer isn't the end of the road, it's merely one more lead you need to track down and investigate.

The hard part isn't finding the red flags—it's recognizing them when you see them and figuring out what to do with them.

Remember that cultural, social, and economic factors influence our decisions and opinions. What might seem suspicious to you might be your subject's normal way of doing business. Consider the following real-world example: A woman from an East African country had applied for a government certification from the agency I worked for. Her paperwork was not in order, but it would have been fairly easy for her to rectify the situation. My co-worker spent almost 30 minutes trying to explain what the woman needed to do, but it just wasn't getting through. My co-worker then asked me to intercede and I spent another 20 minutes trying to explain to the woman what she needed to do. I assumed the language difference accounted for the applicant's inability to understand the situation. She was obviously very frustrated and kept asking if there wasn't something else she could do. In turn, I kept telling her, in very simple English, exactly what she needed to do. Finally, she seemed to understand, thanked us for our help, and said goodbye. After our conversation was over, my laughing co-worker turned to me and said, "We are such idiots. She was offering us a bribe."

Suddenly, the entire conversation made sense. Bribery is an accepted and routine part of business in the woman's home country. When my co-worker told her that her paperwork was not in order, the woman assumed that was merely a pretext to ask for a bribe. When my co-worker called me in to "assist," the applicant figured it was a regular part of the haggling—like when the car salesman tries to get approval from the manager to give you a good deal. So the woman tried to respond appropriately, using vague language to let us know she was willing to pay and trying to find out how much it would take to satisfy us. Her frustration was understandable; we wouldn't tell her how much we wanted! The stalemate was only resolved because she finally accepted our words at face value. We told her exactly what she needed to do to qualify and she had enough trust to simply do what we told her. She eventually got her paperwork in order and qualified for her certification—all without paying any extra "fees" or other "consideration."

The lesson here is not to let your own perspective or cultural values cloud your judgment. Both my co-worker and I assumed that our failure to help the woman understand was due to language difficulties. If we had been more sensitive to the woman's culture, we probably would have realized what was going on much sooner and saved everyone a great deal of frustration. This is an important lesson when conducting investigations: remember to look at actions and events through the eyes and cultures of those involved. People hide assets for many reasons. They may be trying to save face, preserve family or company honor, or ensure a legacy to their children and grandchildren. It may have nothing to do with you or your investigation; your subject may not even realize what they are doing is improper.

It is important to manage expectations related to your investigation. That includes the expectations of management, of a complaining party, and even of yourself. Sometimes the information just isn't out there, no matter how hard you look. You want to make sure you don't set yourself up for failure by promising something you can't deliver. Be realistic and, in the case of bosses or witnesses, explain what your limits are.

Always try to minimize surprises whenever possible. If the subject is likely to complain about you, talk to your boss and prepare them for that possibility. If the subject doesn't understand what your investigation means and what you are going to check, talk with them. If your boss doesn't understand why a particular case is taking so long, explain it to them. Open lines of communication can help smooth over many disagreements and avoid misunderstandings.

Place yourself in the subject's position. How would you feel about being investigated? Who would you trust if you needed to hide assets? What sort of family pressures might induce you to help someone else launder money, disguise income, or hide assets? Your subject is a person, just the same as you. They may even have a similar cultural or educational background. If you think of it, they probably will as well.

Hopefully, these materials have given you enough basic information to start using when you're conducting a financial investigation on the Internet. The same techniques can be used when evaluating businesses or individuals for program eligibility or specialized assistance. More importantly, knowing this information will help you make better determinations and justify those determinations to the subject, your supervisor, agency management, legal professionals, and the public.

Appendix A: Practical Suggestions for Organizing Your Investigation

Financial investigations can produce enough paper to overwhelm even the most diligent filers. Keeping track of the various documents you collect sometimes seems like a monumental task. There is no single best way to organize documents; the best organization system is the one that works best for you. However, here are some suggestions about how to organize the physical aspect of your investigation. If you can't find the exact product I mention, look for something else that serves the same or similar purpose.

Files Folders and Documents

Researching and conducting financial investigations on the Internet has a serious downside: it is far too easy to print out lots of very long (and not always relevant) documents. It almost becomes second nature to hit the "Print" button anytime we find something even remotely interesting. The first strategy you can use to minimize the amount of papers you have to organize is to not print everything. Only print documents that are actually relevant to your investigation. At the very least, try to only print documents that have a high likelihood of being relevant. Once you do hit the print button, you'll need to arrange documents in a way that you can find what you need when you need it.

PARTITION FILE FOLDERS

File folders are how most people choose to organize documents. File folders have a great advantage over other methods: filing cabinets are designed to hold them, and filing cabinets are readily accessible. They are also tidy to look at. Never underestimate the amount of stress that is generated by a messy desk, even if you know where everything is! The first file folder option is partition or "classification" folders. These usually have a heavy colored front and back cover with lighter weight kraft partitions in the middle. A six-partition folder is a very common type, but they also come in four-partition and eight-partition versions. Each partition will have a two-hold punch fastener at the top. These are the type of folder I use for most investigations. I like them because I can organize different types of documents by group and can use different colored folders for different purposes (e.g., green for financial investigations, red for criminal investigations, and blue for licensing investigations). I also use these types of folders because they are easy to get and are very common—there are always some in the supply cabinet.

The different file folder categories you assign will depend on each investigation, but try to keep them consistent. This will make it easier to find things. For example, I always use the first partition (inside the front cover) to store the basic information related to that file, including contact information. No matter what type of file it is, that basic information is always on the first partition. That way I always know exactly where to find a phone number, address, or other important data. For most Internet-based financial investigations, you might consider organizing and labeling a six-partition file using the following categories:

Partition 1: Basic Information

This includes names, addresses, phone numbers, and other key data. I usually put the copy of the investigation plan here as well, including any related lists.

Partition 2: Correspondence

Copies of all letters (and everything else in the file) should be kept in reverse chronological order with the oldest documents on the bottom. Also keep hard copies of any important emails and treat them as if they were letters. While an electronic version of emails is usually fine, you need to ensure that you can produce a copy of important emails even if your computer dies, the server crashes, or the email accidentally is lost, deleted, or misfiled.

Partition 3: Contact Records

I like to keep my written phone notes separate from letters and emails because I tend to look for a document based on how I communicated about it. Make sure each contact record has a date, time, name of the person you spoke with, and a reference to which investigation it relates. It is a good practice to use a contact record to document important voicemail messages. If you expect to use a contact record as evidence, consider typing it.

Partition 4: Corporate and Business Records

This is the partition where I include printouts from the Secretary of State's office, business licensing entities, etc. This is also the partition where I would file any other documents that demonstrate a corporate or other business relationship, including corporate minutes, web pages showing a company's managers, or a printout showing the subsidiaries in a larger corporate family.

Partition 5: Asset Lists and Real Estate Records

Along with copies of deeds and Deeds of Trust, this is the partition where I file reports from the tax assessor's office, reports from Zillow showing fair market value, and printouts showing comparable parcels of real estate in the area. If a subject has significant personal property, I would include the documentation here as well. Assets such as boats, airplanes, vehicles, and collections can all be very valuable.

Partition 6: Financial Records

This partition may include tax returns, financial statements, credit reports, check registers, and any other financial documents. I recommend placing these records in the final partition because that partition is stronger than interior partitions and the fasteners are longer (allowing for more sheets of paper to be kept in this location).

BUCKET FOLDERS

If you don't like partition folders or have too many types of documents to organize in a limited number of partitions, you can instead organize your investigation documents in a series of manila file folders kept in a single "bucket" or expanding file pocket. Bucket folders come in a variety of depths, but a 5.25 inch expansion is a very common size and is more than adequate for most investigations. You do not want expansion folders that have dividers (such as A–Z or 1–31), nor do you want the "wallet" style that completely close; neither of these versions will give you enough room to properly organize all your documents.

  If you choose to use this filing method, make sure to label each manila and bucket folder with the file name and number. Each manila folder should only contain a single type of document, such as real estate records, personal property records, or tax returns. This filing technique may be preferable when you expect to deal with a large volume of documents.

FILE RETENTION JACKETS

These useful pockets can be hard to track down, but are invaluable if you like to keep difficult documents contained. File jackets are a pocket designed for holding a document in a file folder without punching holes in it. There are pre-punched holes in the file jacket instead. These jackets are perfect for filing documents that are too large to punch (such as a company's Annual Report) or documents that you want to preserve and not poke holes in (such as an original bond, Trust Agreement, or Will).[1]

POST-ITS AND SHARPIES

When it comes to organizing documents in a file folder, nothing beats Post-it® Standard Flags. These colored tabs stick to documents without damaging them and are exactly the right size for labeling documents. I place the tabs along the bottom edge of the document with the edge of the colored portion aligning with the edge of the paper. If you align the tabs from left to right, exactly eight tabs will fit across the file. They come in a variety of colors—each investigator in your office can use a different color for easy reference.

  I use the tabs to label each document in the file. I use an extra fine felt-tip pen (Sharpie® Ultra-fine Point pens work very well because the ink dries quickly and doesn't smear). Gel ink pens do not work well on the tabs and should not be used because you

---

1   The pre-punched jackets I use are manufactured by both Smead® and Pendaflex® and I am able to order them from Office Depot® (one brand is available for individual purchase and the other brand comes in a box of 100). I have not found similar folders made by other companies nor have I found other retailers that carry them, but they may exist. Check your local retailers or centralized purchasing agency to see which brands are available in your area.

will end up with ink all over your fingers. Old-fashioned ball point pens work fine, but the tabs can be slightly more difficult to read (depending on what color tab and what color ink you use). I write just enough to make it clear what the document is so I can find it when I need it. For example, a copy of a Letter of Credit dated July 16, 2010 would be labeled with a tab that read "7/16/10 LOC" and a September 23, 2009 email from John Smith would be labeled "9/23/09 Smith email."

Two last minor cautions: first, always write on your tab before placing it on the document and second, be cautious when using tabs in any color other than white. If you use a ball point pen or use a lot of pressure when you write, the colored tabs will transfer your writing to whatever surface the tab is attached to while you are writing on it. Using a felt-tipped pen minimizes this transfer because you tend to use less pressure while writing. I typically place the blank tab on a scrap sheet of paper to write my label to prevent these problems.

OTHER METHODS

If you find file folders difficult to work with, you may want to try another organization method. The other I have used with some measure of success is using a three-ring binder with tabbed dividers. With the invention of easier methods for creating divider tabs, this may be a good way to organize your documents. There are three downsides to using notebooks to organize your investigation documents: first, they don't fit easily and reliably into most filing cabinets, so storage may be challenging; second, holes along the margins may inadvertently cut off information; and third, three ring binders are frequently more expensive than file folders. On the plus side, it is far easier to add documents to or remove documents from a binder than it is a file folder and you don't need to remove documents to access one underneath. It is also easier to assemble a large number of documents into a single binder—far more documents will fit in a notebook than even the largest partition file.

Computer Organization

Properly organizing files on a computer can make your life far more efficient. However, the best way to organize investigation documents depends on what type of documents they are, how often you access them, and how you plan to use them.

BOILERPLATES

A "boilerplate" is a template or form that you use repeatedly and customize each time you use it. Investigation plans, final reports, and requests for additional information are all examples of documents that can be turned into a boilerplate for future use. When creating boilerplates, I recommend saving the original form in whatever folder your word processing program defaults to. (If you use Microsoft Word, your default folder is probably going to be called "My Documents.") I also recommend starting the name of each boilerplate document with a zero, followed by a dot, then the name of your document—such as "0.investigationplan.boilerplate.docx." Why so complicated? Because the computer defaults to displaying files in alphabetical order (unless you tell it otherwise). Putting the zero in front of the file name puts all your boilerplates together (because they now have similar names) and also puts all of them at the top of your file list, making them easier to find. If you omit the zero from the file name above, then you'll have to spend time scrolling through the files to get to the ones beginning with "I." The rest of the file name tells you that the file is for an investigation plan, that it is your boilerplate form, and that it is a word processing document.

To use a boilerplate, open your word processing program and select the option to "Open" an existing file. Highlight the boilerplate you want by clicking once. Then look for the button that says "Open" but don't click on it. Instead, look for a small down arrow that should be next to the word "Open." Click that arrow instead. You should now be looking at choices to open the document, open a read only version of the document, or open a copy of the document. Select either the "read only" or "copy" option. Either of these choices will prevent you from accidentally saving over your boilerplate. If you forget to open a separate copy of your boilerplate, you can also just click on the "Save As" option and give it a new name. That will also protect your boilerplate form.

CHECKLISTS AND OTHER FORMS

In addition to boilerplates for long documents like investigation plans, you can also create shorter checklist forms to help you keep track of documents and websites during your investigation. You might save considerable time if you create a checklist of all the documents that need to be submitted as part of your agency's application. If you include some introductory language at the top and print it on your agency's letterhead, you can simply check the documents the subject failed to provide and send it to them as a request for additional information. That way you aren't required to draft an original letter every time a subject fails to follow all the applicable instructions.

Checklists can also help you verify you've completed all the required steps in your investigation. This acts as a backstop to your investigation plan; even if you forgot to include a particular item in your plan, a final checklist can remind you before it's too late.

CASE SPECIFIC DOCUMENTS

Once you start creating investigation plans, contact records, letters, memos, and other documents, you need a place on the computer to store them. You need to be able to find and access these documents quickly and easily and not confuse them with other documents. The easiest way to do this is to create folders to store related documents. In your default folder ("My Documents" or whatever you have it set to), create a series of folders to handle the different types of things you handle in your job. You might create a "Personnel" folder, a "Miscellaneous Office" folder, a "Monthly Reports" folder, and an "Investigations" folder. If you handle a high volume of files or investigations, you might want to label and organize your folders by date, such as "2010 Investigations" or "2011 Applications."

Each time you begin a new investigation, simply open your "Investigations" folder and create a new subfolder for that company or subject. Everything related to that particular investigation should go in this folder. If you find it helpful, you can create even more subfolders—one for correspondence, one for scanned documents, one for pictures, one for documents found on the Internet, etc. But for most investigations, a single folder is adequate to hold all related documents.

BOOKMARKS AND FAVORITES

Bookmarking websites on the Internet is a very efficient way to find what you are looking for. Investigations have a way of repeating themselves, but seemingly not often enough for you to remember *exactly* how you got there last time. Organizing your bookmarks is as important as organizing your files and folders. Your Internet browser should allow you to organize your favorites; if it doesn't, upgrade the version or choose a different browser that gives you better customization abilities. Just as you would create folders on your computer for different types of documents, create different folders for your bookmarks. I have folders for "Computer Resources," "Dictionaries, etc.," "Financial sites," "Internet Resources," "Law Sites," "Local Sites," "Public Records," "Training Resources," and (because of where I happen to live) "Washington State Agencies." These folders help me manage what might otherwise be an overly long and unwieldy list. Instead, I know exactly where to find the current rates for a 20-year T-Bill or where to look up the meaning of *"ex post facto."*

When organizing your bookmarks, be sure to give them a name you will understand and one that you will recognize when you try to find it again. Sometimes when you set a bookmark, the web site will simply give you a file name or the web site address you are trying to bookmark. Unless that name is fairly descriptive, it probably won't help you find the site the next time you need to access it. Instead, save your bookmark under a name you will recognize instead of a file name or website address. The bookmark will still point to the full website address even if you give it a shorter nickname on your favorites menu.

Your bookmarks are just like any other data on your computer in one key respect: they need to be backed up on a regular basis. In addition to backing up the data on your computer, make sure you regularly back up your favorites. You can do this by exporting your list of bookmarks. If you don't see an export option, select the option to organize your bookmarks. Exporting a list of bookmarks in HTML should be an option from that page. As an added backup, you can email your bookmarks HTML file to your Internet-based email account or even your home email account for safekeeping.

To Scan or Not To Scan?

Although technology has come a long way over the last decade, we are still far, far away from the paperless office. Electronic storage has some significant advantages: it takes up far less physical space, it saves resources and is better for the environment, your agency has to spend less money on supplies and records are easily transported from one location to another with no waiting. But electronic files also have some disadvantages: they are not universally accepted as being reliable (meaning you might not be able to use them as evidence) and they can't be accessed without the right equipment. They are also more susceptible to tampering by mischief makers; a hacker half-way across the globe can delete electronic files where someone would need to break into your office to destroy the paper version. File management software can also be very expensive to purchase and require extensive staff time to convert old paper files to an electronic format.

When it comes to Internet-based financial investigations, there is no distinct advantage or disadvantage to using paper files versus electronic files. Your decision to use one format or the other should be in line with your agency's policy on electronic storage, your state's sunshine laws, and your own personal preferences. The best course of action may be a compromise between the two: maintain paper files but scan copies of key documents so they can be accessed electronically if needed.

Page Sizes

One final consideration is whether to use letter size paper or legal sized paper, especially when it comes to choosing file folders. Legal sized paper is becoming less and less common. I recommend choosing letter size for both file folders and print jobs. The overwhelming majority of documents you find during a financial investigation will be letter sized, and letter sized file folders and binders are less expensive than legal sized ones.

When printing documents from the Internet, check to see if you have the option to print legal sized documents on letter size paper. Documents in Adobe PDF format frequently have this option. If the type is large enough to be legible, printing on smaller paper is best. If the type will be too small, go ahead and print on legal sized paper and simply fold up the bottom three inches of the page up to make it letter sized. If you are trying to put a legal sized paper in a standard three-ring binder, start by folding up the bottom three inches to make the page letter sized. Then take the left turned-up corner and fold it down so that it is even with the bottom folded edge. This will form a small triangle-shaped space that will allow the bottom hole to remain unencumbered and the page will be easy to turn. Do not simply fold up the bottom portion of the paper first and punch it—that will require opening the notebook rings to unfold the page.

Appendix B: 100 Questions to Answer When Telling the Story

Here are 100 key questions you should be able to answer at the end of your investigation. Not all questions will always apply to every investigation, but you should start by assuming they do. A few questions may seem a little strange or irrelevant. They aren't. They are designed to help you figure out whether the situation you're investigating is typical or atypical. Atypical situations should raise red flags for you and warrant further investigation and explanation.

Starting Questions

1. WHO IS THE SUBJECT?

You should be able to clearly identify who your subject is, whether they are an individual, a company, a non-profit, or some other type of entity.

2. IS THE SUBJECT A COMPANY, A PERSON, A TRUST, OR SOMETHING ELSE?

You should be able to clearly and succinctly explain whether you are investigating an individual, a company, a trust, or some other type of entity. If there are multiple subjects or multiple entities related to a single subject, make sure you can clearly identify the nature of each.

If the Subject is a Company

3. WHAT TYPE OF COMPANY IS IT: CORPORATION, AN LLC, LIMITED PARTNERSHIP, GENERAL PARTNERSHIP, SOLE PROPRIETORSHIP, OR SOMETHING ELSE?

You should be able to explain the legal structure of any company you investigate. If your investigation reveals that the alleged legal structure is not the actual legal structure, make sure you can explain both structures and why the purported structure is not an accurate description.

4. DID THE COMPANY FILE ALL THE PAPERWORK THEY WERE SUPPOSED TO FILE WHEN THEY ESTABLISHED THE BUSINESS?

Many companies neglect to complete all the necessary paperwork when they are created, so it is possible the company does not actually exist. If this is the case, you should be able to explain what documents they were supposed to file, which documents they missed, and the result of that oversight.

5. DID THE COMPANY DO OTHER PAPERWORK THEY SHOULD HAVE DONE, EVEN IF THEY DIDN'T HAVE TO FILE THOSE DOCUMENTS WITH A GOVERNMENT AGENCY (SUCH AS CORPORATE BYLAWS)?

Many companies fail to prepare some documents if there is not a government entity that requires they be filed. Even though the Secretary of State does not require bylaws be filed, a corporation should still have them.

6. DO THE COMPANY'S CORPORATE OR BUSINESS FORMATION DOCUMENTS MAKE SENSE, OR DO THEY CONTAIN STRANGE PROVISIONS?

Strange provisions are there for a reason. You should be able to explain that reason in a clear and succinct way.

7. WHAT DID THE COMPANY DO THAT GIVES RISE TO THE INVESTIGATION, FINE, OR PENALTY?

Be sure you can easily explain why you are investigating the subject. Your explanation should be short and, if possible, reference the supporting regulations that authorize your activities.

8. DOES THE COMPANY HAVE A HISTORY OF REGULATORY VIOLATIONS (HAVE THEY BEEN IN TROUBLE BEFORE)?

Are you dealing with a repeat offender? If so, you may need to be able to explain why the company continues to commit violations.

9. WHERE IS THE COMPANY LOCATED?

Be sure you can clearly identify the relevant legal jurisdictions affecting the company.

10. ARE YOU INVESTIGATING A BRANCH LOCATION, OR IS IT THE MAIN LOCATION?

This question goes to understanding the corporate structure involved. Be sure you can explain the difference between a main location, a branch location, and whether you are investigating the corporate parent or a subsidiary. The main location can be a subsidiary.

11. WHERE ARE THEY LICENSED TO DO BUSINESS?

Can the business legally do what it says it does? And can it do so in the location it claims?

12. WHERE IS THE HOME JURISDICTION AND WHERE ARE THEY LICENSED AS A FOREIGN ENTITY?

Irrespective of whether you are in the company's home jurisdiction or a foreign jurisdiction, you should be able to explain where the company's home state is and all other states where it is registered to do business.

13. DO THE BUSINESS FILINGS IN OTHER JURISDICTIONS MATCH THE ONES IN YOUR JURISDICTION?

If the company's officers, directors, managers, members, or other corporate officials differ from state to state, you should be able to identify any and all deviations and find out why those differences exist. (Remember, the registered agent in each state should be different unless it is a company performing that duty for the subject.)

14. WHO ARE THE OWNERS, MEMBERS, OR PARTNERS OF THE COMPANY?

You should be able to identify everyone that has an ownership interest in the company, even if they own only a very small portion. In the case of publicly-traded companies, you should be able to identify any major stockholders and explain which exchange the company's stock is traded on.

15. DO THE OWNERS, MEMBERS, OR PARTNERS OWN ANY OTHER COMPANIES?

This applies to privately-held companies and any major stockholders of publicly-traded companies. When two companies share an owner, they frequently share other things as well. Silent partners and venture capitalist investors are notable exceptions to this rule.

16. WHO ARE THE OFFICERS, DIRECTORS, AND/OR MANAGERS OF THE COMPANY?

This question applies to the company's official paperwork. You should be able to explain who each of the company's officers, directors, or managers (as applicable) are.

17. ARE THE OFFICERS, DIRECTORS, AND/OR MANAGERS OF THE COMPANY INVOLVED WITH ANY OTHER COMPANY?

Similar to the explanation for Question 15, companies that share officers, directors, and managers are likely to share other things as well. This is even more common than companies that share owners, because companies rarely have silent officers or managers. Companies that share officers and managers are likely not independent companies. Serving on a board of directors, however, may be a more passive involvement and may not necessarily indicate affiliation between the companies (especially in publicly-traded firms).

18. IF THE OFFICERS, DIRECTORS, AND/OR MANAGERS OF THE COMPANY ARE INVOLVED WITH OTHER COMPANIES, WHAT IS THAT INVOLVEMENT?

When this situation occurs, you should be able to explain the involvement of the various managers and what their role is in each company. Being able to explain this fact is important to establishing whether the two companies are affiliated or whether they are independent in spite of the common management. (An owner/officer/director of their own company might be a fairly passive director of another company without creating an affiliation between the two firms.)

19. WHO CAN SIGN CHECKS, CONTRACTS, AND OTHER LEGAL DOCUMENTS ON BEHALF OF THE COMPANY?

Signing on behalf of a company is an indication of power and control. That is a responsibility usually entrusted to only supervisors and managers in a company. If a company claims that a line employee can sign on its behalf, they should have a very good reason. Otherwise, it may be reasonable for you to assume that the "line" employee is really a covert manager.

20. WHO DO EMPLOYEES SAY IS "THE BOSS"?

Even when coached, employees frequently slip up and tell you who is really in charge. This is frequently a more accurate description of a company's operations than what the firm puts in writing.

21. WHO HAS THE NICEST OFFICE?

The boss generally has the nicest office. The biggest office, the choicest location, and the newest furniture are all privileges usually reserved for the person who is really in charge. If the alleged owner has a tiny hand-me-down desk in the corner, and their "office manager" has a plush office with a door and comfortable new furniture, it's a pretty safe bet the "owner" isn't really in charge.

22. IS THE COMPANY DEFERRING MAINTENANCE ON BUILDINGS, VEHICLES, OR EQUIPMENT (E.G., PEELING PAINT, LEAKING ROOF, BURNED-OUT LIGHTS, ETC.)?

Preventative maintenance is one of the first casualties of a financially troubled company. A company that is not maintaining its premises and equipment is probably in financial trouble and is cutting expenses wherever it can.

23. DOES ANYONE DRIVE A CAR PROVIDED BY THE COMPANY?

Businesses in financial difficulties should be cutting back on perks given to employees—which may include company vehicles.

24. IF THE COMPANY PROVIDES VEHICLES, TO WHOM?

Company cars are a privilege usually reserved for owners, officers, and upper-level managers. Receptionists and mail clerks don't get company cars.

25. IF MORE THAN ONE PERSON HAS A COMPANY CAR, WHOSE IS THE NICEST?

Company cars are like offices—the nicer they are, the higher up you are in the food chain. If the "boss" is driving a 1992 Chevy and the "office manager" is driving a brand-new BMW, that's another indication the "boss" isn't really in charge.

26. DOES THE COMPANY'S TAX RETURN MATCH THE OTHER INFORMATION THEY'VE PROVIDED?

Tax returns are frequently overlooked when companies try to hide assets. Make sure everything on the tax return matches the other information you have. Is there a deduction for mortgage interest on a property they didn't list as an asset? Does the compensation to officers match the amount reported as salaries? Are the owners and ownership percentages listed on IRS Form 1120S and Schedule K-1 the same as other documents submitted by the company? Look for any inconsistency between the tax returns and other information you have about the firm.

27. DOES THE COMPANY'S TAX RETURN MATCH THE BUSINESS FILINGS IN YOUR JURISDICTION (AND THE HOME JURISDICTION, IF DIFFERENT)?

If you have access to both federal and state tax returns, are they consistent with each other? Or did the company tell the IRS one thing but the state taxing authority something else?

28. IS THERE ANYTHING IN THE TAX RETURNS THAT DOESN'T BELONG THERE?

Key items would be mortgages not reported as liabilities, mortgage interest deductions for properties that aren't supposed to exist, owners that appear out of nowhere, and loans made without the capital to back them up.

29. DO THE ASSETS LISTED ON THE TAX RETURN MATCH (ARE IN THE SAME BALLPARK AS) THE ASSETS LISTED IN OTHER CORPORATE RECORDS?

If the company's balance sheet shows assets of $1 million, you should expect the company's tax return to report somewhere around that same amount (depending on the effective dates of each document). If the balance sheet shows $1 million in assets but the tax return reports $10,000 in assets, that is a discrepancy you need to be able to explain (or at least request the company to explain the inconsistency).

30. IS THE AMOUNT OF DEPRECIATION LISTED ON THE COMPANY'S TAX RETURNS REASONABLE FOR HOW MANY ASSETS THEY'VE REPORTED?

Depreciation should be in line with assets reported. If a company started the year with $1 million of assets, they shouldn't be reporting $5 million in depreciation. Oddly high depreciation may indicate depreciation is being taken on assets not otherwise reported to you.

31. ARE THE COMPANY'S RETAINED EARNINGS GOING UP OR DOWN EACH YEAR?

This is an indication of both the profitability of the company as well as whether the owners are reinvesting in the firm. An owner that does not reinvest in the company may not be serious about growing their firm or may have other issues going on (such as a drug or gambling habit).

32. HAS THERE BEEN A SIGNIFICANT CHANGE IN THE COMPANY'S GROSS RECEIPTS, RETAINED EARNINGS, PRODUCTION/LABOR COSTS, OR DEBT OVER THE LAST FEW YEARS?

Changes such as these can indicate a change in the business—an owner or leader that is no longer involved with the company, changes in supplier or union contracts, or increases in costs for raw materials and other commodities (such as gasoline). If there has been a significant change, make sure you can explain the cause of that change.

33. IS THERE ANYTHING ON THE TAX RETURNS THAT SEEMS STRANGE— SOMETHING THAT "JUST DOESN'T LOOK RIGHT"?

If it doesn't look right, there's probably a reason. Find out what that reason is.

34. DOES ANYTHING LOOK OUT OF LINE COMPARED TO OTHER BUSINESSES IN THE SAME INDUSTRY?

While it is sometimes appropriate for a company's assets, liabilities, and costs to be different from those of their competitors, it is not overwhelmingly common. Profit margins tend to be fairly consistent across industries. Companies that differ significantly from their competitors may have other things going on you need to be able to explain.

35. IS THE COMPANY A SUBSIDIARY OF ANOTHER FIRM?

If you are investigating a subsidiary, make sure you have information on both the parent as well as the subsidiary.

36. DO THE TAX RETURNS ESTABLISH ALLEGED PARENT-SUBSIDIARY RELATIONSHIPS?

Tax returns should clearly indicate whether a company is a subsidiary of another firm. If the company claims to be a subsidiary of another company, but the tax returns do not indicate that is the case, you should be prepared to explain why the documents refute the firm's claim.

37. IS THE COMPANY AFFILIATED WITH ANOTHER COMPANY?

Just because a company claims it is independent does not mean it actually is. It is important to verify whether a company is independent or is an affiliate of another firm.

38. DOES THE COMPANY SHARE OWNERS, OFFICERS, DIRECTORS, MANAGERS, EMPLOYEES, BANK ACCOUNTS, EQUIPMENT, SUPPLIES, BUSINESS LOCATIONS, OR ANYTHING ELSE NECESSARY TO DO BUSINESS?

Affiliated companies will sometimes claim to be independent of each other. However, sharing owners, officers, directors, managers, employees, facilities, equipment, and other resources affects both firms. Even if the owners want the two businesses to be independent of each other, the activities of one will unavoidably affect the other.

39. IS THE COMPANY INVOLVED IN ANY "LESS THAN ARM'S LENGTH" TRANSACTIONS (THAT IS, ARE THEY PAYING FAR LESS OR FAR MORE THAN MARKET RATE FOR LOANS, EQUIPMENT RENTAL, REAL ESTATE RENTALS, MATERIALS, OR SUPPLIES)?

Over or underpaying for supplies, equipment, and leases is not only an indication the two parties are somehow connected to one another, it can also be used as a method for illicitly transferring funds. If the market rate for a business location is $5,000 per month, but the subject company is only paying $1,000 per month, it is likely due to a connection between the parties and the landlord giving the company a break on rent. Conversely, if the company is paying $25,000 per month rent, they may be doing so to secretly divert company profits to the landlord. Either way, there is probably a connection between the two that you should be able to explain.

40. IS EVERYTHING PROPERLY DOCUMENTED—DO ALL LOANS HAVE WRITTEN LOAN AGREEMENTS AND ALL CUSTOMERS HAVE WRITTEN RENTAL OR SALE AGREEMENTS?

Business owners should get everything in writing. When they don't, it is an indication either of very sloppy business practices (always a possibility) or of a relationship between the parties. If you're "selling" something to a company that you secretly own, why would you need to prepare a bill of sale? If you're leasing the property to yourself, why bother with a lease agreement? Lack of documentation frequently indicates a connection between the parties.

41. DOES THE COMPANY USE THE SAME STANDARDS FOR ALL CUSTOMERS, SUPPLIERS, AND SUBCONTRACTORS?

Deviation from the norm needs explaining. If a company makes most customers sign a 10 page contract, but one customer gets by with a one-page form and an handshake, there is probably a relationship between the parties that needs explaining.

42. DO SOME COMPANIES—CUSTOMERS, SUPPLIERS, OR SUBCONTRACTORS—GET "SPECIAL" TREATMENT?

Any company getting better deals than its competitors is getting them for a reason. If this situation is occurring, you need to be able to explain what that reason is.

43. DOES THE FIRM HAVE A REPUTATION THAT MAKES IT STAND OUT FROM ALL ITS COMPETITORS (IS IT "THE BEST" OR "THE CHEAPEST" OR "FLY BY NIGHT")?

In addition to helping you evaluate the company, knowing this information can help you evaluate the firm's financial position in the market.

44. DOES THE COMPANY'S REPUTATION MATCH UP WITH ITS FINANCIAL INFORMATION?

A company's books and tax returns will likely correspond to their reputation. Companies known for making cheap products should have lower materials costs than competitors with good reputations. Companies known for high quality will likely have both higher materials and higher labor costs.

45. DOES THE COMPANY HAVE FOREIGN (NON US) CONNECTIONS, SUCH AS BANK ACCOUNTS, AFFILIATES, LOCATIONS, OR OWNERS WHO LIVE ABROAD?

Companies with connections outside the United States may have opportunities to conceal assets and earnings, especially if the foreign connection is in a tax haven.

46. HAS THE COMPANY PROPERLY MAINTAINED ALL LICENSES, PERMITS, AND REGISTRATIONS REQUIRED BY LAW?

If the company has failed to maintain the proper licenses and permits to do business in your jurisdiction, you need to be able to explain exactly which registrations have lapsed, the regulatory basis for needing the registration, and the legal consequences of failing to maintain the proper documentation.

47. HAS THE COMPANY FOLLOWED APPLICABLE LAWS AND COMPANY RULES, POLICIES, AND PROCEDURES?

Companies that fail to follow the law or their own company policies and procedures may play fast and loose with your regulations as well. A company that cheats on its taxes may be cheating in other areas as well. You should be able to explain what laws or rules the company hasn't followed and how those failures justify additional investigation on your part.

48. IS THERE DOCUMENTATION THE COMPANY HAS FOLLOWED THOSE LAWS AND RULES?

Compliance requires paperwork, sometimes lots and lots of paperwork. A company that has complied with all applicable laws and regulations should have the documentation to back it up. If the documentation doesn't exist, the compliance might not be real.

49. IF FACING A FINE OR PENALTY, HOW WILL THE COMPANY COME UP WITH THE MONEY TO PAY IT?

A company might have sufficient liquid assets to cover a fine or penalty, or they can use one of a variety of other methods. If a company is claiming an inability to pay, it may be worthwhile to ask the company to explain how they plan to pay the fine. Their answer can give you a clearer understanding of the company's financial situation.

50. COULD THE COMPANY PAY A FINE OR PENALTY FROM CASH ON HAND?

While some companies keep sufficient cash on hand to pay a fine or penalty, many others do not. In fact, in some industries it would be very surprising to see more than a very few companies with the ability to pay a fine or penalty outright. Most companies would either need to borrow the money (say from their line of credit) or they would need to liquidate assets to cover the fine. Companies that claim to be unable to pay should have those claims examined with the utmost scrutiny.

51. WOULD THE COMPANY NEED TO LIQUIDATE ASSETS TO PAY A PENALTY?

Companies that don't have access to liquid assets, can't borrow from a line of credit, and have no other way to pay a fine or penalty may resort (or be forced to resort) to liquidating assets to pay a penalty. This is usually a last resort because the assets are usually a source of the company's income and selling them reduces the company's ability to generate revenue in the future. If a company informs you they will need to liquidate assets in order to pay a fine, it is a good indication there are other financial issues at play.

52. DOES THE COMPANY PARTICIPATE IN ANY ACTIVITIES THAT DON'T HELP THEM MAKE PAYROLL? IF SO, WHY?

Businesses, especially smaller businesses, don't have the time or resources to dedicate to activities unless they either generate revenue or are required by law. Businesses don't have hobbies. If you note a company is participating in activities that are not legally mandatory or don't contribute to the bottom line, ask yourself why. Does the company use the activity as a form of marketing and publicity (like sponsoring Little League teams or volunteering in the community)? That's a legitimate business activity. If there's no obvious benefit to the business, there must be some other reason the business is performing the activity. You should be able to explain what that reason is.

53. CAN YOU LEGITIMATELY ARGUE THAT THE "CORPORATE VEIL" SHOULD BE PIERCED IN A CONVINCING ENOUGH WAY TO PERSUADE A JUDGE?

If you cannot adequately explain why a corporate form is a sham and why it should be disregarded, you will probably not be able to convince a judge to allow you to access an owner's personal assets. If you believe it is appropriate to try to pierce a corporate veil, you should be able to explain why in a simple and straightforward manner, detailing all of the examples of how the owner disregarded their corporate form.

54. HAS THE COMPANY EVER DECLARED BANKRUPTCY BEFORE; IF SO, WHEN?

If a company has previously declared bankruptcy, their options for doing so again may be restricted. It is always worthwhile to double-check whether a company or its corporate predecessors have ever declared bankruptcy, when, and under which chapter.

55. HAS THE COMPANY EVER BEEN A PLAINTIFF IN A LAWSUIT; IF SO, HOW LONG AGO?

An occasional lawsuit may not tell you very much about a company's financial status. However, if the company frequently sues other parties (especially for seemingly minor or insignificant reasons), this may be an indication the company is experiencing financial difficulties and is trying to generate revenue through settlement of nuisance lawsuits.

56. HAS THE COMPANY EVER BEEN A DEFENDANT IN A LAWSUIT; IF SO, HOW LONG AGO?

When a subject company has been a defendant in a lawsuit, it may be for reasons reflecting the company's financial situation. For example, if the company was sued for failing to pay its bills or failing to fulfill its obligations under a contract, that can indicate the company is having significant financial challenges. However, lawsuits related to personal injuries (like slip and fall or car accidents) are usually not relevant to a financial investigation because the company's insurance will likely cover any potential losses.

If the Subject is an Individual (including Partnerships and Sole Proprietorships)

57. HOW IS THE PERSON RELATED TO THE INVESTIGATION OR LIABILITY?

You should always be able to explain the nature of the relationship between the person you are investigating and the underlying reason for your investigation. If there isn't a clear connection, then your investigation may not be warranted. Be sure you can clearly explain why you are investigating this person, especially when the main focus of your investigation is a business.

58. WAS THE SUBJECT'S BUSINESS INVOLVED WITH THE ACTIVITIES THAT GAVE RISE TO THE INVESTIGATION, FINE, OR PENALTY?

If you are investigating a partnership or sole proprietorship, the owner's assets may be legally vulnerable when it comes to the company's debts. Just because the company can't cover the debt it incurred or the penalty imposed does not mean there aren't other assets that can be used to satisfy the amount due.

59. WHAT KIND OF PERSON IS THE SUBJECT: A DARING RISK-TAKER, THOUGHTFUL INTROVERT, SOMEONE WHO LOVES ATTENTION, SOMEONE WHO LOVES POWER, SOMEONE WHO LOVES MONEY, A WORKAHOLIC, SOMEONE WHO LOVES TO PLAY, OR SOMETHING ELSE?

Knowing what kind of person you are dealing with can not only help you predict whether they will attempt to hide assets but also the manner in which they might hide them. All business owners are risk takers to some extent—they wouldn't have struck out on their own unless they could handle some degree of risk. Someone who is obsessed with power and money may be more motivated to hide assets than someone who is more cautious.

60. WHAT KIND OF LIFESTYLE DOES THE PERSON LEAD: EXTRAVAGANT OR SUBDUED?

Someone who flaunts their wealth is frequently someone who will be willing to take at least some actions to protect that wealth. The amount of actions they are willing to take to hide assets will be determined in large part by what they think they can get away with. Someone who is extremely confident in their superiority may be willing to take extra risks because they think they can outsmart an investigator.

61. DOES THE SUBJECT HAVE A CRIMINAL RECORD; IF SO, FOR WHAT?

If the subject has a criminal record for sexual offenses, it is good to know that ahead of time, especially if you are a woman. It may be best to assign cases where a subject previously convicted of a sexual crime to an older male investigator. In cases like that, it's important to not be offended by a case reassignment. Avoiding the situation is as much to protect the subject as it is the investigator. A female investigator may be fully capable of handling any situation that might arise, but the situation might never arise if a male investigator handles the case.

The other situation where a previous criminal record may shed light on a subject or an investigation is when the crime is directly related to issues of fraud, theft, or other matters of dishonesty. Subjects that have previously attempted to conceal income or assets should be regarded with special attention to ensure old patterns are not being repeated.

62. DOES THE SUBJECT'S CRIMINAL RECORD GIVE YOU A CLUE ABOUT WHAT TYPE OF PERSON THIS IS?

If a criminal history indicates repeated reckless behavior, then that may play a role in your investigation. While an isolated crime may not be applicable to your investigation, a pattern of behavior may indicate a specific personality type that may affect how you pursue an investigation.

63. WERE THE SUBJECT'S PREVIOUS CRIMES RELATED TO FINANCIAL ISSUES OR OTHER TYPES OF FRAUD?

This is the most important aspect of checking for previous criminal activities. A subject who embezzled from a previous employer might be more likely to try to hide assets from you and may have the financial wherewithal to do so successfully.

64. DOES THE SUBJECT HAVE ANY OTHER BUSINESS ON THE SIDE?

Running a business is a significant commitment. To successfully start and grow a new business may require far more than 40 hours per week. An owner that has another business on the side may not have sufficient time and attention to pay to all aspects of their business and things may get missed.

65. DOES THE SUBJECT HOLD ANY PROFESSIONAL OR BUSINESS LICENSES?

Knowing whether the subject has any professional registrations or licenses not only tells you something about the subject's education and work history, it also gives you a better understanding of how their company may operate. If the subject claims to run an architecture business but isn't a licensed architect, then someone else is really running the business. Business licenses also indicate what work the subject or company is performing (after all, there's no reason to maintain a business license if you're not using it).

66. IF THE SUBJECT HAD TO FIND A NEW LINE OF WORK, WHAT WOULD THEY DO (AND ARE YOU SURE THEY AREN'T ALREADY DOING IT)?

Depending on the nature of your investigation, you may realize a subject has lost their passion for the company's work and may be drifting away from the company, allowing others to fill the void. It may be helpful if you can explain what new profession the subject would choose if they had the opportunity or were forced to do so.

67. WHAT SORT OF CONNECTIONS DID THE SUBJECT MAKE WHEN THEY WERE GROWING UP (IN SCHOOL AND THEIR SOCIAL LIFE)?

The social connections we make throughout our school years have a significant effect on the social connections we maintain the rest of our lives. Social climbing is possible, but can be difficult to accomplish successfully. The connections we make in school, in the military, and in our early work and social life can stay with us the rest of our lives.

68. IS THE SUBJECT USING THOSE CONNECTIONS RELATED TO THEIR BUSINESS?

Many subjects do business with family members, old schoolmates, and military buddies. If there is a social connection between the subject and their business associates, you should be able to identify and explain it. These are the types of relationships that people are willing to exploit to hide assets.

69. DOES THE SUBJECT HAVE A DEMONSTRATED HISTORY OF TRYING TO HIDE ASSETS?

If the subject went through a nasty divorce and illicitly transferred assets to keep them from being distributed to their former spouse, they may well be willing to try it again. This is one of the few times when divorce records might be relevant to your investigation, but tread carefully and don't worry about issues unrelated to their financial dealings. Records from lawsuits related to business dissolutions may also be relevant in these cases.

70. DOES THE SUBJECT'S FINANCIAL STATEMENT INCLUDE EVERYTHING?

If the subject left any assets or liabilities off their financial statements, there should be a very good reason why. Omitting either one should cause you to look extremely carefully at the other items that were included to ensure their values are accurate. While everyone makes mistakes once in a while, mistakes on financial statements are a big warning sign.

71. DO THE AMOUNTS LISTED ON THE SUBJECT'S FINANCIAL STATEMENT SEEM REASONABLE?

If the subject lives in a million dollar house, they probably didn't furnish it at Wal-Mart. If they've been collecting baseball cards since the 1950s, their collection is probably worth more than $25. When reviewing a financial statement, ask yourself whether the amounts listed seem reasonable on their face. Anything that seems grossly out of place always deserves additional investigation.

72. IF SOMETHING COMMON IS MISSING FROM THE SUBJECT'S FINANCIAL STATEMENT, HOW DO THEY GO WITHOUT IT?

If the subject doesn't list a car as an asset or a lease payment as an obligation, how do they get from place to place? Are they an avid biker or do they take public transportation? If they don't list mortgage or rental payments, where do they live? While there can be reasonable answers to questions like these, the subject should have a good reason why they don't list assets or obligations the rest of us take for granted.

73. DOES THE SUBJECT'S FINANCIAL STATEMENT UNDER-REPORT THE VALUE OF SOME ASSETS, OR OVER-REPORT THE VALUE OF SOME LIABILITIES?

Even if the values reported might seem reasonable at first glance, the subject may still be trying to minimize the appearance of wealth. Use the websites suggested in this book (along with any others you find helpful) to establish whether the values of assets as reported by the subject are reasonable for the items in question.

74. IS THE DIFFERENCE BETWEEN ACTUAL VALUES AND REPORTED VALUES SIGNIFICANT?

A little under-reporting here, a little overstating there, and pretty soon they've had a big effect on their bottom line. As a general rule, I tend to look at any under-reporting of value or over-reporting of liability of more than ten percent to be suspect.

75. HAS THE SUBJECT MADE EXTENSIVE RETIREMENT AND ESTATE PLANS?

Estate planning takes time and money. If you don't have significant assets to protect, it's probably not worth it to spend very much time and effort on complicated estate planning documents. While everyone should have some basic estate planning documents like a Will or Power of Attorney, not everyone has enough assets to justify complicated trusts. If the subject reports spending significant amounts on estate planning attorneys and financial planners, it's a pretty safe bet there are significant assets worth protecting. You can check the subject's tax returns to see if they have deducted their attorney's fees. Property (such as the subject's home) owned in the name of a Living Trust may also indicate a more complex estate plan.

76. DOES THE SUBJECT HAVE A LIVING TRUST AND/OR MULTIPLE RETIREMENT ACCOUNTS?

Subjects may establish a Living Trust to conceal assets (instead of for the normal estate planning reasons), and may establish multiple retirement accounts so avoid fully disclosing their assets. Since most investigators aren't going to have access to banking information, the subject may believe they can get away with omitting some assets from their financial statements.

77. DOES THE SUBJECT'S ESTATE PLANS MAKE SENSE IN LIGHT OF APPLICABLE STATE PROBATE LAWS AND THEIR REPORTED WEALTH?

Depending on where the subject lives, having a Living Trust or multiple retirement accounts may be an indication of significant wealth. While some subjects will get a Living Trust because they saw someone on television who said everyone should, most subjects will only go through the time and expense if it's worth it to their bottom line.

78. HAS THE SUBJECT RECEIVED AN INHERITANCE; IF SO, HOW LONG AGO AND WAS IT SIGNIFICANT?

An inheritance can instantly transform a middle-class business owner to a multi-millionaire. While this is relatively unusual, it can sometimes happen. It can also be a logical and legitimate explanation for financial transactions that seem odd, such as an owner not taking a salary for years on end or living in a home they shouldn't be able to afford.

79. HAS THE SUBJECT EVER DECLARED BANKRUPTCY; IF SO, HOW LONG AGO?

Just like for businesses, declaring personal bankruptcy limits your options. If a subject has recently declared bankruptcy, their financial situation should reflect that reality. Bankruptcies more than ten years old, however, may not have any noticeable effect on a subject or their financial situation.

80. HAS THE SUBJECT EVER BEEN A PARTY TO A LAWSUIT; IF SO, WERE THEY THE PLAINTIFF OR THE DEFENDANT?

Many people have been involved in a lawsuit and it has not had any significant effect on their financial situation. However, court records can occasionally help you understand who the subject is and how they view financial matters and transactions.

81. IF THE SUBJECT HAS BEEN A PARTY TO A LAWSUIT, WAS IT RELATED TO BUSINESS MATTERS?

If a subject was named as a plaintiff or defendant in a business-related lawsuit, you should be able to explain why. Was it because the business is a sole proprietorship or partnership and the subject's assets were at stake? Was it because the subject signed a personal guarantee and promised to pay a debt if the business failed to do so? Whatever the reason, explaining why a subject was personally named in a business lawsuit can give you clues about the relationship between the subject and the company.

82. DOES THE SUBJECT MAKE A HABIT OF TRYING TO FORCE OTHERS TO DO WHAT THEY WANT?

In other words, do they use any legal means available to them to get their way? Do they file SLAPP or other nuisance lawsuits to try and force the other side to give up? Do they introduce numerous citizens' referenda or make copious other attempts to change the law? Are they a person who repeatedly introduces recall petitions because they don't like the decisions of their elected officials? These are all indications that the subject is a person who is accustomed to getting their way (or at least trying to do so). Be prepared—there is a high probability that the subject will file complaints or lawsuits against you and your agency if you don't decide the way the subject wants.

83. IS THE SUBJECT SOMEONE WHO IS FOCUSED ON THEIR HEALTH? FOR EXAMPLE, DO THEY BELONG TO A GYM OR SPEND MONEY ON TRAINERS AND EXERCISE EQUIPMENT?

Exercise can be addictive, and subjects faced with budget shortfalls may place a higher priority on these expenses than others. If you are dealing with a subject who is obsessed with organic foods, taking the latest and greatest supplements, or getting to their spin class on time, don't be surprised if you continue to see exercise and health-related expenses even if the subject is in dire financial circumstances. On the other hand, if your subject is someone who goes to the gym only under protest and will skip working out because they have a hangnail, you should expect to see exercise-related expenses to be one of the first things to go in times of economic hardship. If claims of financial distress and exercise-related expenses don't match up, you should be prepared to explain why.

84. IS THE SUBJECT SOMEONE WHO IS FOCUSED ON INDULGENCE? FOR EXAMPLE, DO THEY EAT OUT A LOT? DO THEY SPEND THEIR MONEY ON FINE WINE, EXPENSIVE CARS, AND OTHER LUXURIES?

Giving up luxuries, even the little ones, can be hard. For many of these luxuries, there may be nothing to show for a very large bill except the subject's enjoyment. If the subject eats out a lot, drinks expensive wines, smokes expensive cigars, or fancies themselves a gourmet chef, they may spend considerable funds with nothing objective to show for it. While those funds could also be going to something like gambling debts or illegal drugs, be sure you confirm the subject's claims otherwise before drawing any conclusions about illicit activities.

85. IS THE SUBJECT SOMEONE WHO IS FOCUSED ON INFLUENCE? FOR EXAMPLE, DO THEY PARTICIPATE IN LOCAL POLITICS, GIVE MONEY TO POLITICAL CAMPAIGNS AND CAUSES, OR FREQUENTLY WRITE LETTERS TO THE EDITOR?

True influence costs money. Whether it is campaign donations, lobbyist salaries, or fundraising expenses, influencing politicians and the citizens can be very expensive. When it comes to subjects who are active in politics and social issues, it is a good idea to distinguish between subjects who are concerned about a particular cause and those who are just in it to rub shoulders with the rich and powerful. Be sure you know which category applies so you can adjust your behavior and analysis accordingly.

86. IS THE SUBJECT SOMEONE WHO IS FOCUSED ON THEIR LEGACY? FOR EXAMPLE, DO THEY SPEND MONEY ON PRIVATE SCHOOLS, EXPERT TENNIS OR MUSIC LESSONS FOR THEIR CHILDREN, OR SUBSTANTIAL DONATIONS TO CHARITABLE ORGANIZATIONS AND FOUNDATIONS?

Many of us invest most of our time and money into our children. Ballet classes, soccer camp, and piano lessons are all a normal part of growing up in the United States and parents are expected to spend money on these types of things. But other expenses are less run-of-the-mill. Private school tuition, expert instruction, and establishing or contributing to charitable foundations are all activities that are usually reserved for the more wealthy in our society. If a subject claims extreme financial hardship, they probably shouldn't be able to afford to send their grade-schooler to private school without financial aid. You should be able to explain any large contributions made or expenses incurred.

For all Subjects

87. DOES THE SUBJECT OR ITS OWNERS, OFFICERS, DIRECTORS, ETC. HOLD PERSONAL BELIEFS ABOUT GOVERNMENT OR THE ENVIRONMENT THAT MIGHT DRIVE THEM TO TRY TO HIDE ASSETS?

Some people genuinely believe it's OK to cheat the government. They may have deeply-held beliefs about the lack of government's authority over them. They may oppose all taxes and other support for government. They may believe that environmental issues are "bunk" and just another way for government to control the citizens. Whatever the nature of the subject's belief (no matter how crazy it sounds to you), it is important to view those beliefs as objectively as possible and try to understand how they affect the subject's financial reporting. If the subject believes it's OK to lie to the government, but that it's not OK to lie to God, they may accurately report charitable contributions to their church but under-report their income, making it appear that they donated 50 percent or more of their income to charity.

88. DOES THE SUBJECT OR ITS OWNERS, OFFICERS, DIRECTORS, ETC. HOLD A PATERNAL ATTITUDE ABOUT THE FIRM?

That is, will the subject be motivated to take whatever actions they believe necessary in order to protect the firm and its employees (for whom they feel personal responsibility)? Some subjects will steal or not file taxes in order to free up enough cash to make payroll because they don't want to have to lay off any employees. Remember that hiding assets and engaging in other financial schemes is not always due to selfish concerns about a subject's own pocketbook.

89. DOES THE SUBJECT OR ITS OWNERS, OFFICERS, DIRECTORS, ETC. DEFINE THEIR SUCCESS OR FAILURE IN LIFE BY THE SUCCESS OR FAILURE OF THE SUBJECT COMPANY?

This attitude is more common in some cultures than others. Some subjects are willing to go to great lengths to disguise the fact they are not successful—John Emil List killed his entire family and started a new life to disguise his failure (Benford 2007). Subjects like this are more likely to take extra steps to try to conceal information they'd rather not share. That doesn't mean you should ignore the law or regulations just to make them feel better, but it may require that you think about your investigation and plan it out so that it causes the least amount of confrontation with a subject like this.

90. DOES THE SUBJECT OR ITS OWNERS, OFFICERS, DIRECTORS, ETC. HOLD STRONG BELIEFS ABOUT PUBLIC FAILURE AND SHAME?

Again, this attitude is much more common in some cultures than in others. If the results of your investigation are likely to cause public embarrassment and shame, the subject may be more motivated to conceal unflattering information. In cases such as these, keep all of your options open and in mind. If a subject can simply request their application or complaint be closed or they can stop the investigation process by failing to respond to a request for information, that may be the best outcome for all involved. Sometimes giving a subject a way to save face is possible while still following the law.

91. IF THE SUBJECT OR ITS OWNERS, OFFICERS, DIRECTORS, ETC. HAD TO CHOOSE BETWEEN BEING PUBLICLY EMBARRASSED OR PAYING A FINE, WHICH WOULD THEY PICK?

These attitudes are also frequently based on cultural values. Sometimes it is possible for a subject to quietly pay a small fine and end the matter without it being reported by the local news. If your subject is someone who is deeply concerned about public embarrassment, it may be worthwhile to talk with a supervisor about other legal options for resolving the matter.

For all Cases, Irrespective of the Subject

92. WHAT SORT OF PENALTIES OR REGULATORY ACTIONS DID YOUR AGENCY PREVIOUSLY TAKE IN SIMILAR CASES?

Consistency is a large part of fairness. If a subject has committed a legal violation, how does that violation compare to those of other individuals or businesses? How did you treat the subject's competitor when they committed a similar violation? Failing to be evenhanded in your approach is usually going to be justification for overturning your decision.

93. IS THE PENALTY OR ACTION YOU'RE CONSIDERING PROPORTIONATE TO PREVIOUS CASES; IF NOT, CAN YOU JUSTIFY WHY?

Sometimes there is a good reason that you treat one violation or subject differently than another. Were there aggravating factors involved with this matter? Were there mitigating factors involved in the previous matter? If you're going to penalize a business for illegally dumping dangerous chemicals down the drain, you might be justified in fining one company more harshly if one of the chemicals was far more dangerous than the other. It may be completely appropriate to deviate from previous penalties; but if so, you need to be able to explain why in a clear, concise manner.

94. HAVE YOU BEHAVED IN A COMPLETELY PROPER MANNER DURING THE COURSE OF THIS INVESTIGATION?

It's worth taking a few minutes to think about all the steps in your investigation. If there is anything you've done that was questionable, now's the time to think about it.

95. HAVE YOU DONE ANYTHING DURING YOUR INVESTIGATION THAT A DEFENSE ATTORNEY COULD USE TO IMPEACH YOUR CREDIBILITY?

Any misstep on your part is going to come out in a hearing. Any half-way decent defense attorney is going to bring up your misconduct as a reason for throwing out your determination and all of your work.

96. IF YOU ARE SUBJECT TO PROFESSIONAL STANDARDS OF BEHAVIOR (SUCH AS THOSE IMPOSED ON ATTORNEYS OR ACCOUNTANTS), HAVE YOU LIVED UP TO THOSE STANDARDS DURING THE COURSE OF YOUR INVESTIGATION?

Even if you weren't acting as an attorney or an accountant during your investigation, you may still be held to those professional standards. If you have failed to live up to those requirements, a defense attorney may use it against you.

97. IF YOU ARE SUBJECT TO PROFESSIONAL STANDARDS OF BEHAVIOR, HAVE DO DONE ANYTHING THAT MIGHT BE INTERPRETED AS VIOLATING THOSE STANDARDS?

In addition to having your case dismissed and research ignored, you could also face potential professional sanctions if you've violated applicable standards. At the very least, you could be in for a time-consuming investigation in which *you* are now the subject.

98. HAVE YOU FOLLOWED ALL THE POLICIES, PROCEDURES, AND PRACTICES APPROVED BY YOUR AGENCY?

Policies and procedures are in place for a reason. Some policies may have even gone through an extensive review and public comment period. Policies and procedures are there to not only help you do your job, they're there to protect you from subjects who don't like you or your investigation. If you don't follow those practices, they can't help you.

99. IF YOU HAVE NOT FOLLOWED YOUR AGENCY'S POLICIES AND PROCEDURES, CAN YOU JUSTIFY YOUR DEVIATION FROM APPROVED METHODS?

If you didn't get your supervisor's express permission to deviate from accepted procedures, you might have a tough road ahead of you. "Oh, everyone ignores that rule" isn't a good enough answer. Decision makers are going to want a very good reason why you didn't follow the rules but expect them to punish someone else for not following the rules.

100. HAVE YOU SOUGHT OUT EXPERT ASSISTANCE WITHIN YOUR UNIT, SECTION, OR AGENCY?

If you have a particularly difficult case, you should be consulting with the experts within your organization. Not only can they help you understand and decipher a complex set of facts and documents, they can also provide you with additional investigation leads. More importantly, if a defense attorney asks you if you are an expert in that particular area, you can respond that you consulted with an expert in the field and that consultation guided your investigation.

Appendix C: Writing Internet-Based Investigation Plans and Reports

Investigation Plans

The following boilerplate should be customized for your individual jurisdiction and the types of investigations you do. Use this boilerplate to create a word processing document on your computer. Save it in an easily-accessible location. Each time you begin a new investigation, save a copy of your word processing file in the company's folder. Remember where you saved it because you will need to update it throughout your investigation—investigation plans are "living" documents that constantly need updating.

If you prefer to fill out the plan by hand, add some lines to the word processing document to give yourself a comfortable place to write the answers. Even if you maintain your plan by hand, make sure you type up the final version at the end of your investigation. You may need to produce your plan so decision makers (including judges and juries) can review it—make it neat and tidy and easy for them to do so. Regardless of how nice your penmanship is, a typed form is always easier to read.

Feel free to customize the boilerplate so it meets your needs and is helpful to guiding your investigation. For web sites you use on most investigations, go ahead and fill in the information on the original boilerplate and make it part of your official form. For web sites that you only use occasionally, either type them in to the copy or print out the copy and write them in by hand, whichever you find easier.

Remember this boilerplate is designed for investigations that are primarily based on Internet resources. If your investigation will involve interviewing numerous witnesses, collecting physical evidence, or other non-Internet-based activities, this form should be altered accordingly. In cases where you collect physical evidence, make sure you also incorporate the applicable chain of custody documentation.

[Agency Name] Investigation Plan

DATE

Start by listing the date you create your investigation plan. Leave enough room to add subsequent dates for each time you amend the plan.

FILE NAME/NUMBER

Each file should have a unique identifying number that is unrelated to the business or subject's name or other government numbers related to the business or subject. Using a Social Security Number or Employer Identification Number will help you identify the subject of the investigation and prevent mix-ups between files with similar names. However, using these types of identifiers could lead you to confuse files of unrelated investigations. John Smith's file from ten years ago might be important, but probably shouldn't be confused with his file from today's investigation.

If your office does not use a unified numbering system, of if you are the only person conducting investigations and maintaining files, it may still be worthwhile to create a numbering system. Numbered files can help you maintain order and can help future co-workers or successors understand your completed investigations. You might consider including numbers for the year an investigation was started and the type of investigation it was in addition to any sequential file numbers. For example, the first two or four digits could be the year and then the next number (or letter) could not whether it is a routine licensing check, a complaint investigation, or verification of a subject-initiated request. That would allow a future employee (long after you've retired and moved to a tropical beach somewhere with no phones) to look at the file number 11-a-035 and instantly know that this was an application received in 2011 and was the 35th investigation handled that year.

CROSS REFERENCES

Make sure to list any applicable cross references, such as previous or concurrent files. This is another reason why a numbering system can be useful even if you don't handle many files in a year and could keep track of them by only using subject or company names.

PURPOSE

List the purpose behind your investigation. This should be a simple and unambiguous statement [e.g., "To determine if ABC Company, Inc. is eligible for the agency's small business assistance program" or "To identify potentially liable parties in the XYZ toxic waste cleanup"].

SCOPE AND AUTHORITY

This section of your plan should clearly state the regulatory basis for your investigation [e.g., "49 CFR 23 and 49 U.S.C. 47107(e)"].

STANDARD OF PROOF

Note the applicable standard of proof related to your investigation: such as "Conclusions must be supported by a preponderance of the evidence," or "Conclusions must be supported by clear and convincing/cogent evidence," or "Conclusions must be proven beyond a reasonable doubt."

SUBJECT/RESPONDENT

This is the section where you identify the main subject of your investigation. If you are investigating a business, list both the business and its main owner or manager.

NAMES FOR INVESTIGATION

This list should include the subject, the subject's spouse (if any), and any other family members or business associates that are related to the topic you are investigating. Only list relevant individuals and businesses—the subject's six-year-old daughter is probably not relevant, but the subject's 26 year old daughter who is a Vice President for one of the subject's companies probably is relevant. List all applicable names, including spelling variations. If you are unsure whether a name should be included or not, try breaking the names list down into sections: subject and business partners, family members, and associates with unclear relationships. If you later determine someone doesn't belong on the list after all, don't delete them. Instead, simply note that you learned that person was not related to your financial investigation, why they were not relevant to your determination, and the date when you removed them from consideration as part of your investigation.

FOLLOW-UP QUESTIONS

This list should detail the various questions you feel need additional explanation. This would include application questions that the subject has failed to answer, supporting documents that were supposed to be provided but were not, or responses that don't make sense to you based on what you typically see.

VERIFICATION QUESTIONS

This list is the routine information that you will verify as part of your investigation. If your job entails reviewing routine information, your agency may have a standardized checklist for the information you need to verify on a regular basis. Any information related to the subject or the purpose of your investigation might require verification. Licensing and registration information, property values, and corporate status are all issues that routinely need verification during the course of an investigation.

INVESTIGATION QUESTIONS

This list is the red flags list: documents, actions, and information that needs more research. Information on this list might include a history of ownership of a parcel of real estate, other property or vehicles not included on a list of assets, or the corporate history of a subject company. Anything that seems out of place or otherwise odd should go on this list.

RESOURCES

This is the section of your investigation plan where you start to identify the resources you expect to use to collect documents and verify information. If you don't have a checklist of standard web sites included on your Verification Questions list, consider adding them here instead.

If there is information that is unique to a particular investigation, you may not know what resources you will need to use. If that is the case, simply list the type of resource you need with your initial ideas, such as "Baseball card collection value—start by checking eBay and collectibles sites." While you may not find your verification at eBay, you may find the lead that leads you to your verification. Including these notes in your investigation plan will document how you found the needed information and what resources you considered.

OUTSIDE RESOURCES

This is the section of your plan where you should highlight any non-Internet resources you'll need to access. This might include an interview with your subject, a site visit to a business location, or personal contact with an outside expert.

SPECIAL CONSIDERATIONS

Include any information that is unique to this particular case or subject, keeping in mind the item's importance to your investigation. If the information does not have a direct effect on your investigation, leave it out. Information such as, "Applicant claims to be unable to work due to a mental disability" is probably relevant and should be included. A statement such as, "Applicant is a noted friend of the Governor" is probably not relevant and should be omitted.

AMENDMENTS

If you make a dramatic change or alteration to your investigation plan, you may want to add a brief explanation as to why you did so. This is not applicable to every change you might make. Adding or deleting a related name, adding something new to the "Special Considerations" section, or editing the list of resources you need to consult aren't things that need to be included in this section. Small changes can simply be noted in their relevant section as appropriate. The Amendments section of your investigation plan is intended as a placeholder in case you have significant, unpredictable changes that have occurred since the onset of your investigation. Changing the type of investigation (e.g., an administrative investigation becomes a criminal investigation) or merging two previously separate investigations are changes that may warrant a brief explanation under this heading.

Investigation Reports

At the end of your investigation, you should plan to write a final report. The report should include enough detail for someone else to understand what you did, why you did it, what you found, and why you made the final decision you did. While each investigation and report is unique, the format should be as consistent as possible. In addition, you may be able to develop some boilerplate language that can be copied and pasted into your reports, thus saving time. The following can be used as a template for developing an investigation report:

[Agency Name] Investigation Report

REPORT DATE

Depending on how you plan to use your report, you can either type in the date you finish the report, or insert a date code into your word processing document. If you use a date code that automatically updates itself, this could cause confusion later on if you ever need to verify the report date or if you correct a typo after the report is finished. If you open the word processing document to make even a minor change, the later date will be the date that is printed—not the date you actually finished the report. Automatic dates are convenient but can cause unexpected problems later on, so it may be best to avoid using them.

INVESTIGATOR/ANALYST

List your name and any other investigators that worked the case with you. If applicable, include credentials for each analyst or investigator (CPA, JD/Esq., and CFE would all be worth mentioning—others may also be worthy depending on their relationship to the subject).

OTHER INVESTIGATORS, EXPERTS, AND CONTRIBUTORS

If other investigators assisted on a limited basis, make sure to include them here. Also note the participation of any other experts, consultants, or other contributors to your work. This section is for people who helped you perform your investigation or analyze the evidence you obtained. Witnesses and other specialists go in a later section.

SUBJECT/RESPONDENT

This can be copied from your investigation plan.

CASE/FILE NUMBER

If you have assigned a case number or file number to your investigation, list it here along with any cross-referenced file numbers.

INVESTIGATION DATES

Note the date you started and finished your investigation. Your conclusion date should probably be the same as the date of your final report.

INVESTIGATION PURPOSE

This can be copied from your investigation plan.

INVESTIGATION SCOPE AND AUTHORITY

This can be copied from your investigation plan.

STANDARD OF PROOF

This should be a brief statement clarifying which standard you used in your investigation. This may be a slightly different wording than appears in your investigation plan. Instead of stating that the "preponderance of evidence" standard is required, consider phrasing the explanation in your report as, "Determinations related to this investigation were made using a 'preponderance of evidence' standard."

RESULTS/RECOMMENDATIONS

Briefly explain your final determination or result. This is simply the conclusion, not the underlying explanation for that conclusion. Try to keep this section to no more than two or three sentences. Your entry in this section could be as simple as "The subject is not eligible for the program because they are not a US citizen." Don't try to explain why that statement is true—that comes later.

BACKGROUND

Including a "Background" section in your investigation report can be a helpful way of laying the groundwork to explain your specific findings. For example, you might want to separate out the basis for your investigation from your preliminary information in this section. In other words: if it was provided to you, include it in the background; if you found it yourself, include it in the findings.

DOCUMENTS AND EVIDENCE OBTAINED

This section is merely a list of each document or piece of evidence you obtained, where you obtained it, and when you found/obtained it. A table can be a good way to organize this information. If you can, try organizing this list or table in alphabetical order, instead of organizing by source or by date. Remember, a reader is far more likely to wonder if you collected a particular document as opposed to wonder which documents you received on a particular date or from a particular source.

SPECIFIC FINDINGS

This is the section of your report that will contain the most detail and will take you the longest to write. It will also take you the longest to prepare because there will be many topics, issues, and resources you will need to organize. Every document you find needs a paragraph explaining how you authenticated it, what it demonstrates, why it is important, and what conclusion it supports. For example, if a company lied about when it was established, you might include a paragraph that says:

Certificate of Formation. XYZ Industries, LLC submitted a copy of its Certificate of Formation dated January 17, 2010. However, when I reviewed the copy of the firm's Certificate of Formation on file with the Secretary of State's office, Corporations Division, I observed the Certificate's actual date is January 17, 2000. I spoke with Penny Cooper, Corporations Agent for the Secretary of State's office, and she confirmed XYZ Industries, LLC has actually existed since 2000. A careful review of the document submitted by the firm shows a minor inconsistency in the typeset of the Certificate's date. Based on this inconsistency and the information received from the Secretary of State's office, I concluded the company has existed for more than one year and that the Certificate of Formation provided with the company's application has been altered to make it appear otherwise.

You should also include specific findings for documents that didn't affect your decision either positively or negatively. Even if a particular piece of evidence didn't change your mind one way or the other, you still want to document that you considered it. Although you may find it cumbersome, a narration style is best for this section of your report. Using a table or list simply does not provide sufficient detail to explain your actions and recommendations.

NEXT STEPS

Finally, it is good to conclude your report with a brief explanation of what should come next. This may explain the subject's appeal rights and applicable deadlines or the next stage in the hearing process. If there are statutory or regulatory deadlines, hearing dates, or other mandatory time limits, make sure to include them here.

SIGNATURE

It is a good practice to sign the final version of the document.

Appendix D: Quick Answers to Common Questions

How Do I Find Out if the Subject is Married?

You can check a number of resources to find out whether a subject is married. First, look at the deed for the subject's home and see if it lists the subject as a married person, a single person, or two people as "husband and wife." Of course, the subject's marital status could have changed since the date of the document, so look for a marriage certificate filed with the county recorder in the county where they live or a divorce filing with the county court clerk's office. You can also search newspaper announcements for marriage licenses being issued, divorces being filed, and obituaries listing names of surviving family members. If you have access, you can also try checking social networking sites to see if a spouse is listed.

How Do I Find the Names of the Subject's Siblings?

You can check probate filings to find surviving heirs and obituaries to find surviving family members. Social networking sites may help you find other family members who are "friends" of the subject (you may be able to see who the subject's friends are even though you are not their friend). Also check alumni services to find people with the same surname who are close to the subject's age. Newspaper announcements (especially wedding announcements) may also list the names of siblings.

How Can I tell if Two Businesses are Related?

Check to see if they share any owners, officers, directors, managers, employees, facilities, supplies, bank accounts, addresses (including post office boxes), or phone numbers. Common tax registration numbers, business license numbers, worker's compensation accounts, and other government registrations are also a good indication two businesses are related.

How Can I Tell if the Subject has a Complicated Estate Plan?

Check the deed to see whether the subject owns their home or whether they have transferred ownership to a Living Trust. If you have access to vehicle records and other similar documents, check ownership of those assets as well. If the subject deducted attorney's fees on their personal taxes, it is likely because they had a complicated estate plan. Documents discussing life insurance trusts and Crummey trusts are also indications of a complicated estate plan.

How Do I Find Out Who Owns a Piece of Property?

Check the county recorder's office and find out who was the "grantee" on the most recent deed. That person, persons, or entity should be the current owner. You can also confirm that fact with the county tax assessor's office, who may have listings for both owner and taxpayer.

How Can I Find Out if Someone is Still Alive or Whether they've Passed Away?

Check the Social Security Death Index. You can also search obituaries, either through a national search or through the local paper's web site (especially if they lived in a small town).

References

Alexa Internet, Inc. 2009a. *The Top 500 Sites on the Web (1–20)*. [Online, effective December 29, 2009]. Available at http://www.alexa.com/topsites/global [accessed December 29, 2009].

Alexa Internet, Inc. 2009b. *The Top 500 Sites on the Web (21–40)*. [Online, effective December 29, 2009]. Available at http://www.alexa.com/topsites/global;1 [accessed December 29, 2009].

Alexa Internet, Inc. 2009c. *About Myspace (myspace.com): Social Networking Site*. [Online, effective December 29, 2009]. Available at http://www.alexa.com/siteinfo/myspace.com [accessed December 29, 2009].

Benford, T.B. 2007, September 11. *The Pursuit, Capture and Trial of John Emil List*. [Online]. Available at http://www.associatedcontent.com/article/362109/the_pursuit_capture_and_trial_of_john.html?cat=17 [accessed December 29, 2009].

Brouard, F. 2002. *Note on Financial Statement Analysis*. [Online]. Available at http://sprott.carleton.ca/~fbrouard/teachingmaterial/notefinanstatanalysis.DOP.pdf [accessed December 29, 2009].

Brown, J.G. 2000, September. *Department of Health and Human Services Office Of Inspector General Report: Birth Certificate Fraud*. (Publication no. 0EI-07-99-00570). [Online]. Available at http://oig.hhs.gov/oei/reports/oei-07-99-00570.pdf [accessed November 22, 2009].

Brutsche v. City of Kent, 164 Wn.2d 664, 686, 193 P.3d 110 (2008) *(Chambers, J., dissenting in part)*.

California Franchise Tax Board. 2000. *Frequently Asked Questions: Qualified Subchapter S Subsidiaries (QSub)*. (Publication no. FTB 1093 Rev 05-2000). [Online]. Available at http://www.ftb.ca.gov/forms/misc/1093.pdf [accessed January 1, 2010].

eNotes.com. 2006. *Clear and Convincing Proof*. [Online version of *West's Encyclopedia of American Law*. 2nd Edition. Edited by J. Lehman and S. Phelps. 2005] Available at http://www.enotes.com/wests-law-encyclopedia/clear-convincing-proof [accessed December 2009].

Galvin, W.F. 2009. *Citizen Information Service: Historical Data Relating to the Incorporation of and Abolishment of Counties in the Commonwealth of Massachusetts*. [Online]. Available at http://www.sec.state.ma.us/cis/cisctlist/ctlistcounin.htm [accessed December 31, 2009].

Golden, T.W. and Dyer, M.T. 2006. *A Guide to Forensic Accounting Investigation*. Hoboken, NJ: John Wiley & Sons, Inc.

ICANN 2009. *Internet Corporation For Assigned Names and Numbers Registry Listing*. [Online]. Available at http://www.icann.org/en/registries/listing.html [accessed December 29, 2009].

Internal Revenue Service. 2004, March 22. *Internal Revenue Bulletin 2004-12*. (Publication no. 2004-12 I.R.B.). [Online]. Available at http://www.irs.gov/pub/irs-irbs/irb04-12.pdf [electronic version accessed March 2, 2007].

Internal Revenue Service 2008. *Qualified Subchapter S Subsidiary Election*. (Form no. 8869). [Online]. Available at http://www.irs.gov/pub/irs-pdf/f8869.pdf [electronic version accessed December 27, 2009].

Internal Revenue Service 2009, December 14. *S Corporations*. [Online]. Available at http://www.irs.gov/businesses/small/article/0,id=98263,00.html [accessed December 27, 2009].

Jadad, A.R., Boyle, M., Cunningham, C., Kim, M. and Schachar, R. 1999. November. *Treatment of Attention-deficit/Hyperactivity Disorder*, (Publication No. 00-E005), Rockville, Maryland: Agency for Healthcare Research and Quality (US), available at http://www.ncbi.nlm.nih.gov/bookshelf/br.fcgi?book=erta11 [accessed December 14, 2009].

Kessler, R.C., Chiu, W.T., Demler, O. and Walters, E.E. June 2005. Prevalence, Severity, and Comorbidity of 12-Month DSM-IV Disorders in the National Comorbidity Survey Replication. *Archives of General Psychiatry* [Online], 62(6), 617–627. Available at http://archpsyc.ama-assn.org/cgi/content-nw/full/62/6/617/YOA40303T1 [accessed December 14, 2009].

Law.com Dictionary. 2009. *Corporation (Definition)*. [Online]. Available at http://dictionary.law.com/default2.asp?selected=358 [accessed January 1, 2010].

MetaCrawler. 2009. *About MetaCrawler*. [Online]. Available at http://www.metacrawler.com/metacrawler/ws/about/_iceUrlFlag=11?_IceUrl=true [accessed December 28, 2009].

Miranda v. Arizona, 384 U.S. 436 (1966)

Moye, J.E. 2005. *The Law of Business Organizations*. 6th Edition. Clifton Park, NY: Thomson Delmar Learning (West Legal Studies Series).

North Dakota. 2004, June 1. *Alien Documents 430-05-30-60-35*. [Online]. Available at http://www.state.nd.us/humanservices/policymanuals/foodstamps-508/430-05-30-60-35_ml2921.htm [accessed November 22, 2009].

Orecklin, M., Ressner, J. and Thigpen, D. 2003, May 12. Civil Liberties: Checking What You Check Out. *Time Magazine*. [Online]. Available at http://www.time.com/time/magazine/article/0,9171,1004797,00.html [accessed January 1, 2010].

PACER. 2009. *Public Access to Court Electronic Records Overview*. [Online]. Available at http://pacer.psc.uscourts.gov/pacerdesc.html [accessed December 29, 2009].

Philadelphia Bar Association. 2009, March. *Opinion 2009–02*. [Online]. Available at http://www.philadelphiabar.org/WebObjects/PBAReadOnly.woa/Contents/WebServerResources/CMSResources/Opinion_2009-2.pdf [accessed September 6, 2009].

Silverstone, H. & Sheetz, M. 2004. *Forensic Accounting and Fraud Investigation for Non-Experts*. Hoboken, NJ: John Wiley & Sons

Sonnenfeld, Barry (dir.) (2002) *Men in Black II*.

Uniform Law Commissioners. 2002a. *A Few Facts About The Uniform Limited Partnership Act (2001)*. [Online]. Available at http://www.nccusl.org/Update/uniformact_factsheets/uniformacts-fs-ulpa.asp [accessed November 22, 2009].

Uniform Law Commissioners. 2002b. *A Few Facts About The Uniform Partnership Act (1994)(1997)*. [Online]. Available at http://www.nccusl.org/Update/uniformact_factsheets/uniformacts-fs-upa9497.asp [accessed November 22, 2009].

US Navy Inspector General. 2007. *Investigations Guide*. [Online]. Available at http://www.ig.navy.mil/Documents/InvestigationsGuide/chapter3.pdf [accessed December 18, 2009].

WebCrawler. 2009. *About WebCrawler*. [Online]. Available at http://www.webcrawler.com/webcrawler_stoolbar/ws/about/_iceUrlFlag=11?_IceUrl=true [accessed December 28, 2009].

Index

If you have found this book useful you may be interested in other titles from Gower

Investigation and Prevention of Financial Crime: Knowledge Management, Intelligence Strategy and Executive Leadership
Petter Gottschalk
Hardback: 978-1-4094-0331-9
e-book: 978-1-4094-0332-6

Fraud and Corruption: Prevention and Detection
Nigel Iyer and Martin Samociuk
Hardback: 978-0-566-08699-1
e-book: 978-0-7546-8294-3

Investigating Corporate Fraud
Michael J. Comer
Hardback: 978-0-566-08531-4
e-book: 978-0-566-08959-6

The Anatomy of Fraud and Corruption: Organizational Causes and Remedies
Tomas Brytting, Richard Minogue and Veronica Morino
Hardback: 978-0-566-09153-7
e-book: 978-0-566-09154-4

Visit **www.gowerpublishing.com** and

- search the entire catalogue of Gower books in print
- order titles online at 10% discount
- take advantage of special offers
- sign up for our monthly e-mail update service
- download free sample chapters from all recent titles
- download or order our catalogue